MILTON'S CREATION

A Guide through *Paradise Lost*

MILTON'S CREATION

A Guide through Paradise Lost

HARRY BLAMIRES

METHUEN & CO LTD

11 NEW FETTER LANE, LONDON E.C.4

First published 1971 by
Methuen & Co Ltd
11 New Fetter Lane London EC4
© *1971 Harry Blamires*
Printed in Great Britain by
Richard Clay (The Chaucer Press) Ltd
Bungay, Suffolk

1.1.

SBN 416 65880 6 hardbound
SBN 416 65890 3 paperback

Distributed in the U.S.A.
by Barnes & Noble Inc.

England hath need of thee

Contents

Note on the Text

In quoting from the text of *Paradise Lost* I have used editions of the poem that preserve the original Miltonic spelling. Some recent editions have modernized Milton's spelling; others have modified it so as to accommodate various theories of what the poet's intentions were. I am not convinced that we know enough about the poet's intentions in this matter. For instance, everyone admits Milton's addiction to double meanings, but not all editors have given thought to it before tampering with his spelling. Yet one need only compare Milton's preference for 'faultring' (II. 989; IX. 846; X. 115) with his crucially emphatic use of the word 'faults' (X. 1089 and 1101) to suspect that words are being handled with an innocent Joycean duplicity much practised in the seventeenth century. To replace 'faultring' by 'faltering' is to eliminate in advance the freedom of the reader's own sensitiveness in such matters. Again, it may well be that Milton's preference for 'adventrous' ('adventrous Song', I. 13; 'adventrous Eve', IX. 921; 'Adventrous work', X. 255) represents a desire to fashion an adjective from *advent* as well as from *adventure*. In each of the three contexts cited, such a multiplicity of meaning would be richly relevant – and characteristically Miltonic. The editor who prints the word 'adventurous' is perhaps half-silencing Milton. Or consider the comparable use of 'ventring', for *venturing* (IX. 690), where the word *vent* and the notion of exhalation could well be in Milton's mind. The serpent is boasting of what he has achieved – by heroically venturing 'higher than my Lot', the satanic voice proclaims; by blowing yourself out like a wind-bag, the Miltonic voice perhaps quietly adds. Such may be the force of the word 'ventring'. I do not press these conjectural instances in the present book: indeed there is much work to be done before we can fathom all Milton's intentions in this respect: but we must keep a Miltonic text in use that permits the work to be done and at least allows the reader to make his own acquaintance with the poet; otherwise we may become the generation that has finally silenced Milton in deference to Satan.

Introduction

In escorting the reader through *Paradise Lost*, I have tried
to answer the needs of the student who wants a bird's-eye
view of the poem as a whole and also of the student who
wants detailed help wherever the text is loaded or difficult.
He is generally one and the same reader. He wants to look
closely at what are the richest and most crucial passages, and
not to miss any of their subtleties; he also wants to get a
grasp of their place in the work as a whole. My guide is
designed to meet both of these requirements. To do this task
of guidance well I believe a writer has to escape the idio-
syncracies of his own personal style and to some extent
sacrifice the character of his *feel* for words to that of the
writer he is dealing with. A choicely worded paraphrase is
not necessarily the same thing as an elucidation which
follows the original writer's sentences closely enough to
disentangle and clarify them at a glance. Where the text
requires it, line-by-line interpretation is provided here,
which of itself reveals the shape of Milton's syntactical
complexities and matches his difficult words with modern
equivalents.

The fact that I do not argue with recent critics does not
mean that I think they should be ignored by students, but
my guide is a guide to *Paradise Lost*, not to modern thought.
When I began to write, it soon became clear to me that, if
I was to fulfil my aim of elucidation, there would not be
space within the compass of the book to enter into current
controversy. The decision was not a difficult one for me to
make. I happen to take the view that in *Paradise Lost* Milton
meant what he said, and therefore I have been happy to
concentrate on a straightforward reproduction of what he
said, without devoting space to argument with those who

disagree about what he meant, while agreeing that, whatever it was that he meant, it was not what he said he meant. In this connection my opinion is that B. A. Wright* has said some very good things about where critical thinking tends to go astray, just as C. S. Lewis† did in a previous generation. But my task does not overlap much with theirs. I do not write *about Paradise Lost*. I take the reader into the poem, into Milton's own Creation. There we shall meet not only our great progenitors, but also the Satan who postured as a hero, took in Eve for a time, and (so thoroughly and subtly Milton did his job) is still pulling the wool over the eyes of fallen men, critics especially.

To confess that working on Joyce and Eliot has taken me back to Milton with renewed zest is probably a matter of more than autobiographical interest. The more one reads *Ulysses*, the more aware one becomes of Milton's presence in the background; and of course the work cries out to be matched with other epics. Thomas McGreevy‡ speaks of Joyce as a writer 'with a power to construct on a scale scarcely equalled in English literature since the Renaissance, not even by the author of *Paradise Lost*', and Milton's epic seems to undergird *Ulysses*, both in substance and in structure, as do the epics of Homer and Dante. I am sure that a post-Joycean reappraisal of *Paradise Lost* is needed, indeed that a post-Joycean readjustment in the literary world is overdue; and one of the main requirements is that we should recognize the English Epic (of Milton and Joyce) for the powerful and integrated thing it is. I hope that my present book will serve as a step on the road to that end. I recognize that we have not yet got far enough to place T. S. Eliot's work in this category with the same confidence with which we can place Milton and Joyce: but, as one who has worked very carefully over what begins to look like the last book

* B. A. Wright, *Milton's Paradise Lost* (London, Methuen, 1962).

† C. S. Lewis, *A Preface to Paradise Lost* (London, O.U.P., 1960).

‡ Samuel Beckett and others, *Our Exagmination Round His Factification For Incamination Of Work In Progress*, 2nd ed. (London, Faber & Faber, 1962), see p. 120.

of Eliot's 'epic' (*Four Quartets*, his *Paradiso*), I suspect that the other 'two books', when properly interpreted, may fill out an achievement as integrated and orderly as Milton's and Joyce's, and standing in a direct relationship with them. If this line of thought is valid, academic study of English literature will perhaps have to accommodate itself for some centuries to the poetic dominance of this delightfully compatible epic trinity of three most distinctive geniuses.

Book I

*1–83 The poet invokes the Muse and introduces the subject (–26),
the Fall of Man (–32) and the Fall of the Angels (–44), then
reveals Satan and his followers in Hell (–83).*

In calling upon the Muse to inspire him, Milton lays before
us the subject of his poem, the Fall of Man and the 'Fruit'
(1: it also means *consequences*; cf. IX. 647–8) of the forbidden
tree. The fatal human act ('mortal', 2, covers both adjectives;
cf. III. 214–15) of eating this fruit has introduced death and
misery into the universe, and deprived us of the happiness
of Eden until Christ, the unique man who is more than man
('one greater Man', 4), re-establishes us in happy possession
of our home ('Seat', 5). The muse Milton calls upon inspired
Moses, shepherd (8) and teacher of the Israelites ('chosen
Seed', 8), and supposed author of the account of creation
with which the book of Genesis opens, and which Milton
here echoes ('In the beginning', 9 – Genesis I. 1). We shall
hear more of the revelation to Moses on *Sinai* (7) in the
historical prophecy of Michael (XII. 227; and see pp. 293–4).
The muse also inhabits the brook Siloa, which flows by the
temple at Jerusalem ('Sion', 10), and perhaps finds more
delight in the sacred city and temple. The aid Milton invokes
is for a project more enterprising ('adventrous', 13) than the
classical Muses of Mount Helicon ('*Aonian* Mount', 15,
sacred to the Muses – *Aonides*) were ever invited to sustain,
a hitherto unattempted theme for poetry.

So far Milton has but called upon a 'Heavnly Muse' (6)
to 'sing', and the initial invocation can be aptly paralleled
with those of the great Classical epic poets; but now he
addresses the Holy Spirit specifically. The words, 'Instruct
me, for Thou know'st' (19), speak of a new requirement by
the epic poet whose theme is to involve the redemptive

5

scheme of Christian Revelation. Not only must he have the imaginative range and power to 'sing' with the inspiration of a Homer or a Virgil, he must be nourished with an insight and understanding from the divine source of all knowledge. The sequence moves from the call for poetic impetus to the request for instruction; from the call to a muse in the mountains, then to a muse of city and temple, and now to a spirit who prefers to dwell in the temple of a pure and upright heart (18). The intensification of inspirational requirement culminates in the image of the Holy Dove, mighty wings outspread in an act of impregnation over the 'vast Abyss' (21) at Creation (cf. VII. 233–5). This same brooding (breeding) spirit is called upon so to illuminate the darkness of the poet's limited vision (another creational *fiat lux*) and so to exalt his 'low' (23) level of earthly understanding that he may rise to the height of insight which the higher-than-human subject ('Argument', 24) demands, and do what, without such special divine aid, would be humanly unattainable – that is, establish that a Divine Providence is operative behind the temporal order, and show God's treatment of human beings to be just (for fuller comment on the already implicit correspondence between divine creation and poetic creation, see p. 178).

Now Milton makes it clear, with repetitive force ('Say first . . . say first what cause', 27–8), that attention is to be given initially to Satan in order to make plain how it came about that our primal ancestors, Adam and Eve, fell away from the God who had established them not only in the happiness of Eden but in that overlordship of his new created world (32), which was the favoured status chosen for them. The rhythmically weighted contrast between the 'one restraint' and 'Lords of the World' (32) puts the ban on the forbidden tree into perspective. Indeed Milton's emphatic opening stress on 'Mans First Disobedience', followed by his emphases ('what cause/Mov'd', 28–9) and reiteration (27–32) all indicate that the chronological priority given to Satan's activity in Hell is not to be misunderstood. It is not a logical priority in the structuring of the epic pattern of heroic events. Over against the 'Grand Parents', the 'Lords of the World', Satan makes his introductory appearance in the text as the 'infernal Serpent' (34) who 'first seduc'd them' to 'fowl revolt' (33), a being infected with 'guile', 'Envy' and 'Revenge', and therefore prepared to deceive 'The Mother of Mankind' (36). The contrast between healthy and poisonous connotations is now so firmly planted among the reader's sensitivities that he ought to be proof against the allurements of the devil he is about to meet. He *ought*: but he is not. To the development of that dichotomy in the psychology of fallen man Milton devotes his skill as a poet and his insight as a prophet. In this connection we may note that within the system of hierarchical thinking whose framework persists in the mind of Milton, as it does in the mind of Shakespeare, words like 'aspiring' (38), 'ambitious' (41), 'Pride' and 'proud' (36 and 43), and 'impious' (43) have a force and flavour which they have since partially lost. (For instance, in Spenser, whom Milton valued especially for his quality as a moralist, one finds that in the very depths of the miniature hell over which the demonic Mammon presides, the golden chain-ladder on which those who set foot destroy themselves by covetousness is called *Ambition* – *Faerie Queene* II. vii. 46.)

We find the fallen angels, after their 'hideous ruine' (46) to bottomless perdition, rolling in fire, 'confounded' though immortal; and the word 'ruine', meaning *falling*, is elsewhere Milton's keyword for the collapse of human innocence and virtue. The thought of 'lost happiness and lasting pain' (55) is an additional torment for Satan, and he takes in the dismal scene with eyes which testify to ('witness'd', 57) the magnitude of his own 'affliction and dismay', and to his unbroken pride and hate. Milton is already showing us Hell partly through our own eyes and partly through the eyes of Satan, so that we experience the objective and subjective horrors of the place. Not only do we see Hell, but we savour from within the personality whose proper habitat it is. In each respect we have to adjust ourselves to a new motif, that of self-contradictory disorder wherein fire and flame can exist without light, and where darkness, itself visible, can actually 'discover' (that is, *uncover* or *reveal*) 'sights of woe' (63–4). The paradoxes for the reader are sharp. It is not just that the external world has fallen about our ears, but that the whole regulatory, associative machinery of experience, whereby light and sight go with seeing and spectacle, whereby fire and flood are incompatible (cf. 'fiery Deluge', 68), has been suddenly obliterated. This is so as touching both the experience of the senses and the experience of the mind. As the key principles of all sensitive responses to environment have fragmented away (we spoke of a *motif* of disorder above, to distinguish it from the *principle* of order), similarly that which is basic to all mental being itself has gone; for hope here 'never comes'. 'That comes to all', Milton declaims in our ears at the beginning of the next line (67) in order to stress the paradox. The hopelessness of Hell is crucial because hope is the one thread that gives meaning to consciousness in the midst of affliction and torment. Utter hopelessness represents an inner disintegration comparable to the outer disintegration. For the rebel angels the disintegration is self-induced. It is the only possible and logical outcome of that 'impious War' and 'vain attempt' (43–4) whereby subordinate and derivative being has tried to assert itself against supreme being and source of all being. Contradiction and failure are built into the venture from the start and cannot but extend their corrosive effect over the disintegrators who embrace them. In this condition lie the fallen angels, three times as far from the light of Heaven as the Earth is from the 'utmost Pole' of the universe (i.e. from the *primum mobile*).

84–191 *Satan addresses Beelzibub: he is determined to continue the struggle with Heaven* (–124). *Beelzibub replies, lamenting their changed condition* (–155). *Satan strives to hearten him* (–191).

The 'equal ruin' (91) of persons and cause accepted by Satan makes false the speech which follows. He labours to construct a persona from the wreckage, a persona whose rebellion, viewed retrospectively, was an expression of fixity

8

of mind, high disdain, sense of injured merit (97–8). Defeated duplicity's *post-facto* invention of an imaginary self and an imaginary history has begun. Milton's reproduction of posturing in the retrospective surveys of the unrepentant is penetrating. Satan claims that a battle only ('field', 105), not a war, has been lost, and that there remains in him an integrated personality still by virtue of the allegedly unifying power of persisting obduracy, pursuit ('study', 107) of revenge, and undying hate; to which he adds the 'courage' (108) of not being overcome when you are indeed overcome (109). Then, falsifying the present situation as he has falsified the past, claiming that he is no worse off 'in arms' than he was when he started, and much better off in the faculty of 'foresight' (119) – he could hardly be worse – Satan proposes 'eternal' war and irreconcilability with that power whose omnipotence he no longer questions. After this outburst by Satan, Milton tersely and quietly reminds us that Satan is 'Vaunting aloud, but rackt with deep despare . . .' (126). The thing has been a put-up show, noisy vaunting from a wrecked being in the depths of despair.

No doubt all evil-doing creatures inhabit imaginary worlds. Perhaps it is only on the basis of a falsely conceived self inhabiting a falsely posited personal environment that evil can be plotted and executed. Certainly Beelzibub is at first quick to enter the imaginary world fabricated by his former superior. He, too, reflects backward on the campaign which 'endanger'd Heav'ns perpetual King' (131): and the phrase is self-contradictory, since, if God is the perpetual king then he was certainly not endangered, and if he was truly endangered then the perpetuity of his kingship cannot be assured. Then he speaks of having 'put to proof' God's 'high Supremacy' (132); but granted the supremacy, there is nothing to test, and the pseudo-question whether God's supremacy is upheld 'by strength, or Chance, or Fate' (133) represents a further excursion into illogicality. If supremacy is upheld by something else, then it is not supremacy.

The fallen angels are already weaving from irrationality and illogicality a mental fabric of spurious non-thought in which they posture as integrated beings. Not that they are incapable of facing facts. Beelzibub recognizes the defeat, destruction, loss of Heaven (135–6), but wonders whether there is not some catch in the fact that, being 'Gods' (138, that is, angels), they have not totally perished. Their 'glory' is extinct, their happiness consumed, but the ruin of their being falls short of annihilation perhaps only to the extent that they can be aware of their defeat. To survive defeat and destruction, as a consciousness, only to the degree and to the end that awareness of defeat and destruction is your lot, this is at best a doubtful advantage. Beelzibub is plainly still in danger of lapsing back from unreason into reason. Small wonder that Satan replies 'with speedy words' (156).

The philosophy (or non-philosophy) of evil is briefly summed up. To do anything good is now permanently out of the question. Always to do evil will be the only possible 'delight' (160) simply on the grounds that it negates the will of God. Since God's providence works in such a way as to produce good even from evil, the motif of all action in Hell must be the converse; to pervert the good into evil, a programme which may 'succeed' (166) at least to the extent of grieving God and disturbing those divine plans which it is impossible to thwart. Thus concisely the character of the good is negated. As goodness ultimately consists in doing the divine will, so evil can only consist in *trying* to subvert it. The quiet note sounded here, ringing with a reminder of the ultimate powerlessness of evil, is to be listened to. *Paradise Lost* is a much more cheerful poem than it has frequently been represented to be. The foundations of the whole structure of evil, through which the human race becomes infected, are shown here to be so shaky and insubstantial that the mind savours a kind of laughter in contemplating the irony. And on such foundations are to be constructed all those pseudo-heroic posturings whereby the non-motivated, self-manufactured protagonist pursues his self-contradictory adventures in parodic emulation of the truly purposeful epic heroes of Homer and Virgil. If there is a devastating epic parody in English literature, it is not represented by the journeyings of Joyce's Leopold Bloom around Dublin, but by the empty enterprise of Milton's Satan. Of course he himself would *be* the hero.

See, he says, the divine artillery of cosmic hail and fire is letting up. We must not let the opportunity go by ('slip th'occasion', 178). Let us make for that 'dreary plain' (180), gather together our forces there, and plan how best to assault God, our enemy. The final contradictory reference to hope and despair is the kind of rhetorical flourish to which we become accustomed as we listen to Satan. The words 'hope' and 'despair' are voiced (190–1) in a sequence which has the superficial shape of an epigrammatic rational utterance, but it makes little sense within the context that Milton has now created, for we are placed where hope never comes (66) and what Satan has to say is itself a 'vaunting' that veils despair (126).

192–282 *The poet describes the enormous size of Satan as he lies in the burning lake (–210) and explains why God allowed him to pull himself together (–220). Satan raises himself and Beelzibub follows (–241). Satan declares his delight in Hell (–263) and decides to call his followers together (–270). Beelzibub concurs (–282).*

Satan's horrific magnitude is impressed upon us by comparisons relating to the gigantic and monstrous figures of ancient legend and Classical poetry. Sweeping the literature of the past with darting glances at Greek, Hebraic and Norse mythology, Milton effects that universalization of his material which nothing less than a world-view can compass. Thus the physical sense of Satan's magnitude is reinforced by correspondences that put capsulated areas of human history and experience within the grasp of poet and reader, whose eyes are fixed on the monstrous being and the vast uncontainable theme. Then the poet carefully explains why God leaves Satan 'at large' (213), allowing him to rise from the impotence of inaction. It is not in order that he may do more damage. It is, we may say, in order that the ethos of positive being may be reasserted. God will not be trapped into a denial of his own wholly beneficent creativity by an act of annihilation. Let the negations posture as they will, they shall not gain the advantage of negativity unaware of its own negativity. Milton puts it more concretely. Satan seeks only 'evil to others' (216). The awareness must be kept alive in him (in order that the principle itself shall not be even privately defeated in him) that all such malice can only serve to 'bring forth/Infinite goodness' (217–18), that even his seduction of mankind can but release a new flow of 'grace and mercy' to men, and threefold misery upon himself.

The rising of Satan from the burning lake and his alighting on dry land is accompanied by imagery of earthquake and volcanic eruption; and the very words 'lake' and 'land' mislead, the poet indicates, Satan having but exchanged a liquid for a solid fire. Beelzibub follows Satan. Milton characterizes their new-found upright stance ironically. They attribute it to their own 'recover'd strength' (240). What follows is uproarious. In rollicking mood, Milton displays a pantomimic Satan who surveys the horrific, torment-ridden environment and seems to find it good. Is *this* 'the seat' (243; cf. 'blissful Seat', 5) they must accept in exchange for the light of Heaven? Be it so. God is in charge *now* (246), and can make his own decisions about what is right and what is not right. The further away from him the better. The grotesque performance gathers momentum as Satan opens his arms and his heart, hailing the horrors around him as their 'new Possessor' (252). Entering upon an inheritance of total misery, he declares that the mind is its own place and can 'make a Heav'n of Hell, a Hell of Heav'n' (255). The epigram is powerful: in an appropriate context it might carry the burden of a dignified resignation to undeserved hardship. But, as used here, it is laughably absurd. *See* Satan (for it is not enough just to listen to him). See where he is and what he is surrounded by, and then savour the comic explosions of his pretentiousness. He talks of being 'still the same' (256), implies that he is in everything else equal to God except that God has a store of thunder at his disposal. The implication is that, this little matter apart, the two of them could scarcely have anything less balanced than a fifty-fifty relationship. In a climactic burst of absurdity he declares 'Here at least/We shall be free'. This place of utter desolation which every living thing would shrink from is a place God will not 'drive us' from (260). Here he may 'reign secure' (261). Every emphatic word, 'secure', 'reign', 'choice', rings with irony against the sounding-board of solid and liquid fire, 'stench and smoak' (237) involving the speaker. 'Better to reign in Hell than serve in Heav'n', as here proclaimed (263), is a slogan that covers a monstrous leap into mental unreality. (Like all things satanic, it is parasitically second-hand. See Abdiel's rebuke of Satan during the war in Heaven, vi. 183–4.)

Milton continually makes his fallen angels employ the machinery of discourse to chew away at a non-existent substance. Satan and his followers employ the devices of rationality and articulacy, but under scrutiny their utterance turns out to be operating on the basis of premises which are either false or totally out of keeping with the context in which they are used. We see much more of such unreal mental activity in Satan's coming address to his followers (622–69) and in the great council in Book II, but it is evidenced here as Satan turns to Beelzibub to draw attention to their followers still stretched out in liquid fire, and speaks in an idiom which seems to suggest that it is unjust to leave them 'astonisht' (266) – that is, *stunned*. They should be invited to join the party. The doubtful privilege of being lifted up from a condition of oblivion in order to 'share' (267) with Satan and Beelzibub a fuller awareness of misery is what seems to be at issue. That, and the scarcely more encouraging project of finding out what there is to be 'regained' – or, more realistically, 'what more' there is to be 'lost' (270).

Beelzibub supports Satan in his resolution. The followers have but to hear the voice of their trusted leader and they will resume their courage and revive. Why beings brought to such a dismal state of total defeat and disintegration as the fallen angels are in should be likely to regard the voice of the leader who brought them into this unthinkable plight as either 'their liveliest pledge/Of hope in fears and dangers' (274–5) or 'Their surest signal' (278), Beelzibub does not pause to explain.

283–330 *Satan moves towards the shore (–300), looks on his fallen followers (–315), and calls on them to awake and arise (–330).*

The massiveness of Satan hits us again in Milton's imagery as we see Satan's shield hanging on his shoulders like the moon, as studied by Galileo, the Tuscan astronomer ('artist', 288), through his telescope ('Optic Glass', 288), and his spear handled like a walking-stick, though the tallest Norwegian pine, chosen for the mast of a flagship, would be but a little stick ('wand', 294) by its side. Satan's step is yet an uneasy one over the burning soil ('Marle', 296), though his weapons are so vast that the furniture of earth and sky seem to be within his grasp. He reaches the beach of the flaming sea where the thickly scattered angel forms lie 'intrans't' (301, *enchanted*). They are compared to fallen autumn leaves in Italian woodland ('Vallombrosa', 303) and to the thick sedge of the Red Sea, the sea where Pharaoh and his hosts ('Busiris and his Memphian Chivalry', 307) were overwhelmed by the waves as they pursued the Israelites ('Sojourners of *Goshen*', 309). The story is told in Exodus XIV and is retold in Michael's prophecy to Adam (XII. 195–214). For more on the special significance of this deliverance of the Israelites in the poem as a whole, see the commentary on p. 293 and pp. 295–6.

The fallen angels are 'abject and lost . . ./Under amazement of their hideous change' (312–13). It is the hideousness of the transformation that stuns them. The same hideous change underscores the irony of Satan's opening cry, 'Princes, Potentates,/Warriers, the Flowr of Heav'n . . .' (315–16). How can one grasp the flavour of it? Is it like entering a death-laden, disease-ridden concentration camp, strewn with near-skeletons, and beginning, 'Ladies and Gentlemen'?

Certainly the ironic bite in such titles is sharp, and Satan's succeeding sarcasm lashes smartly. Is this your idea of a rest-cure after battle (318–19)? Or are you practising a new posture for prayer (322–3)? But the final note of Satan's call is a threat, for in the last resort he is a bully. Are you going to lie here till the conqueror becomes fully aware of the advantage he has just gained, and sends out his troops to finish off the rout and polish off the fallen?

331–521 *The fallen angels bestir themselves* (–375). *The chief of them are listed in order* (–521).

The element of the bully in Satan is important. The followers spring up like men who have been caught asleep on duty by someone 'whom they dread' (333). They are not really awake to what they are doing (334). It is not that they are unaware of their misery and affliction, but that they submit in blind obedience to their 'Generals Voyce' (337). This is the obedience to which the abandonment of heavenly obedience has reduced them. Their uprising is represented in imagery which emphasizes the potency of Satan's call and the darkly poisonous character of the hovering multitude; for it is just as when Moses ('Amrams Son', 339) waved his 'Rod' (338) and called up the cloud of locusts to hang like the blackness of night over the realm of Pharaoh (cf. XII. 184–6). The 'numberlessness' (344) and the associations of the ten virulent plagues set the tone for a crowded imaginative sequence in which the uplifted spear of Sultan Satan, with all its overtones of dark pagan power, waves down hordes of Goths, Huns and Vandals from the frozen North (350–1) to deluge the Mediterranean civilization of Rome.

Such is the throng. Yet Milton touches a new vein of emotion now as he notes relics of their former grandeur – 'shapes and forms' still godlike (358), for these are indeed in essence and origin 'Princely Dignities/And Powers' (359–60) that once sat on thrones in Heaven. It is as important that the reader should not underestimate the devils as that he should not overestimate them. If they are absurd in their rebellious reasoning, they are not negligible in the character of being God gave to them. Our Great Mother was not taken in by something so patently contemptible that any mediocre intelligence might have been expected to see right through it. We see already how difficult a course Milton has set for himself. The more he plays up the irony of Satan's idiocy (which he cannot afford to ignore), the less easy will it be to maintain the dignity of our Grand Parents whom that idiocy deceived. Hence he cannot afford *not* to remind his readers, episode by episode, of the grandeur that was these angels. But their names are 'blotted out' from the heavenly Books of Life (362–3).

They have not yet acquired the names by which they are known in human history, and under which they have corrupted men to worship them in the various idolatries of paganism. Milton lists them with enough detail to convey an impression of a crowding formidable host to match the resounding catalogues of ships and warriors in Homer and Virgil. There are the false gods against whom the jealous Jehovah of the Old Testament protects his chosen people: Moloch, destructive sun god of the Ammonites, one of those to whom Solomon, under persuasion by his wives, built high places on the Mount of Olives (392–405); Chemos (or Peor), similarly honoured, 'obscene' (406) god of the Moabites because of the orgies that marked his worship (406–18). With these Milton lists 'Baalim and Ashtaroth' (422), giving plural collectivity to the various manifestations of Baal and Astarte, male and female, sun god and moon goddess of the Phoenicians. That 'Spirits' can assume what shape or sex they please enables them to fulfil their good or evil purposes among mankind, Milton notes (423–31). Then, after recalling how often the Israelites were led astray by such devices to the worship of 'bestial Gods' (435), he moves on to name Astarte again, moon goddess 'with crescent Horns' (439), linked with Aphrodite, and also acclaimed by the 'uxorious' Solomon (444). The full significance of these first two references to Solomon (400–3 and 444–6) will emerge later. In anticipation of what is to follow we should note that his uxoriousness enables him to be 'Beguil'd' (445) and 'led by fraud' (401). (See IX. 442–3, 797 and 1018. See also the commentary on pp. 221 and 236.) Thammuz (446) is the Greek Adonis, slain by a boar in Lebanon, from whose wound blood pours afresh annually to redden the river that flows from his burial place. As the '*Syrian* damsels' (448 – the '*Tyrian* Maids' of *Nativity Ode* 204) mourned him, so Ezekiel saw, in his vision of abominations, the daughters of Zion themselves (453) lamenting him at the gate of the Lord's house (Ezekiel VIII. 14). Once more this is an allusion whose significance is to be enriched later on (IX. 439–40: and see p. 221). Next comes Dagon, national god of the Philistines, whose statue fell on its face before the Ark of the Covenant (459–60) so that the 'palms of his hands were cut off upon the threshold' (1 Samuel V. 4) ('grunsel', 460 – threshold). Next is Rimmon, Syrian god of Damascus. Then follow the nature deities of the Egyptians, animal or semi-animal in form, at the mention of whom the poet reminds us how the rebellious Israelites made a golden calf to worship in the wilderness (Exodus XXXII) and how Jeroboam, rebelling against Solomon's successor Rehoboam, made two golden calves (1 Kings XII. 28). Last comes Belial who, in *Paradise Lost*, is a fallen spirit representative of lust. Milton uses this invented deity as a type of effeminacy and lechery to balance the ferocity and cruelty of Moloch. The outburst here, against wantonness in courts and palaces and streets, is no doubt especially appropriate against the background of permissive Restoration London. Thus ends the catalogue of 'chief' devils, extending from lines 381 to 505. A brief glance at the also-rans follows. It takes in gods of Greek mythology whom, though alien to Christianity and therefore fitly included here, cultured Milton had probably no wish to smear overmuch with the tar-brush of devilry. The point of the roll-call cannot be grasped except by reference to Michael's prophetic survey of history in Books XI and XII, where the evils first encountered here in Hell are seen at work upon the human scene. That the list is not an arbitrarily selected one will there become clear.

522–621 *Satan calls his followers to order* (–530) *and raises his standard* (–540). *The army acclaims him* (–549) *and moves into*

formation to the sound of music (–567). Satan surveys them (–587)
and the poet describes his appearance and state of mind (–621).

Milton defines the condition of the fallen angels with great
care. Their looks are, not surprisingly, 'Down cast and damp'
(523), but there is also 'Obscure some glimpse of joy' (524).
There are two reasons for this glimmer of false hope. The
first is that they have found their chief 'Not in despair' (525).
But Milton has assured us that he *is* in despair and only
pretending not to be (126), so that the first basis of the
devils' hope is a false one into which they have been tricked
by their 'trusted' leader. And the second reason for the
glimmer of hope is that the fallen angels have found
'themselves not lost/In loss itself' (525–6). In other words,
they are surprised that amid the ruin and disintegration they
themselves subsist to savour the ruin. We have already explained why it is logical that God should deny them the full
dose of disintegration.

It is a frail basis on which to build a new plan of action
and Satan's face wears an understandably dubious expression
('doubtful hue', 527) at the spectacle before him, but gathering together ('recollecting', 528) his habitual pride, and
using lofty rhetoric, which is high-sounding but meaningless ('Semblance of worth not substance', 529), he is able to
lift their spirits a bit. Whereupon he orders the raising of his
standard. Azazel unfurls it. There is music – a flourish of
brass, a great shout, and the sudden upraising of ten
thousand banners and a forest of spears. The packed helmets
and locked shields of an army in close formation are im-
pressively pictured. As they begin to move, the accompanying music (woodwind this time) is such as was used to rouse
heroes of old to a mood of noble courage (552). We must
not miss the irony of the implicit contrast. The same music
breathed 'Deliberate valour' (554), courage weighed and
rational, not empty 'rage' (553), in the noble heroes to whom
the reference applies. Moreover music also can make mellow
the troubled mind, removing worry and sorrow by its
sweetening touch. Under its influence the fallen angels taste

some fixity and unity of mind and are so 'charm'd' (561, enchanted) that they can drag their pained feet over the burnt soil (562). The music seems to drug them as Satan's rhetoric drugged them, and soon they stand in ranks bristling ('horrid', 563 – Latin, *horridus*) with spears 'in guise' (564) of warriors.

They are not in brute strength a despicable gathering. On the contrary; the force gathered ('imbodied', 574) here would make any gathering of human warriors look like a pigmy host (575) by comparison, even though the gathering took in the whole mass of notable mythological and historical armies from the legendary giants and epic forces of the ancient world to the great chivalrous armies of medieval romance (European and Arthurian, 580–1) and history. To that extent these gathered powers exceed any conceivable muster of might at the human level. There must be no mistake about the sheer magnitude of either angelic or demonic power, which might fasten its grip on the creatures of earth.

The 'Arch Angel ruind' (593) is vastly more awesome than a ruined man. The obscuring of that excess of light in which angelic face and form outshine in glory what men can face (cf. Donne, *Aire and Angels*) can only be compared to the morning sun behind a mist or the sun eclipsed in a sudden wayward darkness that threatens disaster to nations and kings. The note of cosmic immensity, thus sounded in expressing the faded satanic grandeur, is carried forward in the image of the thunder-scarred face. Behind is that thoughtful ('considerate', 603) vengeful pride which is biding its time: there is also, for all the cruelty, a glimmer of pained remorse in noting that the partners of his crime – or rather those whom he led into crime ('the fellows . . . the followers rather', 606) – whom he once surveyed in heavenly bliss, should now be condemned to eternal pain, millions deprived ('amerct', 609) of heaven for *his* fault (609), cast out from splendour because of *his* revolt (611), yet standing here 'faithful' before him. The withered glory of the host is like that of oaks burnt and stripped by lightning.

622–669 *Satan addresses the fallen angels and puts new heart into them.*

Satan flatters his listeners. They are 'Matchless' (623) except against God. Who could possibly have anticipated that a force so great as theirs could ever be defeated? (If they reply that anyone might have foreseen it, then they depreciate themselves.) Or who indeed can even now believe that a force like theirs, so great that their ejection from Heaven must have virtually 'emptied' (634) the place, will be incapable in their own strength of recovering their true home? (In fact we know that Satan himself believes the truth he here declares impossible to believe: cf. 245–9.) Having directed attention from himself as possible author of their misery to themselves as virtually undefeatable, Satan now turns God into the object of his followers' anger. God, he implies, was until their rebellion simply upheld by 'old repute/Consent or custom' (639–40). Empty tradition, as it would be called today, alone sustained God's power. God kept up his outward show of royal pomp ('Regal State', 640). He also deceptively (it is implied) concealed the extent of his real strength, thereby leading rebellious-minded angels into temptation ('Which tempted our attempt', 642), and thus himself bringing about their fall. Notice carefully what is being said by Satan. It is first implied that God sat 'secure' (638) on his throne – until the rebellious angels acted – upheld by empty tradition; in short that God's power and authority were bogus. Having pinned bogusness on to God for not being as strong as he pretended to be, Satan now pins deception on to God for always ('still', 641) concealing from them how strong he really was. Within the same sentence God is under fire for falsely displaying strength and falsely concealing strength, and the hinge on which the two contradictions flap noisily in the ear is the worn slogan about 'old repute' utilized in every age. Now, Satan goes on, we know God's power (the falsely displayed power or the falsely concealed power?) and we know our own (the powerlessness Satan has already admitted?) so that we are not likely either to provoke more war (then what is the speech all about?) or to fear more war if it is thrust upon us (643–5). The better plan is to try to achieve by secret planning and deceptive intrigue (646) what force failed to achieve, so that at least God can be taught the lesson that the person who defeats his foe by superior strength alone has only half defeated him.

There follows the first news ('fame', 651 – report) of that new created world, our own. Distantly, as it were, it swims into our view, its favoured inhabitants as the objects of demonic interest. On this hint Satan calls for a full discussion. Since peace is out of the question, for the reason that submission is out of the question, war – whether overt or secret – must be the subject of discussion and resolution.

The fallen angels, victims all to Satan's oratory, acclaim the announcement with drawn swords waving, a clashing of shields, and shouts of anger against God (notice that the use of the word 'rag'd' here, 666, justifies our reading of the contrast between 'rage' and 'Deliberate valour' above, 553–4).

670–798 *Mammon directs the building of Pandaemonium (–751). Satan's heralds summon the fallen angels; they throng to the gates (–776) and the council assembles (–798).*

A band of demons makes for an area where volcanic smoke and the blackened scaly surface ('glossie scurff', 672) give evidence of mineral deposits. They are equipped with spades and pick-axes like a pioneer corps, and they are under the command of Mammon, the least exalted of all the fallen angels, for even in Heaven his thoughts and his head were bent downwards upon the pavement, as he marvelled more at the gold beneath him than at the blessed vision of the Divine. It was Mammon, Milton tells us, who first taught men to abuse their mother Earth by rifling her 'bowels' of 'treasures better hid' (688). One should not be surprised ('Let none admire', 690) to learn that such treasures are to be found in Hell: indeed the soil of Hell is the most appropriate place for a menace so coveted.

Mammon represents an aspect of evil which today we loosely call *materialism*. His mind and heart are set on things below, even in Heaven. As Milton expands his concept of Mammon a new theme is added to that critique of human society and civilization contained in *Paradise Lost*, which, of course, has a significance extending beyond its seventeenth-century application. Milton himself presses home the human relevance of what is happening here in Hell. Let those who boast of human achievements in the field of architecture please note, he says. The most monumental triumphs of human strength and skill (such as the pyramids, for instance, 694) are easily overmatched by worthless devils who, in that direction, can knock up in an hour what it takes numberless human hands an age of toil to construct. The word 'boast' (693) is crucial. It is human boasting, a state of mind, that is under fire: there is no direct denigration of human achievements as such, only a reminder of their proportionate significance within the compass of a vision that surveys things eternal. The vastness of the angelic power and the angelic field of activity, by comparison with the human, and the absurdity of miniscule human pretensions, are laid open momentarily before us.

A second band of devils taps the lake of liquid fire and leads it by sluices to cells where the ore is melted; and a third band channels the molten mass from the cells to moulds where it is shaped and cooled. The process is aptly compared to the feeding of wind into a cluster of organ pipes. The verbal detail here, and the implicit correspondence between constructing a great temple-like building and creating a huge musical fabric of sound together take the mind forward to the cultural achievements prophetically foreseen in Adam's vision (XI. 558–73), and to Michael's judgement upon them (XI. 607–12) as being the work of men who do not acknowledge their Maker's gifts (see pp. 281–2). Milton's direct comparisons here are with the architectural triumphs of idolatrous Babylon and Memphis ('Alcairo', 718, as it later became). The binding together of what is happening in Hell here, and elsewhere in Book I, with what

22

goes wrong in human history as later represented in Book XI is characteristic of the overall unity of *Paradise Lost*. It should scarcely need to be said that, such is the complexity and unity of Milton's design, piecemeal study of individual books of *Paradise Lost* is no more satisfactory than piecemeal study of individual acts of *Othello* would be.

There is no lack of grandeur about the building itself which the devils construct. Its dignity (722), amplitude (725) and general magnificence are impressed upon us, and the multitude, crowding in, marvel at it ('admiring', 731). Milton underlines the point we have already made: the same architect, Mammon, was responsible for many a high structure in Heaven, duly put to healthy angelic use by those exalted princes whose authority is properly exercised within the hierarchical system ordained by God himself. The value of a good building, put to its proper purpose, is thus no more to be depreciated than the assertion of angelic power properly sustained under the divine authority is to be discountenanced.

In order to extend the scope of his historic and cultural inclusiveness, Milton here equates Mammon with the Greek Hephaestus and the Roman Mulciber (or Vulcan) whom Zeus (Jupiter, 'Jove', 741) angrily threw out of Heaven for taking his mother's part in a parental quarrel (Jupiter and Juno). Milton's wording takes us back to Homer's account of the story in the *Iliad*, but he discounts the Olympian legend as a false version of the ejection of the rebel angel whose architectural achievements in Heaven 'availed' (748) him nothing once the rot had entered into him. He and his 'industrious crew' (751) from that point could fitly build in Hell alone.

Milton, inventing a word, calls the new building Pandaemonium (home of all the demons). Satan's heralds (Milton has an aural partiality for the Italianate 'Haralds', 752) announce the forthcoming assembly of 'Satan and his Peers' (757), calling together 'the worthiest' (759) from each band and regiment. The chiefs, each pursued by an enormous retinue, come to Pandaemonium, which of course cannot cope with the crowd. The spacious hall, compared to a 'covered field' (763), enclosed by barriers, for chivalrous encounters between rival champions, the porches, and the gates, are all blocked by the throng. The massing is as thick as the pouring out of bees in spring (the image has a conventionalized epic flavour due to its prior use in Homer and Virgil). But, at a signal, the devils exercise their power to assume what shape they will (cf. 1. 423 ff.), and shrink to minute stature, such as one hears of from travellers who have seen pigmy tribes beyond the Himalayas, or from peasants who have seen (or imagine they have seen) fairy elves in the moonlight. Thus the packed hall accommodates the enormous multitude. But Satan and the great seraphic lords are not reduced in size. 'In their own dimensions' (793) they hold their secret meeting 'far within', a numerous ('frequent', 797) gathering enthroned on golden seats.

Book II

The throne on which Satan sits in state outshines in magnificence the wealth of Ormus, a marketing centre for the traffic in eastern jewels, and of those Oriental capitals where kings at their crowning are powdered with gold dust and have pearls strewn at their feet. Satan deserves to be thus uplifted in the perverse topsy-turvydom of Hell, where the worst will be exalted above the worse. On this pinnacle of badness it seems that he has deceived himself by his own deceptions. Deluded, he no longer faces the fact of despair, but aspires higher. He has learned nothing from the outcome ('success', 9) of his rebellion, and his speech puts on show the conceited fantasies of his ungoverned imagination.

Milton's emphasis on 'proud imaginations' and his use of the word 'displaid' (10) are important. Satan is like the actor who reconstructs himself for every situation as it comes, centring himself and his interests in mid-stage. He then loses himself in each successive role, however contradictory, to the point at which nothing can be received from him as emanating from a stable or coherently developing being. It is questionable whether one ought to speak of Satan's *character*. In a sense there is no satanic character, only a persistent satanic will, bent on evil.

His speech is an exercise in unreality. He addresses the fallen by their unfallen titles, but devils in Hell are no more 'Deities of Heavn' (11) than the contents of the dustbin and the pig-trough are beef-steaks and trifles. Since no depth can put out the spark of life in an immortal being, even when fallen, he does not account Heaven as lost (11–14) – but in fact he has already said farewell to Heaven and accepted Hell (1. 242–63). New fantasies are now to be built on this pre-annihilated premise: first, that the power ('vertue', 15) of celestial being will somehow, when it has re-achieved Heaven, be more glorious and awesome than it would have been had there been no Fall, and that therefore the re-arisen heavenly beings would have such trust in themselves as not to fear a fall again. Aspects of the doctrine of Redemption are here parodied. As the fashioning of the New Man in Christ more than compensates for the fall of the Old Man in Adam, and as therefore the re-arising of man to salvation brings an even richer humanity to Heaven than would have existed had not man fallen and Christ redeemed him, so Satan suggests here that a re-arisen devil will be more glorious and secure than an unfallen angel. But the fall of the angels differs from the fall of man in that no external evil came to tempt Satan as Satan comes to tempt mankind. Moreover man is saved, not in his own power, but by the redeeming act of Christ. Satan's emphasis is upon the capacity of the angels acting in defiance of God, wholly reliant upon their supposed inner independence of being. The words 'trust themselves' (17) make the satanic fallacy plain. They turn upside down the theology of restoration, which is rooted in the necessity for human repentance and divine grace. There can be no equivalent for the fallen angels of the thankful cry, *O felix culpa* (O happy sin – of Eve's transgression) by which man redeemed and restored acknowledges that his last state is better than his first state of innocence (see XII. 469 ff. and p. 299 for the working out of this theme).

Satan claims leadership of the devils under three titles; the 'fixt laws of Heaven' (for which he has no respect), their 'free choice' (how exercised we cannot guess since Satan has admitted that he led them into rebellion, 1. 606), and the fact of his outshining them in council and battle. He sees his throne as safe, because not enviable. No one in Hell will be so foolish as to covet a superiority of status which exposes its occupant to the first shots from God's armoury, and to invite the largest share of any subsequent retribution (he said it was better to reign in Hell than to serve in Heaven, I. 263; now he suggests that it is better to serve in Hell than to reign in Hell). So another principle is formulated. Where there is no good thing to be striven for, the evil strife of competition cannot arise. Satan again manages to bring off the propagandist's trick of assuming an air of moral superiority under the shelter of a slogan (cf. I. 259–60, 641–2, 647–9). There is no one present, he argues cogently, who is so dissatisfied with his meagre helping of immediate discomfort that he will be greedy for more.

Another theme has come full circle. The 'present pain' that is tormenting them all has been proved to be their great 'advantage' (35) in that it secures them in unity and mutual trust such as could not exist in Heaven. The irony gets sharper. The satanic mind is now establishing virtues like 'union, and firm Faith, and firm accord' (36) on the basis of a shared dread of retribution for evil-doing, which makes a mockery of the virtues named. The satanic mind is parodying reason and good sense in every utterance, every phrase. Satan is now talking of returning to claim a 'just inheritance of old' (what price the mockery of the 'old' now? cf. 38 with I. 639) as though he were at the head of a band of suffering martyrs or penitent prodigal sons. At the basis of the new venture and the new confidence lies the absurd pseudo-paradox that there is a surer way of prospering than by prospering (39–40). Nothing succeeds like failure. It remains only to decide which route to failure to adopt.

The description of Moloch already given (I. 392–6), as one who was worshipped with human sacrifice, accords well with the ruthless ferocity registered here, 'now fiercer by despair' (45). Recall the erosive potency of the Spenserian Despair, which totally upsets the mental balance sustained by reason and temperance (*Faerie Queene* I. ix). Moloch must be 'deem'd/Equal in strength with God' (46–7). There is a firm emphasis on 'deem'd'. It is the personal recognition he is after, not the reality. The subjective corruption goes deep. It is not so much that he desires a strength worth having, as that he lusts after the reputational boost that feeds the vanity. To have anything less than this supreme self-recognition is worse than annihilation. Total egocentricity is reached here; and it is marked by total indifference. God, Hell, annihilation – in other words, bliss, misery, being, non-being – are not to be differentiated: they are all equally meaningless if the ego cannot stand at the peak of all evaluation. *That* is why he speaks as he does, Milton tells us ('thereafter', 50 – *accordingly*).

He advises open war ('sentence', 51 – *verdict*). Being less experienced ('unexpert', 52) in 'wiles', he will make no claims in that direction. Beings who need to go in for that kind of contrivance can get on with it as their need arises; but this is not the time for it. For if the schemers settle down to their armchair work, what about the rest of us, the armed millions waiting and longing to get back to the fight? Must they linger imprisoned here in this dark and shameful dungeon, sustaining by their delay the continuing rule of their tyrannical persecutor? It is better to turn the things that torture us to use against our torturer. The vain dream of using the thunder and fire of Hell to consume the throne of God (64–70) presents the objective parallel to Moloch's subjective condition – the lust for supremacy or nothing; the peak of paranoia that leads on earth to padded cells and bunkers under Berlin.

Moloch forestalls a possible objection – that the odds against you are too great when you are making an uphill assault. The natural, easier movement for angels is upwards: downward flight is toilsome. Within the ordered hierarchical universe of medieval cosmology, the natural movement of a thing (its 'proper motion', 75) is towards the place natural to it. A stone will fall downwards through air to earth; fire (flame) will rise upwards through air to regions above. We recall how a state of unnatural disorder in Shakespeare is represented as much by fire coming downwards from heaven (lightning) as by imagery in which stones (the lowest of things) 'rise and mutiny' (*Julius Caesar* III. ii. 232) or assume the character of animate, rational beings far above them and begin to 'prate' (*Macbeth* II. i. 58) of the rebellious regicide's 'whereabout'.

It may seem odd that Milton here should use Moloch thus to remind either the devils or the reader of the proper character of angelhood. But it is appropriate and logical that fallen angels, eroded in thought and being, should have lost, or be in danger of losing, all conception of what true angelhood is. If the essential need of rational man is to know himself (cf. Sir John Davies's *Nosce Teipsum*), how much more requisite is it for the angelic being, higher in the scale of creation, possessing a pure rationality disentangled from the natural and animal affiliations which hamstring human rationality, to know himself.

There is more to be said yet. In reminding the fallen angels of the universal hierarchical principle whereby it is easier for them to rise than to fall, Moloch is appealing to the very principle which his immediate proposal flouts. He is pinning his argument to the regulatory system of due observance of degree; but against that system he is in a state of total rebellion (see 46–7), as his present proposal proves (60–70). The inconsistency of the diabolical mind and the irrationality of evil are of crucial importance in the poem. If we do not fully savour the *badness* of the corrupted intellect in Milton's Hell, we may fail to respond to that heavenly and paradisal Good of the Intellect that is so important in later books of the poem. The negativity of evil is what the poem is about. There is much in the great scenes in the Garden to illustrate and develop the theme of evil corrupting good in terms of God's bounty and man's gifts betrayed and abused. Anticipating those scenes are the scenes in Hell and in Heaven, where we see the corruption of good in terms of reason and intellect abused and eroded, and the corresponding beauty of good in terms of intellect and reason fruitfully exercised.

We return to Moloch's immediate argument. He has proved the ascent easy (81); what else is to be feared – the outcome ('event', 82)? That if we again provoke God he may find some 'worse way' of destroying us? There *can* be nothing worse than this exile from bliss, this condemnation to utter woe where endless torture calls us to penance. One more turn of the tormenting screw, and we should be annihilated. We have nothing to fear because we have nothing to lose, since annihilation is preferable to continuing torment (and, by implication – for Moloch does not linger on the point – torment is better than penance, 92). It appears that we have now learned from successive diabolical voices that it is better to reign in Hell than serve in Heaven, better to serve in Hell than to reign in Hell, better not to exist than to be in Hell at all. The only thing worth being is God. That, or non-being.

Explicitly Moloch concludes that they have reached the worst point short of annihilation and, with a final blast of unreason, argues that by virtue of experience already tasted ('by proof', 101) they feel their power adequate to 'disturb' Heaven and 'alarm' God. The evasive emotive quality of the two words blurs from his hearers the admission of inevitable ineffectiveness in real action which follows: for God's throne is impregnable ('inaccessible'), his sovereignty unshakeable ('fatal', 104).

106–228 *Belial rises (–118), he argues the futility of war against the Almighty (–151) and the dangers of provoking God further (–186). He advises resignation (–208). They must adapt themselves to Hell (–228).*

The previous picture of Belial (1. 490–505) has prepared the reader for something very different from the 'frowning' (106) fury of Moloch. Belial's bearing ('act') is altogether more gracious and courteous ('humane'), but the fair exterior conceals interior emptiness and falsehood. His utterances are so plausible that they can deceive even wise men against their better judgement; but his real thinking is vicious and cowardly. Belial is the representative of debauchery and lust and is therefore outwardly alluring. Nor is there anything bogus about that alluring beauty in itself – for a 'fairer person lost not Heav'n' (110). That the sensuous, assiduously pur-

sued and cultivated (cf. 'to vice industrious', 116), has power
to de-rationalize the mind of even the maturest and the
wisest is the theme of many a poet and thinker. The theme
is directly relevant to the later confrontation between the
fallen Eve and the yet unfallen Adam. Once more Milton is
anticipating at the purely intellectual level what is to happen
at the human level. The study of Belial is relevant to the
study of Eve, not in the puritanical sense that sensuous
beauty and experience are evil, but in the sense that what
goes wrong at the human level, even where culpability is
slight, even where human beings retain great lovableness
and call out the maximum compassion, is after all, in the
Miltonic Christian view, derivative from falsities, which in
their full intensity are rebellious and diabolical. Milton's
power of organization is remarkable. We are being prepared
for Eden all the time.

The first part of Belial's speech seems to answer Moloch
point by point. Being no less hostile to God than Moloch,
he would like him press for open war, were it not that the
main arguments used by Moloch to support his case prove
to be the best of reasons against his case, and indeed create
a most dismal forecast of the outcome (123). The being
whose special excellence lies in feats of arms ('fact of arms',
124 – *en fait d'armes*) has apparently come to the point of
doubting whether anything can be achieved by their use, and
therefore bases his case for their use on despair, advertising
annihilation as the ultimate goal – after some dreadful act of
vengeance. But in fact revenge is out of the question because
of Heaven's impregnability. The watch kept is too strong;
and even if they could let loose all Hell in Heaven, God
would still remain in royal incorruptibility, and the angelic
beings would quickly be healed of any temporary injury or
damage.

The prospect offered, then, is another and final repulse.
We are being urged to irritate God to the point of losing his
temper and finishing us off, Belial says mockingly. That will
put an end to our troubles ('be our cure', 145). But who
would rather lose all power to think or feel or move than

continue to have a mental existence, however painful? And anyway, if annihilation *were* preferable, as Moloch argues, could God grant it? And if he could, would he? Belial doubts whether God could, but he is sure that God wouldn't. The divine wisdom would certainly not falter in a fit of temper so as to give his enemies the very thing they were hoping for – an end to their troubles. If in his anger God has doomed us to endless punishment, he will certainly not in his anger remove that doom.

The warmongers argue that we have nothing to lose, that there can be no worse suffering than we already endure. But here we are, sitting in council, armed. Is not this a good deal better than fleeing in headlong rout from the armoury of Heaven or lying chained on the burning lake? Suppose God were to turn on again the full force of Hell's spouting 'cataracts of Fire' (176). Or suppose (the sarcasm is intensified), while we are sitting here, armchair warriors planning a glorious campaign, a sudden hurricane of fire should fling us out to be impaled on rocks or submerged in the boiling ocean, there to endure a hopeless eternity of groaning misery, deprived of all remission, sympathy, or alleviation ('Unrespited, unpitied, unrepreav'd', 185). That would be far worse.

Belial's verdict is against war, 'open or conceal'd'. Neither force nor intrigue ('guile', 188) can achieve anything, for as you cannot defeat the omnipotent, so you cannot deceive the omniscient. God is even now listening to their discussion with its useless proposals ('motions', 191). He is watching their council with contempt. Almighty, he can defeat their might. All-wise, he can frustrate all their plots (this point destroys in advance Belial's own proposal, which, however cunningly presented, is in its own way a 'plot' and a 'motion vain': see 210 ff.). As for the question whether they must accept, heavenly beings that they are, this cheap downtrodden life of exclusion and torment (194–6): better that than something worse – and anyway they have no alternative, being up against omnipotence. They have a certain measure of strength: they can employ it passively or actively, either in putting up with torment or in renewing battle. The principle behind that balance of alternatives is a just one. It was built into their project from the start, part of the known gamble – if there was any sense at all in taking on so powerful an enemy, the risk being what it was (203).

Belial mocks those who are bold in battle and then, if defeated, become cowardly before the foreseeable penalties of defeat. The Conqueror has passed judgement on them. If they can put up with their punishment, then perhaps God's anger will be relaxed. If they keep quiet in their remote corner, perhaps God's attention will be diverted from them, perhaps he will feel satisfied with what he has already done to them and will fail to keep up the pressure of the torment (the notion of an inattentive God giving them what they want through sheer forgetfulness is, of course, on a par with Moloch's notion – already harshly ridiculed by Belial, 155–9 – of an angry God giving them what they want through sheer bad temper). In that case they could expect the fires to burn lower. Moreover they could expect their own reviving vitalities to resist more effectively the damaging vapours and gradually to become immune to them. The promise held out by Belial is of a slow adaptation of angelic being to its hellish environment. This interesting excursion into evolutionary thinking ends with the picture of fallen angels for whom familiarity with Hell has made Hell more tolerable and adjustment to Hell has rendered Hell less hellish. The prospect of darkness becoming light and horrors ceasing to horrify is dangled before them as part of the hypothetical improvement to come. In conclusion Belial half-commits himself to the doctrine of inevitable progress. There is always the hope that the future will bring a change for the better. By any measure of happiness their present lot is a pretty bad one, but they well know that by any measure of misery they are not quite at rock-bottom: they could be worse off if they were to go out of their way to ask for it.

Milton was right to warn us of Belial's superficial plausibility. His persuasiveness lies in a cunningly varied blend of oratorical idioms and subjective appeals. He employs argument, ridicule, sarcasm, emotive menace, illusive promise, and all the tricks of the persuader's trade.

229–298 Mammon, too, argues that war against God cannot succeed (–237) and that they do not want restoration to Heaven (–249). He urges the establishment of an empire in Hell (–283). The idea appeals to his audience (–298).

Mammon opens his speech with an apparent sharpness of cut-and-thrust logic which disarms listeners. There could be but two conceivable purposes for renewing the war – either to dethrone God or to re-establish ourselves in Heaven. God cannot be dethroned, so the first purpose cannot be achieved. That being so, the alternative purpose cannot be achieved either, since so long as God remains undefeated there can be no place for us in Heaven. Mammon brushes aside the hypothetical third possibility that they might get back through God's relenting rather than through their defeating him. The prospect of accepting his pardon in exchange for a promise of 'new subjection' on their part is held up for ridicule and disdain. How could they humble themselves anew in his presence, submit to his laws again, and tune up their voices in compulsory worship, while he sits there smugly enjoying their servility (239–46)? They must not strive to get by force what force cannot win. They must not try to recover that condition of magnificent slavery in Heaven, which, if they got it by God's permission, they certainly would not want. Rather let them seek their 'own good' for themselves (253), living their own lives on their own basis, free and accountable to none, preferring liberty in harsh conditions to slavery in splendid and pretentious ones (257).

They will prove their greatness by tackling their wholly disadvantageous situation and making something positive and productive out of it. Wherever you are, you can by 'labour and endurance' turn what is bad to good account. Why should they fear Hell's darkness? Even God almighty in Heaven often chooses to wrap his glory and majesty around with a veil of darkness. If the darkness of Hell is simulated in Heaven, why should not the light of Heaven be simulated in Hell? There is no lack of mineral wealth hidden under the soil of Hell; and they have the skill and knowledge required to exploit it in construction of buildings that could match Heaven's in magnificence (273).

In conclusion Mammon reiterates Belial's argument that the passage of time may familiarize them to the environment of Hell, its pains becoming endurable through their habituation to them and through the adaptation of their own machinery of sensibility. Everything points to a policy of peace, establishment of order, and consideration of how best to tackle the immediate problems while realistically acknowledging their situation.

Mammon's speech is fully in line with the account of him given in Book I (678-88). As the one who seems to embody aspects of materialism familiar to us, it is interesting that he throws off glib slogans that we are tempted to swallow (e.g. 'Hard liberty' rather than 'servile pomp', 256-7) and mocks the things about Heaven we ourselves want to mock (e.g. endless compulsory hymn-singing). No less does he ridicule notions of God that our own age never tires of ridiculing (the comfortably enthroned deity sniffing up the incense of adoration). It all makes us feel rather uncomfortable, if we are sensitive readers. We begin to shift in our seats. What is Milton getting at? How subtle, how ironical is he? Why does Belial sound to us like a twentieth-century professor (146-51) and Mammon like a current radical theologian (239-54)?

It would be a mistake to think that Milton ever forgets what he is doing. We shall see later how, in design and shape, as well as in substantial detail, the debate in Hell parodies the corresponding debate in Heaven. Meantime one should scrutinize the text here with care. Mammon's talk of the 'greatness' of making 'great', 'useful' and 'prosperous' things out of 'small', 'hurtful' and 'adverse' things respectively, and of how they may 'thrive under evil' and 'work ease out of pain' (257-61) should be pondered. Milton has been careful to use a series of emotive terms that fog clear thinking. 'Great' over against 'small' is not good over against evil, nor is 'useful' over against 'hurtful', nor is 'prosperous' over against 'adverse', nor is 'ease' over against 'pain'. There is no evaluative moral term here, only a series of rather ignoble preferences for bigness, utility, prosperity and ease, as against what is small or what is in various ways uncomfortable. The give-away phrase amid this blur of pseudo-antitheses is, of course, 'Thrive under evil' (261). This is the one aim and desire no just being can conceivably have – to *thrive* under evil.

Milton brings Belial to the point of recommending that the fallen should come to terms with Hell and settle down in it, and Mammon to the point of recommending that they should build there a rival empire, a secular civilization ignoring the kingdom of Heaven. Each of the two has to buttress his case with a significant recourse to temporal thinking, both laying emphasis on the hypothetical future (221–3 and 274–5).

The murmur of approval which greets Mammon's speech is associated with lingering rumbles of wind after a violent and exhausting storm. The fallen angels, the tempest of battle behind them, are like seafarers worn out with a sleepless night of struggle against the elements. The humanizing touch presses deeply. If men and devils are linked in dread of thunder and sword, are they not linked, too, in the desire to build a 'nether Empire' in emulation 'opposite to Heav'n' (298)?

299–416 Beelzibub rises (–309). He mocks the peace policies of the last two speakers (–335). Continued struggle is inevitable (–340). It could take the form of some kind of assault on the newly created Earth (–378). The proposal meets with approval (–389), and Beelzibub asks who shall undertake the dangerous first journey to the Earth (–416).

We have already met Beelzibub (1. 84 ff.) as Satan's 'next Mate' (1. 238), his 'bold Compeer' (1. 127), next to Satan 'in power, and next in crime' (1. 79), who in Heaven outshone the bright myriads (1. 86–7) and was so united with Satan in the planned rebellion as to share equality of hope and risk (i. 88–9). In the gospels Beelzibub is called the 'prince' or 'chief' of the devils. The name appears to mean 'lord of the flies'. In the fine visual portrayal here, Milton's emphasis is on the ruin of what has been mighty and majestic. We are to learn later that Beelzibub has already collaborated with Satan in planning the debate and pre-arranging its outcome (ii. 379–85 and 466–73). His task is not an easy one because, though we were not told how the audience reacted to the speech of Moloch, the 'hawk', the two 'doves', Belial and Mammon, have won a sympathetic response for the peace policy and left a great sense of relief behind.

The picture of Beelzibub's slow rising, gravity of expression, and dignity of bearing (300–9) must not be considered in isolation. If Beelzibub's face shines with 'Princely counsel' (304), it is while he is about to plead his 'devilish Counsel' (379). In his rising he may have 'seem'd' (301, *sic*) a pillar of state, but his intention turns out to be absurdly negative (370–6), and his introductory performance cannot be taken seriously. Beelzibub knows the tricks of the trade (as Milton had good reason to know them from his parliamentary experience). Audience-reaction begins from the moment the speaker begins to rise from his seat. The sage elder-statesman act works beautifully, for 'his look/Drew audience and attention' (307–8).

Beelzibub rings off the former titles of the unfallen angels and then catches the devils on the hook – Or do you now want to exchange these titles and be called 'Princes of Hell'? Either they must say to themselves, Yes, we do, or they must move out of the mood that the two previous speakers have induced in them. Thus Beelzibub mocks them for apparently wanting to be styled by such a low title as 'Princes of Hell' (313) and the next moment mocks them for imagining that God will allow them to have any status so comfortable as princedom in Hell. The double sting of the sarcasm bites too quickly for the *non sequiturs* to be sorted out. It is a fantastic dream for them to forget that they are in a 'dungeon' (317: then why first flatter them with their former titles?) and can choose to 'exempt' (318) themselves from God's imposed penalty ('high juridiction', 319) of 'strictest bondage' (321: then why mock them for wanting to renounce their former titles, 312?). They have no freedom of decision of movement, being held under an 'inevitable curb' (322) as a 'captive multitude' (323) by a God who, 'be sure,/In highth or depth, still first and last will Reign/Sole King' (323–5). But if God's sovereignty is so wholesale, what is the point of the proposal about to be made? Beelzibub's speech is the usual patchwork of successive inconsistencies and falsehoods.

God will lose no part of his kingdom by their revolt (325–6), Beelzibub continues. Hell will be as much within his empire as Heaven, iron rule matching golden rule. They have no choice as between peace and war. War has already frustrated them irreparably (330–1), and peace is not available: no one has offered it, no one has sued for it. Enslaved as they are they can expect no peace, only punishment; and grant no peace, only hostility and rejection to the limits of their power. But – we may well ask Beelzibub – if the enslavement is as total as he proclaims, how can their 'Untam'd reluctance' (337 – emotive blur-words again) breed 'revenge', however 'slow' (337)? Beelzibub, of course, is now effecting the *non sequitur* he has castigated his predecessors for employing. He is moving from emphasis on impotence to a proposal of action which impotence renders unavailing in advance. 'Revenge' has somehow been conjured out of 'reluctance', and now 'plotting' is made to produce imaginary results. But the plotting of the impotent and the incarcerated is as powerless to affect the sole-ruling, eternally reigning deity (324 ff.) as are all those alternative proposals which Beelzibub has ridiculed. To blur his way through, Beelzibub now cunningly lays his emphasis, not on an objective result achieved, but upon God's subjective response to what will happen anyway. They cannot deny God his conquest, but they can plot how least he may 'reap' it and how least rejoice in their sufferings.

There will be no lack of opportunity (341), Beelzibub argues, having now effected the blurred transition whereby 'plotting' (338) begins to connote carrying out a plan rather than just conceiving it. There will be no need for any 'dangerous expedition' (342) such as invading Heaven (cf. the coming emphasis on the immense dangers of the proposal he eventually makes, 404 ff.). So direct attack upon Heaven, after being ruled out by Beelzibub as impossible (330), is now being argued out as 'dangerous'. He recommends an 'easier enterprize', knowing how well his words will fit the mood of his audience (see 291–5). The devils, as they ponder the 'danger' of the 'perilous attempt' (420–1) a few moments later, can be relied upon to have forgotten that they were induced to vote for it as an 'easier enterprize' (345).

Beelzibub unfolds the plan to damage God's newly created race 'call'd *Man*' (348). Satan has already hinted at this design (I. 650–6) and we are to be soon reminded that only Satan could have conceived a plan so devilish (II. 380–5). As Beelzibub's phrase 'prophetic fame' (346) takes us back mentally to Satan's prior reference to the 'new Worlds; whereof so rife/There went a fame in Heav'n' (I. 650), so Milton's cunning use here of the highly charged word 'seat' (347) takes us back mentally to the opening of the book with its summary of the main substance of the poem in terms of 'loss of *Eden*' and the ultimate regaining of the 'blissful Seat' (I. 4–5). The network of verbal links shows a careful craftsman at work, who is conscious of the unity of his own design. The subject proposed at the beginning of the poem remains at the centre of his thinking. The reader's eyes are intermittently cast upwards from Hell to Earth as later they are to be cast downwards from Heaven to Earth, for it is on the Earth that the conflict is to be played out.

That Beelzibub should describe God's new creatures as 'less' than the angels in 'power and excellence' (350) is no doubt just ('What is man, that thou art mindful of him? . . . For thou hast made him a little lower than the angels, and hast crowned him with glory and honour.' Psalm VIII. 4–5); that he should speak of man as 'favour'd' by God also does justice to the psalmist's words; but that Beelzibub should throw in the word 'more' ('favour'd more/Of him who rules above') adds just such a touch of diabolical perversion as we now expect from Milton's fallen angels. The word makes God sound irrational (favouring the inferior being) and partial.

That God's creation of the world and man was confirmed 'by an Oath/That shook Heav'ns whole circumference' brings the great supernatural act into line with the decisive supernatural decrees of Classical epic. It is thus that Homer's Zeus and Virgil's Jupiter make the whole of Olympus reverberate to their nod ('adnuit, et totum nutu tremefecit Olympum', *Aeneid* ix. 106). But the reader should note that the image has a more immediate impact than that caused by the epic associations. As his eye looks up from Hell to Earth, it is a fine touch that at the same time brings to his ears the reverberations of a decision first trumpeted in Heaven. As 'all our thoughts' (354), under Beelzibub's guidance, 'bend' towards the Earth, it is appropriate that the pointing diabolical finger should be accompanied by the distant rumbling of the divine Voice.

The plan is to learn the characters of the new creatures, what capacities they are endowed with ('endu'd', 356), and whether it will be better to assault or to seduce them (358). The suggestion that God, though sitting comfortably 'secure', keeping his gates firmly shut against diabolical invasion (358–60), may nevertheless have left this new world dangerously 'expos'd' on the periphery of his kingdom, is calculated to smear God's image with insinuations of greater concern for self-protection than for the defence of his creatures (362). But recall that a moment ago God was being smeared by Beelzibub for favouring these same creatures *in excess* of their due status (350–1).

Beelzibub's proposal is either to lay waste the new world with Hell fire and give the new race a taste of the violent expulsion from bliss that they themselves have just experienced; or so to seduce them to share their own rebellion that God may turn in anger against his own creatures and, regretting their creation, destroy them. This would constitute a novel mode of revenge in that God's present joy in the casting out of evil from Heaven would be broken (371–2) by a new worry, and the joy of the devils consequently increased by the 'disturbance' (373) of the divine happiness and composure. No small disturbance, to see the 'darling Sons' (373), the members of the new race, cast into Hell and cursing the frailty of their first parents ('their frail Originals', 375). The forward-casting of the mind here, through the word 'darling', to the future reign of Sin upon the Earth (II. 868–70) and the implicit correspondence between men, the sons of God, and Sin, the daughter of Satan ('thy daughter and thy darling', II. 870), is another instance of Milton's careful planting of key words. The vastness of the effects to arise from the 'devilish Counsel' here proposed is present to the mind both in the implicit forecast of the reign of Sin and in the implicit image of the human family tree involved in the fall of the 'one root' (383), Adam. We see 'Earth with Hell' together entangled, and the whole scheme, growing before our eyes, is 'done all to spite/The great Creator' (385). Fortunately diabolical spite always operates but to increase the divine glory (385–6) (for more on 'spite' see p. 241). As for Adam, the angel Raphael is to give him fair warning of what is here being plotted against him (VI. 900–12).

Beelzibub's proposal meets with general approval and is adopted. Whereupon Beelzibub feels free to dangle before his audience's mind the kind of delusive hopes which he formerly sarcastically castigated them for cherishing – hopes of perhaps getting back nearer to their 'ancient Seat' (394), maybe to a new residence with sight of Heaven's boundaries, near enough perchance to snatch some opportune moment for slipping back inside Heaven (how fiercely he has previously insisted on the impossibility of so doing! – 327–8, 343–4, 358–9). Or perhaps they may find a new residence within range of the light and healing air of Heaven. The emphasis on 'soft delicious Air' (400) breathing balm no doubt appeals eloquently to beings in the grip of 'corrosive Fires' (401).

Finally Beelzibub puts the question, 'Whom shall we send/ In search of this new world?' (403). The stress is on the hazards of the journey, on the resources required to test ('tempt', 404) the bottomless abyss, to find a way through the unknown ('uncouth', 407) yet tangible blackness ('palpable obscure', 406), to carry one's weight over the wearisomely vast gulf ('abrupt', 409) between Hell and the world; and then on the power and ingenuity ('art', 410) or subtlety ('evasion', 411) needed to penetrate the thick outposts of angelic guards watching over the world. The 'happy Ile' (410 – that is, the whole universe as it hangs in the void) seems remote and small indeed when its picture is dangled tantalizingly among the images of perils so immense and strange. The reader's sympathies reach out compassionately towards it. And the contrast between its smallness and its centrality in the whole drama, the immensity of its importance, is powerful. But the minds of the devils are working otherwise than ours. Beelzibub has scarcely need now to stress how careful they must be in selecting the right person to carry the burden of all their hopes for escape.

417–505 *None dares to offer to undertake the exploratory journey to the world till Satan rises (–429). He stresses the dangers of the journey, then offers to go himself (–456). He then puts an end to the discussion (–473) and the council is dissolved, the devils rejoicing humbly in their leader (–496). The poet draws a moral for man from this unity of the devils (–505).*

Sitting down, Beelzibub stares about him with a look of suspended anticipation. The devils are impressed by the account of the likely dangers of the journey, and see in one another's eyes signs of the shared dread. They are 'mute' (420, a Miltonic key word: see p. 242) and they are stunned ('Astonisht', 423). None is bold enough to undertake the lonely venture, though in fact they are the very 'choice and prime' (423) of champions who have presumed to wage war against Heaven itself.

Satan arises and addresses the fallen angels by their lost heavenly titles, noting their 'silence', but kindly labelling

their hesitation 'demurr', not dismay (431-2). He underlines
how long and hard the journey will be in words that echo
Virgil. The associative link is a notable one, for the Sibyl is
warning Aeneas how easy is the descent into the Underworld,
but how arduous and toilsome the return –

> 'sed revocare gradum superasque evadere ad auras,
> hoc opus, hic labor est.'
>
> *(Aeneid* VI. 128-9)

The imagery by which we learn here again, from Satan's lips
this time, of the hellish environment, might be criticized for
being vague, confused, imprecise, in its appeal to the senses;
but clearly it would be wrong to attack it for failing to do
what Milton had no wish to do. Unlike Dante's Hell,
Milton's Hell is a pre-human Hell. It has no former human
beings inhabiting it. One of Milton's aims appears to be to
keep it out-of-bounds in respect of normal human responses
to what can be seen, felt, smelt or savoured by ordinary
human experience. The environment of Hell must have
neither the familiarity nor the ready conceivability of that to
which human senses and sensibilities readily respond, of that
which the mind aptly cottons on to. One of the characteristics of Milton's Hell (in fact it would be better to say
non-characteristics, or by some other verbal device clinch the
notion that, like the 'characters' of the devils, the 'character'
of Hell is to be chaotically characterless in terms of what is
recognizable by the machinery of human response and con-
ceptualization operating as it does in daily life) is its disorder,
its juxtapositioning of irreconcilables, its non-categorical
mingling of categories. This is the right environment for the
intellectual chaos of irrationality which the debate reveals.

Thus words which suggest the scenic, 'huge convex'
(vault, 434) are unfittingly juxtaposed with terms incongru-
ously appropriate to tactile experience 'of Fire' (434); terms
of the clearly picturable like 'gates' have their clarity immediately cancelled out by the qualification 'of burning
Adamant'. The process of confusing and overwhelming
the machinery of literary response is surely intentional.

43

'Outrageous to devour' (435) is a phrase that introduces the note of an irresistibly savage threat more bestial than scenic, while 'immures' (435) and 'Barr'd' (437) introduce the association of physical imprisonment and of frustration. The conscious design to confuse the senses and discomfort the mind is intensified as the environment of Hell is exchanged for what one would like to call the non-environment of Chaos. Thus, here, as Satan anticipates the journey through Chaos, the vocabulary takes a further leap into the listing of the uncategorizable. It will be a journey through the deep nothingness ('void profound', 438) of substanceless ('unessential', 439) Night, yawning (like monstrous jaws) to receive the would-be traveller, with the menace of annihilating submergence in the vast womb which does not create, but aborts.

Satan professes it his duty to accept the perils as well as the authority, dignity and responsibility ('sov'ranty . . . splendor . . . power', 446–7) of leadership. (Note the emphatic, egocentric 'Me' of 1.450. Milton has used the identical device already, II. 18. Contrast these arrogant satanic pronouns with the fourfold self-sacrificial 'mee' of the Son's corresponding offer in the council in Heaven, III. 236–8 (see p. 77).) His acceptance of superior status and power duly obliges him to accept comparably more testing trials. The challenge thus briefly accepted, Satan tersely dismisses the devils with an over-polite throwaway compliment ('Terror of Heav'n', 457) scarcely earned by their dismal showing when a volunteer was called for. Consider ('intend', 457) at home (the best place no doubt for such unadventurous spirits – for a lot may be read into Satan's choice of words here as elsewhere, a lot detected in the tone of voice suggested by Milton's metrical music) how best to reduce our misery here so as to make Hell endurable. Seek out whatever medicinable devices there may be to provide mitigations of misery, distraction from it ('deceive', 461 – to beguile into forgetfulness), or alleviation of pain. Preserve a continuous watch against the enemy ('intermit no . . .', 462 – double negative). These brief orders given, Satan takes the whole enterprise upon his shoulders alone, and quickly rises, fore-stalling ('prevented', 467) any possible come-back. He takes this precaution (is 'Prudent', 468) because he does not want others, under the impetus of his own determination, to offer now to accompany him, thus (since they would know their offer sure to be declined) earning cheaply a reputation for courage comparable to his own, without having to undergo the trials that would justify it (467–72).

The devils, however, stand just as much in awe of Satan's forbidding voice as they do of the adventure he is under-taking. They rise, and we hear once more the reverberation of distant thunder as another act of supernatural decisiveness (and immense consequence for the human race) is signalled (cf. II. 352). They perform their ritual act of praise and worship before him, as do the angels before God in Heaven. And there is an element of good in this, Milton reminds us, in that they are actually praising courage. Damned spirits do not lose all their 'virtue' – all good, in the sense of their positive efficacy (indeed, if they did, as we have already argued, they would be non-existent). Milton's purpose in inserting the reminder here seems to be the didactic one of preventing his human readers, after savouring the full evil of Hell, from indulging a detached feeling of comfortable moral superiority to the devils. Thus he reminds us how bad men boast of apparently courageous deeds, which are the product of desire for reputation, or of ulterior lust for self-aggrandizement that masquerades as enthusiasm.

The unified rejoicing, however, strikes a refreshing note after the muddled and murky argument in council, so re-freshing that Milton records it with a fine extended rural simile (488–95). And having so changed the key, he abruptly shifts through a new modulation to turn in prophetic anger on the wickedness of men. Even devils in Hell can reach agreement. As for men, while God proclaims peace ('God proclaiming peace', 499 – a syntactical Latinism; cf. *God willing*), they hate and fight one another. The irony, as well as the wickedness of internecine human hatred and warfare lies in the vivid evidence the poet has just given us of the

strength and number and virulence of man's external supernatural foes who plan his destruction. This fact in itself
ought to unite us in harmony ('induce us to accord', 503).

506–628 *The decision of the demonic council is publicly announced
and acclaimed* (–520). *The demons disband to occupy themselves,
until Satan's return, in various activities – athletics and feats of
arms* (–546), *music* (–555), *philosophical discussion* (–569), *and
exploration of Hell* (–628).

Satan leads out his chief counsellors with a pomp imitative
of the ceremonies of Heaven (511). A compact band ('globe',
512 – Latin *globus*) of seraphim encloses him around with
colourful heraldry ('imblazonrie', 513) and bristling
('horrent') arms. ('Of their Session ended', 514 – another
instance of a Latin construction anglicized; as in the phrase
construction anglicized.) After the proclamation of the council's
decision, and its generally favourable reception, the minds of
the assembled leaders are relieved, and they are heartened
a little by false hope. They disperse, and then individually
attach themselves to others for group activities which seem
most likely to set their bewildered thoughts at rest and while
away ('entertain', 526) the tedious time till Satan returns.

That there are accounts of mass sports and games in both
Homer and Virgil comparable to what follows here lends a
formal epic character to Milton's description. Perhaps most
interesting is the specific verbal echo of Virgil in the dupli-
cate use of the word 'Part' (528 and 531) and in the emphatic
word 'contend' (529) –

> '*pars* in gramineis exercent membra palaestris,
> *contendunt* ludo et fulva luctantur harena;
> *pars* pedibus plaudunt choreas et carmina dicunt.'
>
> (*Aeneid* VI. 642–4)

Though Virgil is here describing the activities of souls in
Elysium, the allusion is significant because the guiding
Sibyl's warning to Aeneas has already been echoed from the
same book (see p. 43). The passage we are here dealing with
is rich in Classical allusions of many kinds. Book VI of the
Aeneid will be recalled again (577 ff.).

As some of the devils contend in aeronautics, uplifted ('sublime', 528) by their wings, others have races like those at the ancient Greek athletic festivals, the Olympic games and the Pythian games held at Delphi in honour of Apollo. There are chariot races as well as mock battles. The more violent demons tear up rocks and hills and 'ride the Air/In whirlwind' (540–1). Notice that the comparisons with the great Grecian festivals have left behind such a flavour of the heroic and the civilized that it is thus desirable to remind the reader of the massive savageries of which these beings are capable – and in particular of their destructive preternatural habits – in an idiom that calls to mind the activities of witches and works of demonology. The story of Hercules ('Alcides', 542) receiving from his wife Deianira a robe dipped in what she believed to be a love-potion, intended to restore him to her, but was in fact a poison that burnt his flesh in agony, has been a favourite with our poets from Shakespeare (*Antony and Cleopatra* IV. xiii. 43) to T. S. Eliot (*Little Gidding* IV: see *Word Unheard* p. 168 ff.). Hercules took the unfortunate Lichas (545) who had brought the robe to him, and hurled him into the sea. Then he climbed Mount Oeta (545) and immolated himself.

Devils of a milder disposition withdraw into a valley and sing their 'own heroic deeds' and tragic fall, romanticizing them with false laments over how the force of destiny overpowers independence and courage. The substance is prejudiced but the music is ravishing. Sweeter even than this music (for music appeals but to the senses, while meaningful eloquence speaks to the soul) is the discourse of those who retire, not to the sheltered valley, but to the hill, there to lift their minds to the higher things and argue over the great doctrinal issues thrashed out in academic controversy. They cover the well-worn ground – whether the doctrine of divine providence and omniscience is reconcilable with creaturely freewill, for instance – and lose themselves in the customary circularities and paradoxes (559–61). They then argue on the character of good and evil, of happiness and misery, and on suffering and stoic detachment ('Passion and Apathie', 564)

47

and the rival claims of what seems to lead to glory and what seems to lead to shame. All this philosophical discussion is vain and false. Of course it is, since it is carried on by devils in Hell who have forfeited the right to bandy 'good' and 'evil' at the conceptual level by virtue of their prior and total commitment to evil. It does not mean that the Milton who wrote, 'How charming is divine Philosophy' in *Comus* (476–80) has changed his mind. In any case the philosophical discussion referred to here (II. 562–5) is non-theological and is thereby to be distinguished both from the doctrinal discussion described above (II. 555–61), which is 'discourse . . . sweet' (555) and the '*divine* Philosophy' applauded in *Comus*, where the subject is the praise of 'saintly Chastity'. In Milton's eyes there would appear to be a lot of difference between theology and secularized philosophy. Quite apart from that, there is no virtue in discussion itself, however lofty the topic, if the discussion is motivated by a desire to blind yourself to realities of what you are actively involved in when that involvement is wholly evil in purpose. Even so the dangerous power of philosophical discussion remains: it can delude the mind and the emotions (–569).

Other demons go off in small detachments and dense companies ('Squadrons and gross Bands', 570) to explore the geography of Hell, in the hope that there may be climatically more comfortable areas to dwell in. They go in four different directions, following the course of the rivers of Hell, named as in the topography of Virgil's Underworld: Styx, the river of hatred; Acheron, the river of sorrow; Cocytus, of wailing; and Phlegethon, of burning. Far away from these is the fifth river, Lethe, the river of forgetfulness. (Once more the direct indebtedness to *Aeneid* Book VI emerges.) The frozen waste beyond Lethe, for ever beaten with storm and whirlwind, hail and snow, as treacherous as the Serbonian Bog (Lower Egypt) which once swallowed up part of an invading Persian army (592–4), is another area in which the torments of frost and fire are paradoxically conjoined, the extremes alternately intensifying the agony.

It looks as though Milton is casting his eyes forward and

thinking of damned human beings when he tells how 'all the damn'd' (597) are brought intermittently to the torments of this region and are ferried backwards and forwards across the Lethean strait ('Sound', 604), but are prevented from reaching Lethe itself, one drop of whose waters of forgetfulness would be enough to soothe their minds with oblivion. The gorgon Medusa, the sight of whose face would turn a man to stone, stands guard over the river (cf. *Aeneid* vi. 290–2); in any case the water itself flees human lips as it fled the lips of the tormented Tantalus, punished by Zeus, who placed him in a lake in such a position that a bunch of grapes hanging above him and the water beneath him each swayed out of his reach as he grasped or bent to satisfy hunger or thirst.

Thus, for the first time ('first', 617), the demons inspect their allotted environment, whose miserable character Milton sums up in a passage which is both descriptively powerful (618–21) and philosophically apt (622–8). The place is in all respects the opposite of the world. As a 'Universe of death', it was 'Created evil' (623) – a self-contradictory phrase, as Milton, well read in St Augustine, must have intended it to be. After its shock use, Milton glosses the phrase, 'for evil only good'. All that God creates is good: all God's creativity is good: the making of this place is good in that it is good for evil (which God did *not* create) to have it to dwell in as its appropriate place (its allotment, for 'lot', 617, is a carefully chosen word), a place not so much of this or that quality as of all qualities confused, and therefore of *no* quality; a place whose character (or rather *characterlessness*) can best be represented by saying that 'all life dies' there and 'death lives' (624). Milton is representing an environment of dis-creation matching the condition of the satanic mind and personality. It is a place where 'nature' (and the connotation of the word is that of abundant and ceaseless fertility) 'breeds' only in the perverted sense that wholly *unnatural* freaks ('monstrous . . . prodigious . . . abominable . . . inutterable . . .') issue from it. This placeless place of unnatural nature and characterless

49

character, strictly non-created by an act of non-creativity ('by curse', 622) is Hell. We ought to stretch our brains to the maximum to try to catch up with Milton's vision. We have our twentieth-century imaginative explorations of the paradoxical and the absurd, even our contemporary literary attempts to clinch notions of total meaninglessness or negativity. And though, admittedly, most of these must seem rather tame when they are put alongside Milton's Hell, they will at least help us to get to grips with certain aspects of Milton's excursions into the joint descriptive-and-philosophical representation of Hell, its functionless functions, its death-dealing life, its negative productiveness, and its meaning rooted in meaninglessness.

629–726 Satan sets out and reaches the gates of Hell (–648). There he meets Sin (–666) and Death (–680), whom he challenges (–687). Death's reply is hostile (–703) and the two prepare for combat (–722), but Sin intervenes (–726).

Satan's solitary flight is first described in exploratory images as he scours the limits to either side, skims ('shaves') the depths and soars to the heights (631–5). The picture of an East Indian trading fleet spied from a great distance adds – by the remoteness of England from the Oriental marketing centres named (638–9) and the vastness of the shipping routes (641) – to the sense of Satan's strange and adventurous isolation. A quick mental switch is effected as a far-sailing fleet on the wide open sea gives place to ninefold gates of brass, iron and rock, before which sits Sin.

Milton's picture of Sin recalls Spenser's Error –

> 'Halfe like a serpent horribly displaide,
> But th'other halfe did womans shape retaine'

from whom there breed

> 'A thousand young ones, which she dayly fed
> Sucking upon her poisonous dugs.'
> (*Faerie Queene* I. i. 14–15)

Like Spenser's, Milton's purpose is to exploit the symbolic potential of a being who has a deceptively attractive side, but who in reality is incessantly breeding and nourishing horrible multiplications of her nastiness. The common origin of the two pictures is the Classical descriptions of the monster Scylla in Virgil (*Aeneid* III. 424 ff.) and Ovid (*Metamorphoses* XIII. 730 ff. and XIV), as Milton here testifies (659–61). It is Ovid who tells how Circe, in jealousy, threw magic herbs into the sea where Scylla bathed (660) and transformed her into a monster. The allusion to the 'Night Hag' who comes 'riding through the Air' and delights in 'infant blood' (662–4) brings associations of witchcraft and black magic to bear upon an already packed cluster of horrors.

The symbolic figure of Death is drawn to fit a comparably allegoric motive, and is reminiscent of Spenser.

> '*Death* with most grim and griesly visage seene,
> Yet is he nought but parting of the breath;
> Ne ought to see, but like a shade to weene,
> Unbodied, unsoul'd, unheard, unseen.'
>
> (*Faerie Queene*, VII. vii. 46)

The negative insubstantiality of death, with its black mystery, its terrors, and its menace, is sharply summed up in one of Milton's most concentrated descriptive studies. As one notes the crucial final Miltonic touch – that Death wears the 'likeness of a Kingly Crown' – one is confronted again with that insistence upon inextricably blending description or narrative with theology, which demonstrates the tight yet ranging economic unity of imagination and thought. Like other kingly crowns, this one is a borrowed, a spurious, an illusory one. The one kingly crown belongs to the sovereign who has defeated death (XII. 420–1). Death's sovereignty may look pretty frightening, even tangible, at the ninefold gates of Hell. But there are forces against which even those gates shall not prevail.

Satan addresses Death with scorn as a 'hell-born' (687) being who would be foolish to undergo the painful experience of learning not to obstruct 'Spirits of Heaven'. But Death recognizes Satan as the leader who gathered rebel angels together in conspiracy ('conjur'd' – sworn together,

693) against God. He mocks the defeated Satan as 'Hell-doomed', no longer to be reckoned among the 'Spirits of Heaven' (696) but rather under *his* dominion – for Death himself claims the sovereign lordship of Hell (698–9).

In his anger Death – who comes in many shapes and strikes in many different ways – grows ten times more awesome and hideous ('deform', 706). Over against him the incensed Satan stands ready for combat with the terrifying cosmic stature of a burning comet whose trailing fire threatens pestilence and war to nations and men (711). The correspondence is an apt one, and the feel of a war-torn universe, of cosmos and kingdom in strife, is carried forward in the imagery of clashing clouds in the sky and clashing armies beneath, all compressed into the Miltonic shorthand ('Heavn's Artillery . . . rattling on . . . front to front . . . signal . . . dark Encounter', 715–18). That they stand so equally 'matcht' (720) intensifies the suspense. Never 'but once more' (721), Milton adds, is either likely to meet 'so great a foe' (722). That foe will be Christ. But the combat is forestalled, for Sin rushes between them (see IV. 985 ff., where Satan confronts Gabriel, prepared again for a combat which is forestalled).

727–870 *Sin calls Satan father and Death his son (–734). Satan pauses, astonished (–745). Sin recalls her birth (–761), the birth of their son, Death (–789), and of the monstrous progeny of Death and herself (–809). Then she warns Satan of Death's power (–814). Satan explains his mission to Sin (–839), and promises Sin and Death a share in its fruits (–849). Sin agrees to co-operate (–870).*

The words in which Sin addresses Satan ('O Father . . . thy only Son', 727–8) parody the language of Heaven. The blasphemy intensifies Sin's ironic mockery of Satan in pointing out that he is in danger of starting a quarrel in his own family, which can only bring joy and laughter to God. Sin sharpens the torment in Satan's mind to the maximum by stressing that God has 'ordain'd' him 'his drudge' (732), thus bitingly blending the stately word 'ordain', used of promotion to high civil office in Milton's time, and the scullery word, 'drudge'. In the eyes of Sin God's execution of justice is the indulgence of bad temper (732–3).

In reading this passage, we recall how often in literature the tables are turned by a sudden discovery of an unexpected relationship. The discoveries of family relationships at the end of Elizabethan plays like *The Winter's Tale* and *Pericles, Prince of Tyre* are instances of joyful conclusions, matching, in their various ways, the climactic re-establishment of the family of three (father, mother and son) at the end of the *Odyssey*. Considered in this context the Satanic family reunion is hilarious. Was ever creature faced by the sudden discovery of relations such as these? In all the age-long recounting of fatherhoods revealed in a flash of drama, lost daughters hurled into the arms of astonished warriors, unanticipated sons presented to amazed and grateful parents, and long-mourned wives coming home to share memories of early days of love, is there anything which does not help by contrast to give a laughable flavour to Satan's face-to-face meeting with his long-lost daughter, one-time mistress, and unimagined son by incest – not to mention the grandchildren (if that is the right term) which their too intimate, over-devoted family affections have produced?

That is one aspect of Satan's encounter with the least personable family that ever hero or warrior was asked to acknowledge for his own. It is not surprising that he does not mince his words. He never 'saw till now/Sight more detestable' (744–5). There is not a glimmer of recognition. He declares this their first meeting (742) and wants to know, contemptuously, 'What thing' (741) Sin is.

He learns. She recalls how she was born out of the head of Satan when the rebellion was planned in Heaven. The birth matches that of the goddess Athene who sprang from the head of Zeus. Classical and medieval traditions are blended once more. For as Scylla and Athene are in the background of Milton's thinking, so too are Spenser's Error and Death. And the detailed allegorical thinking that associates the birth of Sin from the head of Satan with the origin of disobedience and rebellion in the mind of Satan is as clearly in line with medieval symbolism as are the visually personified representations of sin and death.

Description, action, and morality are closely woven. Sin, on the first encounter by the righteous, is something from which they recoil (759). Indulge a little familiarity with sin and it (or she) begins to give pleasure, to allure, eventually to win over the heart (–764). That Satan is enamoured of Sin by the fact that he sees his own 'perfect image' (764) reflected in her indicates that self-centredness is the root of evil (we shall have to take note later of the fact that, as Sin is the perfect image of Satan, so the Son is the perfect image of the Father, and Eve of Adam – see p. 56). The incestuous union of self with self's image (contrast Eve's glimpse of her own reflection in the lake. iv, 460–71) in the act by which the other is exploited to indulge self-love cannot be fruitful in the making of a truly living and itself creative being, but the abandonment of the self to sin certainly makes sin pregnant. As Sin conceives and gestates with a 'growing burden', there is war in Heaven and the rebels are cast out, Sin with them. The key of Hell is delivered into the hand of Sin (774–5), and then the offspring of the ghastly coition between self and self's product, image, and only-begotten is brought forth. It is Death. What else could it be, after all that has been said (or implied) by Milton about being and creativity, over against non-being and negativity? And Death lusts after the Sin that engendered it, the intercourse of the two producing a monstrous progeny 'hourly conceiv'd', 'hourly born' (796–7), wholly nourished on sin, inseparable from sin (799–800) and goaded on by death (804) in their feverish cycles of tormenting and tormented activity, which are totally introvert within the diseased 'family' of evil and negation. Thus sin breeds. And death cannot destroy sin.

Sin's final warning to Satan that his own arms, though 'temper'd heavenly', would be powerless against the deadly blow ('mortal dint', 813) of Death's dart, must be taken with a pinch of salt.

Satan quickly sums up the situation, his lesson ('lore',

815) soon 'learned'. He has changed his tune since he was threatening to teach Death *his* lesson (cf. 'learn by proof', 686). Indeed he manages now to address the 'thing' (cf. 741) before him as 'Dear Daughter' (817) and to acknowledge the 'execrable shape' (681) with its 'miscreated Front' (683) for his 'fair Son' (818) and (for there is always something to be said for flattering the mother, however unblessed her children in form and feature) the 'dear pledge' of their former sweet 'dalliance' (819). The comedy shrieks aloud here. We have all had our experience of the need suddenly to adapt our social conversation to the new realization that we are speaking to a person already linked to us, that we are talking of persons related to those we address. Satan's hasty self-adjustment here is a caricature of all such specious self-adaptations by contradiction of what has already been implied. Satan's new politeness is ironic cartoonery.

He plays the injured victim of just claims ('pretenses', 825) rejected, and the lonely avenger of a vast injustice done alike to the fallen angels, and to Sin and Death. He reveals the plan – to find the foretold new world on the outskirts ('Pourlieues', 833) of Heaven, with its 'upstart' race of new creatures, no doubt destined for the places left 'vacant' (835) in Heaven by their fall, though kept at a sufficient distance to ensure that there will not be any risk of an overcrowded ('surcharg'd', 836) Heaven which might become a breeding ground for further factious turmoils ('broiles', 837) (we must reckon at all times, of course, with the fact that Satan is a liar).

The courtesies and the self-justification completed, Satan finally bribes Sin and Death with the prospect of a new and vastly more comfortable home to dwell in and of innumerable creatures to feed on. Sin, who has nothing to thank God for, concurs, addressing Satan finally with profane variants of the terms in which the Son fitly addresses the divine Father (864–5). The climax of this profanity is reached when Sin pictures herself reigning eternally, seated at the 'right hand' of Satan in ease voluptuous, world 'without end' (868–70: cf. VI. 892). The echoing of Bible and liturgy at last make Milton's intention clear. The family relationships between Satan, Sin, and Death represent a sharp parody of that network of relationships which bind in one the persons of the Trinity. As the Son is the only begotten of the Father, 'begotten not made' (Creed: cf. v. 603–4), so Sin is begotten of Satan; and as the Holy Ghost 'proceedeth from the Father and the Son' (Creed), so Death, Milton's unholy ghost, is the issue of Father and Daughter, Satan and Sin. The inner completeness of the two families is what strikes home. The Son is the image of the Father as Sin is the 'perfect image' of her Father, Satan (764). The use of the phrase 'thou my Author, thou/My being gav'st me' (864–5), in Sin's address to Satan, pre-echoes not only Michael's address to Satan as 'Author of evil' (VI. 262), but also Eve's address to Adam as 'My Author and Disposer' (IV. 635). Thus we have an early intimation of a further correspondence which will make the human family an image of the divine family, as the diabolical family is a parody of the divine family. Milton himself has not yet given us this intimation, of course. The correspondences are to be gradually built up from the repetition of key words (such as 'Author') whose use we shall have to note several times yet (see p. 53 especially). The reader should take note, however, that as the Son is the only begotten of the Father and Sin is begotten from the head of Satan, so Eve is extracted from Adam's side.

The concept of a diabolical 'trinity' matches in moral and imaginative power the equivalent parodic correspondences of the Joycean Hell in the *Circe* episode of *Ulysses*. There is need to stress the closeness of these similarities in terms both of artistic method and of spiritual judgement.

871–967 *Sin opens the gates of Hell* (–889). *Satan stands and surveys the outer scene* (–927), *then passes through and eventually reaches the throne of Chaos* (–967).

The opening of the massive gates, themselves a parodic caricature of the gates of Heaven (for all Hell is one vast caricature of Heaven, as all evil in the last analysis is an absurd and grotesque caricature of good), is, like other decisive acts of tremendous moment, accompanied by preternatural thunder which reverberates down to the lowest deeps beneath (883). Sin can open the gates, but cannot close them. And, once open, there is space for a battled and bannered army, horse and foot and chariot, to march through. Flame and enveloping ('redounding', 889) smoke pour out as from the mouth of a furnace.

The view of Chaos now opened up shows a battlefield for those uncomposed bases of which the elements are compounded and all things fashioned. That is to say, 'hot, cold, moist and dry' (898) are as yet unbound in those elementary relationships from which the work of creation might start. For hot and dry conjoined would constitute the element fire; hot and moist, air; cold and moist, water; cold and dry, earth. These are the basic elements of which the cosmos is made. Likewise, in the human microcosm, hot and dry conjoined would constitute the humour choler; hot and moist, blood; cold and moist, phlegm; cold and dry, melancholy. These are the basic humours of which the human being, the little world of man, is made. The disorder here is not like the disorder pictured in Shakespeare where elements or humours conflict in disproportionate or misplaced relationships, but a pre-creative disorder at the level of anarchy as between particle and particle – at a pre-molecular stage, if one may stretch an image. And the arena in which embryonic 'atoms' (900) thus merge and swarm uncohesively is 'illimitable' (892) and dimensionless, a locus that antedates Nature itself, timeless and placeless. No one can be said to rule it. There is no 'rule'; there is no 'it'. But the precursors of Nature (Night and Chaos) 'stand' there – not by definition, not by occupancy, but 'by confusion' (897). We said there is no 'rule'. There is instead a parody of rule, an umpire whose function destroys his identity, for the more decisions he makes, the more he embroils the contestants in further 'fray' (908) – so he is an umpire who is *no* umpire. Likewise there is a governor who is no governor, an arbiter who is no arbiter, and that is Chance, the chaotic nature of whose functioning cancels out the identity and definition he has been given in the name 'Arbiter' (909).

Into this non-water, non-earth, non-air, non-fire (912), womb, and perhaps grave, of the whole natural order, Satan stares, and he takes thought. We have seen and felt something of what faces him. Now we hear it too, and the sound is like the full-scale seige of a capital city in the age of gunpowder. But that is to compare the immense with the minute. It is more like the tearing apart of the total fabric of the cosmos by such a mutiny of elemental matter as the mind of Milton might prophetically envisage and the age of nuclear fission might more readily dread (920–7).

Satan spreads his wings ('Vannes', 927) and takes off. It is fitting that the wings should be 'Sail-broad', which suggests a vessel in the sea rather than a bird in the air, for this journey is through no definable element or atmosphere, and though Satan may be riding at one moment, at the next he encounters a 'vacuitie' (932) in which his wings ('pennons', 933) flutter vainly. He is rescued from a sudden drop, ten thousand fathoms deep, by a raging cloud charged ('Instinct', 937) with explosive ('Nitre' – saltpetre, 937). But soon he is dragging himself through a quicksand, ('*Syrtis*', 939), half-walking, half-flying.

Milton compares Satan to a griffin ('Gryfon', 943), a 'fabulous animal having the head and wings of an eagle and hindquarters of a lion, believed by the Greeks to inhabit Scythia and to guard its gold' (*O.E.D.*). The Arimaspians (945) were reputedly a tribe of one-eyed creatures whose habit was to steal the gold from the griffins. Milton would be aware of Spenser's picture of the griffin (*Faerie Queene*, I. v. 8) and of Dante's use of it* as a symbol of the twi-natured being in *Purgatorio* XXXII, for we find him decisively echoing Dante immediately afterwards in the phrase 'dense

* The reader may be aware of Eliot's comparison of the Church to the winged hippopotamus (*The Hippopotamus*) and of Joyce's double-edged reference to the image in connection with the heavenly/hellish femininity, the sapphire-lit 'womancity' (*Ulysses* 600) and the sapphire-slipped 'exhibitionististicicity. In a word. Hippogriff.' (*Ulysses* 629).

or rare' (948) ('rari e densi', *Paradiso* II. 60; 'raro e denso', *Paradiso* II. 67; 'rara et densa', *Paradiso* XXII. 141). The association of the two contradictory but conjoint terms with the idealized figure of Beatrice and with the radiance of the divine reinforces one's sense that the parodic aspect of Milton's Hell, Chaos, and diabolical studies is a constant and unifying principle in *Paradise Lost*. Milton's exploration of disorder, disintegration, and negativity at the hellish and diabolical level counterbalances a strong awareness of order, harmony, affirmation (and sheer joy) at the heavenly – and, by derivation, at the human – level.

Satan 'swims or sinks, or wades, or creeps, or flyes' (950) till his ears are assaulted by a 'universal hubbub' and he makes towards it. It is thus, in pursuit of further confusion and hubbub, that he reaches the throne of Chaos. The list of personifications here has a Classical base: it adds to the growing number of indebtednesses to *Aeneid* VI (see the description of the palace of Pluto, *Aeneid* VI. 273 ff. 'Orcus' here, 964, is in fact the name of Pluto used by Virgil, *Aeneid* VI. 273). In view of what we have already said about indebtedness to Spenser, it is perhaps more interesting to note a marked similarity to the collection of personifications gathered around the approaches to the realm of Pluto in *Faerie Queene* II. vii. 20 ff., because the medieval and the Classical literary traditions meet and merge in Spenser's blend of allegorical personifications and miniature-epic framework as they blend in Milton's own work. The reference here to 'the dreaded name/Of Demogorgon' (964–5) brings together memories of Spenser's Abyss of the three Fates who dwell

> 'Downe in the bottome of the deepe *Abyss*,
> Where *Demogorgon* in dull darkness pent,
> Farre from the view of Gods and heavens blis,
> The hideous *Chaos* keepes, their dreadful dwelling is.'
>
> (*Faerie Queene* IV. ii. 47)

and his Hermitage of Hypocrisy where Archimago takes the Redcross Knight and Una as 'drooping Night' creeps fast on them. Here it is that Archimago, framing diabolical spells,

'bad awake blacke *Plutoes* griesly Dame
And cursed Heaven, and spake reprochfull shame
Of highest God, the Lord of life and light;
A bold bad man, that dar'd to call by name
Great *Gorgon*, Prince of darknesse and dead night,
At which *Cocytus* quakes, and *Styx* is put to flight.'

(*Faerie Queene* I. i. 37)

Milton's various verbal recalls here are unmistakable, and we must add that the encounter of the Redcross Knight with Archimago follows hard upon the encounter with Error already firmly recalled in the description of Sin (see p. 50).

Two final points may be added. The association between music and order in the universe, between harmony and the act of creation, makes the climactic emphasis here upon hubbub and discord logical. And Milton's group of personifications carefully mingles the moral aspects of oral and aural evil with the more obvious miseries and distresses of discord and tumult. The damage done by the unruly tongue, implicit in the references to 'Rumor' (965) and the 'thousand various mouths' of Discord (967) is something to which those who had lived through the Miltonic decades of civil strife must have been acutely sensitive.

968–1055 *Satan explains his mission to Chaos (–987), and Chaos, recognizing that he is bent on the pursuit of havoc and ruin, speeds him on his way (–1009). Satan continues his journey until Heaven and the universe are distantly in sight (–1055).*

The spectacle and sound of Satan's apologetic politeness before the grim throne set in the midst of unmitigated nihilisms is surely not without its ironic humour. After all, he can never be 'less than Archangel ruin'd', and this is a visual and aural jungle. Courtesies are always that much more embarrassing in the near presence of pile-drivers or howling competitive demonstrators. Satan's approach is as comic as his situation. He assures Chaos that he has not come to spy (970), to explore, or even to 'disturb' (971) the remote corners ('secrets', 972) of his realm. What purpose or motive could conceivably be served by the laughable projects of furtive espionage, exploration, or trouble-making in the nethermost hide-outs of maximal derangement he does not pause to explain, but the reader should have time to savour the absurdity. With a cool and flattering mention of Chaos's 'spacious Empire', Satan moves on to explain how he seeks a path to some point where the realm of Chaos borders on ('Confine with', 977) Heaven – or, he adds, no doubt aware that he may be approaching a delicate topic and therefore employing a casual, tentative 'if' (977), perhaps to 'some other place' recently created by divine theft from the chaotic terrain. Should he reach such a place, Satan assures Chaos that it is his intention to expel the usurpers and restore the usurped terrain to the dominion of Chaos. Thus Chaos will reap the territorial gains of the venture. 'Yours be th'advantage all, mine the Revenge'. The posture of the heroic, the altruistic, and the self-sacrificial is assumed by Satan in anticipatory diabolical parody of the role of the divine Son. But the evil flavour of the blasphemy does not preclude a piquant accompanying taste of sheer farce – as the vocabulary of usurpation, of rival claims on territory and governance, is bandied about at the heart of a region dedicated to rampant convulsion.

Chaos answers with speech appropriately 'faultring' (989 – a Miltonic key word: see IX. 846, X. 115, and p. 244) and discomposed ('incompos'd', 989). He recognizes Satan as the rebel whose defeated host fled through his domain 'not in silence' (994). One may add that if the noise of the Fall was audible here, where volume would surely have to be measured in megabels (recall the 'universal hubbub wilde/Of stunning sounds and voices', 951–2, and the nearer discord of 966–7), it must have been worth remembering. Chaos was himself impressed by the 'ruin upon ruin, rout on rout,/Confusion worse confounded' (995–6), and we feel that he should know. He has experience in this field.

Comic as is the interchange of ambassadorial phrases about rule and usurpation in a context like this, perhaps even more preposterous is the talk of 'frontiers', 'residence' and the 'Scepter' (the most crucial symbol of ordered sovereign authority, 1002) in reference to the essentially ungoverned and ungovernable by the arch-upholder of non-government, who laments that his arena of non-governing has now been successively 'encroacht' upon by the establishment of Hell and the creation of the world. Milton enjoys his chuckles. It is a moment of wry farce and spurious dignity as the stuttering Anarch bids Satan good speed.

Satan launches himself again to fight his way between the contesting elements. His course is more testing than that of Jason and the Argonauts, who had to sail their vessel, the Argo (1017), between the clashing ('justling', 1018) Cyanean Rocks at the entrance of the Euxine Sea. The rocks were supposed to come together and crush vessels that were passing between. His course is more testing, too, than that of Ulysses who had to steer his way between the rock of Scylla and the equally perilous whirlpool of Charybdis. The currents here (between Italy and Sicily) were so strong that it was hazardous to try to steer clear enough of the one menace without falling victim to the other.

Milton employs a telling device for re-universalizing the action (which has perhaps begun to seem rather remote amid the grotesqueries of the court of the Anarch) and restoring its existential status. The labour and difficulty of Satan's journey, he reminds us, no longer obtains. The fall of man is to produce a 'Strange alteration' (1024). Sin and Death follow Satan and construct a broad highway, so that it is now easy for the perverted devils to come to tempt human beings and carry them back; easy, that is, except in the case of those men and women whom God and his good angels protect by the divine 'grace' (1033). The construction of the highway from Earth to Hell is to be described in detail (x. 293–324).

With the mention of 'grace' we catch our first glimpse of the distant light of Heaven. We have reached the outermost border ('fardest verge', 1038) of the realm of Nature, a border from which the tumults of Chaos withdraw as does a beaten foe from outer fortifications ('outmost works', 1039). Thus Satan moves more easily, as a storm-tossed vessel makes for ('holds', 1043) harbour. Through his eyes we glimpse the light from the walls of Heaven that 'shoots' (1036) the first glimmer of a dawn into the night of surrounding blackness. Through his eyes again, as he is poised more at leisure, we see Heaven itself 'extended wide/In circuit, undetermined square or round' (1047–8), the perfect square and the perfect circle conjoined, indeed a 'box circle', as our remotest glimpse of its shape back in the garden of our childhood *Burnt Norton* hinted, towers and battlements adorned with 'living Saphire' (1050). Milton does not let us forget this. He is to tell us later that at the time of Adam and Eve's rapturous retirement to their nuptial bower the firmament glows with 'living Saphirs' (IV. 605). Of course the *living sapphire* matches *la viva luce* of Dante, which unites the holy smile of Beatrice and the radiance of the beatific vision.

The reader will perhaps appreciate why we noted (see p. 58, footnote) the network of connections between great poets, which the recurrence of certain images establishes. The two-natured Zoe of Joyce's heaven-parodying hell, whose role of harlotry in the lost city of spurious 'exhibitionististicicity' is carried on in sapphire slip (*Ulysses* 629) (though to the accompanying blare of 'The Holy City' from the gramophone outside, 623), remains potential Beatrician image (like the harlot of Eliot's *Rhapsody on a Windy Night*), potential image of a pure 'womancity' (linked by Joyce with the New Jerusalem, *Ulysses* 600) under a sapphire sky. We but touch the periphery of an immense harmony of associations that hide behind the most powerful of the Miltonic key words. And Milton is not a poet operating in isolation. The image of the living sapphire threads its way through glimpses of the *Urbs Beata*, heavenly city and womancity, from Dante's *Paradiso* to Milton's Eden, from Joyce's *Ulysses* to Eliot's *Burnt Norton*.

It remains to add what would scarcely need to be added were it not that ignorant people keep on telling us that our own century has only just discovered what a minute little world we live in over against the unspeakable magnitude of what surrounds it; namely that Milton seems to know nothing of the small three-decker universe that modern writers have foisted on to the thinkers of the past. Here we see the whole universe ('This pendant world', 1052, *not* the Earth only) hanging from Heaven in a golden chain. To get an idea of the relative size of the whole universe and of Heaven, you must picture, in the night sky, the minute pin-prick of the smallest discernible star in relation to the moon (1052–3). That is what Milton has to say about the size of our universe as a whole. At the heart of it, surrounded by sphere upon sphere of planets, lies the tiny earth.

Book III

1–55 *Address to Light* (–55).

Milton speaks of light as the first offspring of Heaven because the book of Genesis records God's 'Let there be light' (Genesis I. 3) as his first utterance; but he then makes the alternative claim to define light as beaming co-eternally from the Creator because 'God is light, and in him is no darkness at all' (1 John I. 5) and must have dwelt eternally in light. Or would light rather be called an 'Ethereal stream' from a source unnameable (7–8), since it existed before God made the sun (Genesis I. 14) or the sky ('Heavens', 9: see Genesis I. 7–8)? Milton worries at this matter because God's creation of light, of Day and Night, and of the rising 'world of waters dark and deep' (11 – an exact quotation from Spenser, *Faerie Queene* I. i. 39) in Genesis I precedes his creation of the lights of heaven, sun and moon, which give us our earthly day and night, and because the phrase 'God is light' gives light a status prior to either creative act.

The formal address to light is appropriate. The poet naturally wishes to mark the end of his gloomy visitation ('obscure Sojourn', 15) of Hell ('the Stygian Pool', 14), as also of his imaginative 'flight' (15) with Satan through the realms of Chaos and Night. The personal note that enters into his glad return to regions of light is an especially moving one, however, because though as poet he is glad to return 'safe' (21) from the dark descent into Hell and even harder re-ascent from the depths (he echoes *Aeneid* VI. 126–9 here, 20–1), as blind John Milton he feels his eyes rolling vainly in search of light's piercing ray. The personal note rings even more loudly when one recognizes lines 25–6 as alternative seventeenth-century diagnostic descriptions of the optic malady afflicting Milton. 'Drop serene' (Latin, *gutta serena*) is a disease of the optic nerve; 'dim suffusion' (*suffusio nigra*) is blindness in general, whether from neural defect or cataract. Not that he is less given to reading poetry (or hearing it read), Milton adds (26–8). Especially he loves the psalms (songs of '*Sion*', 30) and returns to them night by night. He often recalls other poets and prophets smitten with blindness, *Thamyris* of Thrace, who claimed that he could surpass the Muses in song and was punished by blindness and inability to sing, *Homer* ('blind *Maeonides*', 35), *Tiresias* (prophet of Thebes whose fate it was never to be believed: see Eliot's *Waste Land*) and *Phineus*, the Thracian prophet whom the Argonauts liberated from the tormenting Harpies. The personal tone lingers as Milton tells how he feeds on nourishing thoughts, which of themselves breed rhythmic poetry ('voluntarie move/Harmonious numbers', 37–8). He is like the unsleeping nightingale, which sings hidden away in the dark. So, though the seasonal round continues, Milton never tastes the return of daylight, the visual delights of dawn or sunset, spring or summer, or of the human face – 'divine' (44) in that God's image is stamped there especially. In place of that book of knowledge that one reads in seeing the works of Nature, he is presented with a 'Universal blank'. Thus for him 'one entrance' (50) of those by which wisdom comes into the mind of man is closed (i.e. eyesight). All the more need has he for the light of wisdom to illuminate his mind and all its faculties from within, to plant eyes and clear vision there that he may speak of what is invisible to men's outward sight.

It is interesting to compare the sad lines in which Samson bemoans his blindness in *Samson Agonistes* (67–101) with this passage; and more especially to contrast the practical problems of the blind man 'expos'd/To daily fraud, contempt, abuse, and wrong,/Within doors or without, still as a fool,/In power of others, never in my own.' (*Samson Agonistes* 75–8), which Milton must have felt keenly, with the corresponding sense here that the blindness may itself be turned to good in that the deficiencies of outward sight may be divinely compensated for in an inward illumination, which will enable him to describe more revealingly the things invisible that he must now turn to. Just as the earlier lines of this introductory address constitute an objective preparation for the violent change of scene and subject, so these moving lines of personal prayer and dedication constitute a fit subjective preparation of the poet, in mind and heart, for what he must now speak of. As such, of course, they are intended to infect the reader with a like purification of mind and heart for the imaginative entry into Heaven. The poet's bending of his own will, his act of humility and self-offering, is an existential one for the reader to share.

56–134 *God in Heaven looks down on the new Earth and then on Hell and on Satan's mischievous journey (–79). God speaks to the Son, declaring Satan's plan and man's vulnerability to it (–134).*

God in Heaven is surrounded by the angelic hosts enjoying the bliss of the beatific vision (61, 'from his sight' – from sight of him). The Son, enthroned at his right hand, is here 'the radiant image of his Glory' (63), as in the Epistle to the Hebrews (I. 3) he is 'the brightness of his glory, and the express image of his person'. As the reader enters into the heavenly scene, Milton gives him a quick God's-eye view of the earth below where 'our two first Parents' are living in the 'joy and love' (67) of innocence, then of Satan who is now 'coasting' along the boundary of Heaven uplifted ('sublime', 72) on his wings in the half-light ('dun', 72). (We read how the light shoots from the walls of Heaven into the realms of Night, II. 1034–6.) From this position Satan sees, from above, the universe ('World', 74), which at the end of Book II he saw from beneath, hanging in a golden chain (II. 1051). The outer convex of the universe, seen from Satan's position, looks like a shell of 'firm land' (75). He cannot see through to the spheres and the 'firmament' within – still less to that Garden over which God's watchful eye is even now playing. Our glimpse of what the all-seeing eye can behold is also a reminder that 'from his prospect (point of view) high' (77) God holds 'past, present, future' (78) together within his oversight.

God's prophetic summary, here addressed to the Son, of
what is happening, what is to be, and what the creational
basis has been by which such events have been made
possible, is necessarily theological. We must beware of falling into the trap (into which some critics have fallen) of
isolating God the Father's utterances, summing up their
content and character, and then labelling the 'persona' that
emerges from this artificial exercise Milton's God. Within
the context of *Paradise Lost* Milton has preserved an impersonal orthodoxy. He is a trinitarian, of course. God the
Son is God, too. We have not heard what God has to say
until the Son has spoken as well as the Father. The divine
activity is that which emerges in the joint action of Father
and Son (for convenience of argument there is no need to
introduce the Holy Spirit at this particular point). You cannot, unless you are a polytheist (and Milton certainly was
not), have one God who punishes and another God who
saves. If justice and mercy, authority and compassion, meet
and mingle in the interchange of dialogue between Father
and Son, they do so in the unity of a single Godhead. If the
withholding of a compulsively restraining inhibition, which
might have prevented man from falling, is matched in the
intertwining of paternal act and filial act, with the costly and
loving self-sacrifice that rescues man from the consequences
of his own freedom exploited and abused, then it is the
totality of that intertwined pattern of action which shows us
the nature of God, the 'character of God'. Milton was an
educated Christian. He was not a fool (for immediate
corroboration of the point see, for instance, III. 139–43,
III. 169–70, VI. 680–3, VI. 720–1).

This said, we may note that God's first observation on the
Satan whose performances we have studied with some relish
in Books I and II is about the 'rage' that 'transports' him
(80–1). Seeing Satan's purpose, to try ('assay', 90) to destroy
or pervert mankind, and foreseeing that his deceptive
('glozing', 93 – *glossing*, providing a *gloss* upon, as in *glossary*)
lies will bring about man's transgression and fall, he declares
man's own culpability in that he (God) made man 'just

and right' (98) with sufficient virtue to have remained so.

It is important to scrutinize the text carefully hereabouts. Milton keeps our minds on the Garden of Eden and the coming transgression of Adam and Eve up to line 94. Then there is a change from the historical to the more mythological idiom –

'So will fall
Hee and his faithless Progenie' (95–6).

We are no longer listening to God's observations on the events in the Garden of Eden: we are listening to his judgement on the human race, of whose character and conduct the Eden story provides but symbol and summary. Mankind as a whole lies under judgement for two defects represented by the two words 'ingrate' (ungrateful, 97) and 'faithless' (96, carrying, I take it, the firm theological connotation, *lacking in faith*, as well as the weaker subsidiary connotation, *disloyal*). Suddenly, once more, the poem has ceased to be a story about our remote forefather and mother, and becomes an account of our doings as their 'Progenie'. We were made 'free to fall' (99) as were the angels, Satan among them. Freedom is a word that attaches equally to the action of the angels who did *not* fall and to that of those who did (102). Had the angels (and men, too, for as the argument develops it plainly applies to both equally: see 129–30) not been free, what proof could they have given of sincere loyalty to God, firm faith and love for him, when their actions would have evidenced not what they wanted to do but what they could not help doing (103–6)? What commendation could have been given by God to his creatures for doing what they *had* to do, and what delight could God himself have taken in the response of beings simply acting under the force of necessity (106–10)? The key to the argument lies in the character of 'Will and Reason' (108), the two faculties given pre-eminently to angels and men alike. For if will is the force determining action, reason is the judgement whereby the exercise of will is directed. And just as *unfree Will* would be a contradiction in terms, so *unfree Reason* would be a contradiction in terms ('Reason also is choice', 108). God cannot take away from man with one hand what he gives with the other. He cannot endow a creature with the twin gifts of will and reason and then prevent those faculties from operating; otherwise he would have destroyed his own creation. Moreover, a human (or, for that matter, angelic) creature whose will and reason had thus been rendered 'useless', 'vain' and 'passive' (by being 'despoiled' of freedom, 109) would in supposedly serving God *not be serving God at all* but be serving 'necessitie' (110). This aspect of the argument has been too often neglected or ignored. It is often said, as here, that a man compulsorily serving God would not really be a man at all. Milton makes the point (if we may press the implicit logic to an explicit formulation) that just as a compulsorily-serving man would not be a man, so a compulsorily-served God would not be God. To put it another way (even though it means straining utterance almost to absurdity), God's nature as well as man's is at issue. God would destroy *himself* as well as man if he, *per impossibile*, 'created' such a situation as has been hypothetically described. Later on Milton is at pains to make clear that man (Adam) fully understands the divine dispensation by which he has life and lordship over the earth, and the character of that will and reason, which are the twin endowments of his status (IX. 351–8). That 'true Libertie' and 'right Reason' are inseparably 'twinn'd' is also emphasized by the archangel Michael when he has cause to recall to Adam the character of his own lapse (XII. 82–5).

In the rest of the argument God underlines his creatures' culpability again. The fallen can blame neither their 'maker', their 'making', nor their 'Fate' (113). The freedom that they abuse in their falling is built into their 'making'. (If one may press the point further than Milton presses it, in order to achieve the maximum clarification of the doctrine at issue, the faculty and capacity they would complain of, if they complained, would be the faculty and capacity exercised in complaining.) There is no question of a 'Predestination' condemning them in advance to fall. The divine fore-knowledge that foresees what man will do is a power of discernment not an act of compulsive decision with an 'influence on their fault' (118). Take away the divine fore-knowledge that foresees what is going to be and you do not affect the course of free human behaviour at all (117–19). Thus the trespassers, angelic and human, act 'without least impulse or shadow of Fate' (120) and are 'Authors to themselves' (122), utterly free in respect alike of their reasoning and their action ('Both what they judge and what they choose', 123); for the essential gift of freedom was given to them by God in their making, and the only way by which they can lose freedom is by throwing it away (it would not *be* freedom if it could be *taken* away from them). In short, they alone can enslave ('enthrall', 125) themselves. It is an eternal and divine decree that made them free: such a decree is by definition unchangeable, irrevocable. Only a creaturely decision, emerging within the framework of that divinely ordained situation, can pervert the character of what obtains within it, and 'ordain' a 'fall'.

Even so, God makes a significant distinction between the act of the 'first sort' (129), the rebellious angels who fell 'self-tempted, self-deprav'd' (130) and the fall of man who is first 'deceiv'd' by Satan. For this reason man 'shall find grace'. The divine glory involves an excellence of both mercy and justice (displayed in Heaven and Earth alike), but mercy outshines justice.

135–216 *The Son praises the Father for his declaration that man shall find grace and mercy (–166). The Father explains how his grace will work in men to bring them to repentance (–193), and how the gift of conscience will guide them (–202). But the need for some willing victim to atone for broken human allegiance will remain, if justice is to remain untampered with (–212). Who will answer this need? (–216).*

As the beloved ('elect', 136) spirits rejoice, the Son outshines all in glory, for the Father's nature and character are visibly expressed, so that the 'Divine compassion' of the Father, and

'Love without end' of the Father, and the 'Grace – without measure' of the Father can actually be *seen* in the Son (140–2). Unless we fully grasp the doctrine of the consubstantiality of the Father and the Son, we shall misunderstand Milton and misrepresent the conception of God that *Paradise Lost* sets before us. If we *see* in the face of the Son what we cannot detect in the unfaceable face of the Father, if we *hear* in the words of the Son what the Father's words do not seem to say, this is no justification for characterizing the Father separately from the Son. The two are one (cf. III. 169–70). If there is a dialogue between the demands of justice and those of love and mercy, it is *not* a dialogue in which the Son is arrayed against the Father. It is a dialogue within a single personality.

The Son praises the utterance ('word', 144) that has brought to an end the Father's judgement ('sentence', 145). It is 'gracious' to grant 'grace'. It would not be consistent with the character of the Father (note this, 153–4) if man, his beloved 'creature' and 'Son' (151) were to be finally lost, tricked by a fraud, that fraud abetted by his own folly. Satan cannot be allowed thus to achieve his purpose, accomplishing a kind of revenge in the corruption of men, or indirectly causing God to undo what he has done (to cancel out an act of creation by an act of destruction). The point of the easily misunderstood lines, 165–6, is that the devils must not be allowed to get away with it, as we should say. Their blasphemous attempt to *probe* and *test* God's greatness and goodness (such is the force of the word *question*, 166) by such provocation as might lead him to destroy corrupted mankind in anger, must be *answered in action* (such is the force of the word *defence*, 166). They must be thwarted. In short, the necessity for the plan of loving redemption by which man is to be saved is based not only on the mercy of God towards men as expressed by the Son, but also upon the rational need to uphold the justice and authority of God, over against the challenge of evil, a need equally cited by the Son. Man must be saved out of love and mercy: man must also be saved lest evil go unpunished and justice be betrayed.

The Father's reply begins with the clear assertion that the Son is not only his 'chief delight' (168) but also –

'My word, my wisdom, and effectual might' (170).

All the words that the Son speaks are in fact the thoughts of the Father, all the products of the Father's eternal purpose. There is no conflict, no dialogue except as within the mind of a single being, balancing emphasis against emphasis. The discussion is a verbal dance not a struggle; a counterpoint of woven themes, as in music. To try to turn it into something approaching oral fisticuffs is crudely insensitive.

Man will not be lost. Those who will to be saved shall be saved – not by the power of that willing but by the grace freely on offer in God himself. God will renew man's claims (entitlements – 'powers', 176), which have lapsed (run out, we might say) and been rendered null through the forfeiture of his rights in the act of enslaving himself by sin to unpermitted evil desires (175–7) ('exorbitant' – outside the range of what is proper, 177). Thus man will be restored to the position of being able to match strength with strength over against Satan, but the strength will be wholly of God's sustaining, so that man will realize how frail he is of himself and owe his deliverance solely to God (178–82).

God concedes now that there will be those whom his special gift of 'peculiar grace' will elect for the highest calling – presumably to sanctity, martyrdom and heroic self-sacrifice. He does not explain this but says, 'so is my will' (184). The rest of mankind will hear his call, will be warned of their sinfulness and of the need to appease God's wrath while yet his grace is on offer to save them. God promises that he will provide all that is needed to clarify whatever their 'senses dark' might render confused, and to soften their hard hearts to repentance and obedience. He will be quickly responsive to any sincere endeavour in the way of prayer and repentance. Moreover he will grant them the inner guidance of conscience, and the more they allow themselves to be enlightened by its guidance the clearer will be the light of the guidance it offers. (The neat summary, 195–6, of the doctrine of the cumulatively increasing enlightenment to be provided by the developed conscience, which matures through use, is an instance of Milton's sureness and subtlety in the field of moral theology as well as of his powers of epigrammatic concentration.) This is the way – by persevering to the end – to salvation; and those who ignore or scorn the patience of God in so long keeping the way open, will never taste it. Indeed as the effect of attending to the voice of conscience is cumulative, so the effect of hardness of heart and blindness to its light is cumulative. The hard heart shall be further hardened, the ignoring eye increasingly blinkered and blinded, to further stumbling and a deeper fall. But only such as thus harden and blind themselves shall be cut off from mercy.

We have followed the course of the argument closely thus far because the lines now before us (203–12), defining the need for an atoning victim, need to be understood within the context of the freely offered grace and the mercy available to penitent man. In man's act of disobedience there has been something more than (and distinguishable from) the offence against a person which a person can forgive. There has been a questioning of the very framework of things within which even the person forgives. Let us try to grasp this point by analogy – crude and inadequate though all analogies must be. If you slap your brother across the face in anger, it is probably satisfaction enough to apologize and ask forgiveness. If, as a witness in a law-court you go up and slap the judge across the face there is something more than a personal injury which the judge as a person, man to man, can simply forgive. There is an offence against some system of authority which, as a person, even the judge himself *has no right to overlook*. For, if he overlooked it, he would be letting down the very system within which he operates. Indeed it would be selfish of him (self-indulgent, even conceited) to imagine that there is nothing in the affront which his own personal predilection cannot immediately wipe out.

Now plainly we are dealing with a vaster and profounder issue here. But God's point is that man's sin has turned topsy-turvy the very fabric of relationships which constitutes the ordering of Heaven and Earth. To break creaturely 'fealtie' and virtually subvert the supremacy of Heaven is to try to play the God and thus to ruin everything: for it is an act that parallels the satanic act in being essentially *discreational*: that is to say, it is an act that has *reversed* the pattern of things (the Creatorly-creaturely pattern) by which the Creator created the world and man within it. The man who has sinned is one thing: he shall be forgiven. The reversed pattern, the creational order turned in the direction of discreation is another: it won't turn back of its own accord. You can put a new element in an electric fire or a new lamp in a socket to replace burnt-out ones. But if the burning-out blew a fuse in the fuse box you will not thus bring back heat or light. Mechanical analogies perhaps hinder as much as they help, and there is something unsavoury in paralleling the atoning Son of God with a fuse wire, but the strain that the fuse bears in crucially sustaining the redistribution of light gives the image a certain aptness. We have renewed our burnt-out human lamps; who shall be the living fuse, bearing in substitution the full strain of what burnt out the now darkened system? Improper self-assertion turned creation discreationwards. Willing self-sacrifice alone can turn the discreational back into the creational grooves. As the creature usurped the Creator's authority and the human dislodged the divine, so the divine must put on the creaturely humility and willingly assume the human. Which of the beings of Heaven has charity equal to the task?

217-343 *The hosts of Heaven are silent (–226) till the Son offers himself as the atoning victim, ready to assume humanity (–238), to die (–249), and return victorious over death to Heaven (–265). The hosts are raptly attentive (–273) as the Father accepts the Son's self-offering, not only to restore man and redeem him from sin (–304), but also to exalt his manhood in bringing it back to Heaven (–320). God also foretells the judgement and the coming of a 'New Heaven and Earth' (–343).*

Milton's emphatic line-endings, 'mute' and 'appeerd' (217

and 219), help to remind us that we have reached the parallel point in the heavenly council to that reached in the hellish council in II. 417 ff. (cf. 'appeerd' and 'mute' ending lines II. 418 and 420).

The company about the throne is silent: no one offers to plead ('patron', 219 – advocate) or mediate on man's behalf, or to accept man's penalties on his own head in man's place, till the Son, in whom dwells the 'fullness . . . of love divine' renews that process of 'mediation' which is the 'dearest' of all things between Father and Son. For this is surely Milton's point in lines 223–7: not that stern Father would send man to Hell while loving Son would forgive him – any notion of such a distinction would be alien to Christian thinking. Rather the 'dearest' thing of all in the consubstantial relationship of Father and Son is the active reflection back to the Father of his own love living in such fullness as to overwhelm what divine judgement in isolation might otherwise determine. There *is* no divine judgement in isolation, for we are dealing with a triune God.

The Son's offering of himself is couched in terms that maintain the theological flavour and emphasis. The Father's word has already been given that 'man shall find grace' (227). Correspondingly the 'means' by which grace reaches man will be readily available. This must be so by the very nature of divine grace itself – which is always freely given, unanticipated ('unprevented', 231) and unsought; such is its joyful character as a gift to man. It must be so also by the very character of man's fallen status. The status of disaffiliation to which disobedient man has inevitably committed himself is a status from which no fit approach could be initiated and no bargain struck, for man has nothing left to bargain with. Having nothing to offer, man can make no valid move towards expiation. He is, in short, wholly dependent for possible recovery of creational status on some movement starting outside himself and then involving him and carrying him back with it into the orbit of dialogue with divinity from which sin totally and logically has cut him off. The thoroughness of Milton's explication here has once

76

more the effect of universalizing the situation. If the reader feels that he is being preached at, it is because he *is* being preached at. This is a sermon. That it is also recognizably a day in the life of the Trinity may not make us feel hungry to share in the joys of Heaven, but we are fallen men and perhaps cannot be expected to relish such high delights: at least it makes us fully aware of what our human condition amounts to.

In the Son's words of total self-sacrifice on man's behalf the reiterated emphatic 'mee' of lines 236, 237 and 238 echoes the parodic egotistical 'Me' of Satan's corresponding self-offering (II. 450) in the council of Hell, and once more emphasizes the antithetic balance between the two councils. A more authentic personal note intrudes occasionally (276–9), but the prevailing tone here seems to be set by Milton's determination once more to expound the doctrine of the Son's acceptance of man's punishment by substitution, and his conquest of death by freely submitting to it a being in divine essence and character alien to its authority and uncontainable within its grasp. One strains again after helpful analogies. In accepting divinity as his 'prey' (248), Death feeds on that which it can neither digest nor utterly consume. Spoiled of his spoil, Death will thus be deprived of that comprehensive capacity to consume and devour which constitutes its authority and strength. It will be rendered weaponless (253). The Son will bind the powers of Hell. The symmetry of thought is neatly preserved as we foresee, through the prophetic words of the Son, that the evil foes of freedom will themselves be finally fettered and that Death's will be the last corpse consumed by the grave (259), while the multitude of those redeemed by the Son will be taken before the face of the Father, now unclouded by that anger which the spectacle of evil provokes.

Milton's picture of the Son (266–72) again presses upon us, point by point, the parodic aspect of Satan's supposed distinctive character. Satan's bold front and utterance were, after all, but the false negation of the Son's meekness and eloquent silence (267), his undying hatred of men but the

77

negation of the Son's 'immortal love' (267) for them, his unyielding spirit of rebelliousness but the negation of the Son's 'filial obedience' (269), his unremitting vengefulness but the negation of the Son's glad self-offering as he is wholly attendant on the will of the Father (271). If there was any mistake as we read Books I and II, there can surely be no mistake now, when Milton hammers into our minds the realization that there never *was* a satanic character after all – nothing but a set of empty parasitical postures assumed in the vain attempt to parody what is real.

The Father replies to the Son as the only guarantor of peace for men, who would otherwise be under judgement, and likewise (and for the same reason) the only guarantor of his own (and their mutual) joy (such is the force of the word 'complacence', 276). So dear is mankind to the Father that delight in the Son's presence must be foregone for a time in order that the otherwise lost race may be saved. Only the Son can redeem man, by assuming man's nature and uniting it with his own. The forecasting of the Incarnation is in line with every other universalizing aspect of the sequence. It is necessary for the Son to stand in the place of Adam, as a second or substitute root of the human family, for, as we have seen, Adam's sin (being in line with the satanic disobedience) will turn the new creation discreationwards and living men deathwards. The reversal of this process demands a new and living divine root to turn what is moving discreation-wards and deathwards once more into the way of life (–289: cf. p. 146).

It is a corrupted human family with which God has to deal after the sin of Adam – not just an erring individual. The shared sinfulness of humanity is not quite the same thing as an aggregate of individual offences. Membership of a family alienated at the paternal and maternal root from the God who created it with a now betrayed purpose involves men in a guilt at once personally less culpable but generally more erosive than what can be charged to an individual's account. This shared guilt of the race, which each man willy-nilly inherits, must be washed out by a shared virtue, which men cannot individually purchase or as a family receive from external endowment. The need is for a positive righteousness inserted by an act of new creation into the life-stream of the race. Milton's image here is that of a transplantation (293), oddly apt, perhaps, in the day of experimental surgery such as ours. The Son will in this very precise sense beat a new flow into the human family blood-stream. The Son is the willing donor, giving his life.

The one act is at once a satisfying of the demands of justice, which closes the drama of man's disobedience and fall (for man's voluntary acceptance of the discreation that man's disobedience has purchased completes the cycle of justice in action), and a renewal of creation at a higher level of being, in that the human nature that closes the drama is a divinely inhabited one, which, in rising beyond death, brings the ransomed family to a state of being as infected with divinity as the fallen family was infected with sin (-297).

Too much has been made of the alleged dryness of the argument hereabouts. It is true that the reasoning is abstract, but surely the astonishing symmetry of the sequence is notable both intellectually and aesthetically. The thinking dances with a mathematical poise and precision; there is a musical shapeliness in the balanced interweaving of contrapuntal ideas. Heavenly love is to outdo hellish hate (298), yielding ('giving', 299) to death, and dying to redeem costingly what hellish hate cheaply destroyed. The play of word and thought here is as much like a ballet as it is like a lecture or a sermon. In and out, notion weaves with notion as concept is interchanged with counterconcept. It is impossible to read and dwell on the lines that build up the climax of the argument here without sensing the curve and sway of verbal and conceptual sequence as moving in patterned rhythmic flow that pulses with vitality. Thus the Father's voice declares how the Son, by descending and assuming man's nature, will not decrease or degrade the divine nature. The voluntary loss (the verb 'quitted', 307) of the heavenly status enables him to save the world from 'utter loss' (308). The enactment establishes in a new dimension (the dimension of creaturely behaviour, which is meritorious or non-meritorious) that Sonship of God which is already his by birthright. The dancing parallelisms are intensified. It is because the Son excels in goodness even more than in greatness (310–11), overflowing with love even more than with glory, that the going down ('Humiliation', 313) shall bring manhood up even to the throne. Balance and correspondence, descent and ascent, paradox and counterparadox, divinity enfleshed, manhood divinized, yielding and winning, . . . idea and word dance to a final harmony of utterance in which 'Both God and Man' (316) reign together, and the 'Son both of God and Man' is 'universal King'. The poetry of theology mounts to a climax as the Father foresees the ascended Son supreme over all things in Heaven and Earth, bringing to judgement ('Doom', 328) the living and the dead, the latter summoned ('cited', 327) from history by the 'peal' (329) of the last trumpet (1 Corinthians xv. 52). In the 'New Heaven and Earth', which shall arise from the ashes of the burnt-up universe, 'golden days' abounding in 'golden deeds' (337) will succeed under the sway of Joy, Love and Truth, for the authoritativeness ('Scepter', 339) of regality will no longer be necessary (340), God himself being 'All in all' (1 Corinthians xv. 28).

The extent to which the Paradise in Eden images the joys here pictured of Heaven (as Hell perverts and parodies them) will emerge later; but in view of what has already been said about the earthly family of relationships imaging the divine family (as contrariwise the satanic family parodies it), one should point the reader's mind forward here from the triumphant climactic lines –

'here shalt reign
Both God and Man, Son both of God and Man' (315–16)

to the lines that come at times of terrestrial delight in Paradise, addressed by Adam to Eve –

'Daughter of God and Man, accomplisht *Eve*' (IV. 660)

and

'Daughter of God and Man, immortal *Eve*' (IX. 291).

(For further discussion of these parallels see p. 113.)

344–415 *In adoration the angels sing a hymn of praise* (–371), *which celebrates the Father's omnipotence and mystery* (–382), *and the Son as the agent of creation* (–390), *the victor over angelic rebellion* (–396), *and the Redeemer of mankind* (–415).

At the close of the council in Hell the fallen angels split up into groups and went off in pursuit of a variety of diversified interests (II. 521 ff.). At the close of the council in Heaven the angelic hosts join together in acts of prolonged adoration and worship. Bowing before the thrones of Father and Son, they cast down their crowns, as in Revelation IV. 10 and in many Christian hymns, but a notable Miltonic difference is that the crowns are not just golden but 'inwove with Amarant and Gold' (352). Amarant, the unwithering flower, 'first' (356) grew in Heaven and was planted in the garden of Paradise to bloom 'fast by the Tree of Life' (354), but when man sinned it was removed back to Heaven. Thus the symbolic journey of the amaranth, in which what is unspoilt of the eternal once planted in the natural order is restored to the Heaven from which it sprang – to be interwoven with the gold of heavenly glory – matches the patterned movements of divinity and humanity already fully explicated (see XI. 77–8, where the Sons of Light hasten 'from thir blissful Bowrs/Of *Amarantin* Shade' to hear God's judgement on mankind). The odyssey of the amaranth is a miniature of the central thought and action in the same sense that, say, the odyssey of Bloom's lemon-scented soap is in *Ulysses*. Amid all the jewelled splendour of the Johannine Heaven (cf. 362 ff. and Revelation IV), enriched by the flowery bliss of legendary Classical Elysium (358–9), the 'immortal Amarant' (353) carries what grew in the earthly soil at the foot of the Tree of Life to the glittering pavement before the throne. Moreover the association between

Amaranthus and the 'purple gore' established by Spenser's account of 'that Paradise' in the Garden of Adonis must have been known to Milton (see *Faerie Queene* III. vi. 43 and 45). The point is interesting because the word 'Impurpl'd' (364) seems to hint at royal self-sacrifice and the price of salvation. Re-crowned, the hosts take their harps to play an overture ('Preamble', 367), then burst into harmonious song. No one is 'exempt' (370), for there is not in Heaven an unmusical ear or a voice incapable of sustaining its melodic line ('part', 371).

They first hymn God the Father, omnipotent King and Creator of all being. He is the 'Fountain of Light' (375 – as they are the 'Sons of Light', XI. 80), invisible and inaccessible in the unfaceable and unsearchable brightness of his presence, except when he draws around himself a shading cloud, which veils his central blaze and enables the brightest seraphim not to gaze with the naked eye (for round the fringe of the cloud the excessive brightness still dazzles and blinds, 379–81), but to approach with eyes covered by the double folding of both wings (382: Isaiah VI. 2). The light that fringes or *skirts* the clouded central brightness of the divine glory provides Milton with one of his recurrent symbolic themes (380: see XI. 332 and 882). (The imagery here is of course closely paralleled in the Light/Dark, Sun/Cloud imagery of Eliot's *Four Quartets*.) Next the hosts hymn the Son in whose face the unclouded likeness of the Father can be actually looked at by God's creatures, though the full radiance of the divine glory rests on him and the full amplitude of the divine Spirit flows through him (385–9: cf. VI. 680–3 and 703–4). By the Son the Father's creative decrees were enacted; by the Son his rejection of the rebellious angels was realized; by the Son likewise – but conversely – the Father's deep policy of pity (402), 'Mercy and Grace' (401) towards fallen man was perceived and effected, at the price of bliss disregarded (408) and death embraced. This unmatched act of love, hymned by the angels, evokes from the poet a postscript of personal dedication (410–15).

416–539 *Satan reaches the outer sphere of the universe, where he walks alone (–443) on the empty uninhabited surface, the Limbo later to be populated by cast-offs and drop-outs (–497). Eventually he comes to the bottom of the stairway that leads to Heaven (–525) and next to it the passage that leads down to the Earth (–539).*

The outer sphere of the universe is the *primum mobile,* solid and dark, which separates the nine spheres within ('luminous inferior Orbs', 420) from Chaos. Here 'Satan alighted walks' (422) – and the phrase is a striking rhythmic parallel to 'Satan exalted sat' (II. 5). Though the vast universe, seen from vaster distances, is a 'Globe', it is a 'boundless' plain to the being who alights on it; waste, exposed, and comfortless too, except on the side that picks up a 'small reflection' (428) from the distant shining wall of Heaven. As Satan walks, thoughtfully bent on the destruction of his human 'prey' (441), he is fittingly compared to a watchful vulture waiting to swoop down from snowy mountain heights on flocks in the valleys below. The Oriental geography perhaps suggests an especially sharp contrast between frozen heights and rich valleys (the 'canie Wagons' of 439 are sail-carts driven by the wind).

Emphasizing Satan's solitude and the cheerlessness of the place, Milton holds up the action to tell how this uninhabited region is later to be a Limbo, well populated by a 'store' (444) of beings 'from the earth'. The 'Paradise of Fools' (496) here pictured (444–97) is fittingly placed on the cheerless and exposed outside surface of the universe. It is to be furnished and populated by a flying upwards from the earth of things and beings essentially empty (the word 'vain' is reiterated, 446–8), too trivial and light to keep their grounding below. (They come up like 'Aereal vapours', 445: cf. Shakespeare's 'trifles light as air'.) Men who have in life rooted their foolish ('fond', 449) hopes, ambitions and efforts in the empty ideals of earthly fame and happiness (or indeed in selfish prospects in 'th'other life', 450) will find here 'fit retribution, emptie as thir deeds' (454). It is notable that the sheer emptiness of the setting is what makes it appropriate;

also that the phrase 'painful Superstition and blind Zeal' (452) would seem to cover extremes of popery on the one hand and covenanting fanaticism on the other. Freaks and misborn products of Nature are 'dissolvd' (457) of earthly substantiality and in their emptiness wander here, and not in the lunar sphere (where Ariosto places them in *Orlando Furioso* XXXIV; and Pope, too, for that matter in his *Rape of the Lock* V. 113–14). Milton reserves the lunar sphere for solider and worthier beings, more appropriate ('likely', 460) to its 'argent Fields' (460) – 'translated Saints' and creatures whose nature is midway between the angelic and the human (the strict philosophical and cosmological fitness of this argument is notable).

Other beings of peculiarly unnatural or mixed creational status will come here, the 'Giants' (464) of Genesis VI. 4, and those 'ill-joynd' (463) offspring of the 'sons of God and the daughters of men', also referred to in Genesis VI, whose conduct is later to be reviewed and judged by Michael in his prophetic revelation to Adam (XI. 683–8). (Indeed the list of creatures here, 444–97, should not be treated in isolation. It has a detailed connection with the review of man's moral history contained in Michael's prophetic survey in Books XI and XII.) Then there are the builders of the Tower of Babel (see XII. 38–62) who dwelt in the land of Shinar ('Sennaar' here, 467: see Genesis XI. 1–9). Individuals who typify the same vanity of human ambitions are added to the list – Empedocles, the Greek philosopher of the fifth century B.C., who plunged into the volcano on Mount Aetna from ambition, some say, to be thought a god (see Matthew Arnold's *Empedocles on Etna*), and Cleombrotus who was so lured by the prospect of Elysium that he drowned himself. To these are added misborn foetuses, idiots, hermits and friars ('White, Black and Grey' – Carmelites, Dominicans, and Franciscans), those whose mistaken notions of religious duty induce them to go on pilgrimages in idolatrous pursuit of holy places on Earth, such as Golgotha the hill of the Crucifixion, rather than to set their minds on the living Christ in Heaven (477), and those who put friars' habits ('weeds', 479) on when they are dying in the hope of passing into Heaven in disguise (a category scarcely worth mentioning, one would think, since the genuine friars have already been consigned to this Limbo, 474–5).

All these shallow creatures float upwards past the seven planetary spheres, past the eighth sphere, that is the firmament of the 'fixt' (481) stars, past the ninth or 'Crystalline' sphere whose balance determines the much-discussed 'trepidation' (cf. VIII. 130–40), and through the *primum mobile* ('first mov'd' sphere, 483) on whose external surface Satan is now moving and the empty beings will eventually find a place. But first the full symbolic significance of their ambitious emptiness is to be tasted and lived through as they continue to aspire heavenwards and even set foot on the stairway that leads to St Peter's gate. There is not weight or solidity enough in them to make the climb. A sudden 'cross wind' (487) blows them off course ('Into the *devious* Air', 489 – the epithet is transferred). They are whirled away along with all the trappings of their vanity, over the 'backside' of the Universe and into the spacious Limbo 'now unpeopl'd' (497).

A gleam of distant light in this desolate region eventually draws Satan to the bottom of the stairway which leads up to the magnificent gate (505) in the wall of Heaven. It is like the stairway on which Jacob saw 'the angels of God ascending and descending' (Genesis XXVIII. 12) when, having robbed his brother Esau of his father's blessing, he left home to go to his grandfather's house at Pandan-aram (513 – Genesis XXVIII. 2) and dreamed of the gate of Heaven as he slept in the 'field of Luz' (513), thenceforward called 'Bethel' (Genesis XXVIII. 19). Milton tells us that each of the stairs has its mysterious symbolic significance (516) and also that the stairway is not always there but may be drawn up to Heaven.

At this same point where the heavenly ladder touches the outer shell of the universe there is a gap in the shell through which is visible below the surface of the ninth, crystalline sphere (cf. 482), a 'bright Sea ... of Jasper, or of liquid

Pearle' (518–19). Human creatures later drawn up to Heaven come either 'sayling' (520) on this surface, 'wafted by angels' (perhaps this is an allusion to what we learn from the parable of the beggar, Lazarus: see Luke XVI. 19 ff. and 22 especially), or fly over the liquid surface in a 'chariot of fire' reminiscent of Elijah's (2 Kings II. 11). That the heavenly stairs should be 'let down' (523) at the time of Satan's exploration may be, Milton suggests, either to test his bravado by an apparently 'easie ascent' (524) or to press upon him his exclusion from bliss.

It is from the base of this stairway that a passage leads down to the Earth. The opening in the shell of the universe is directly above the Garden of Eden (527). The passage is 'wide' so that there is all the evidence of an easy commerce between innocent man in his newly created home and Heaven itself. Indeed, Milton assures us, the passage is 'wider by farr' (529) than the later one that is to lead down to Mount Sion and to the Promised Land. This passage, associated with the comings and goings of angels between Heaven and God's chosen people (his 'happy Tribes', 532), likewise suggests an easy commerce under the Old Covenant between Heaven and Jerusalem, the holy city. Indeed God's 'eye' (534) with special watchfulness ('choice regard', 534) frequently surveys the full stretch of the Holy Land from Dan (later called 'Paneas', 535) in the north where the Jordan rises, to Beer-sheba ('Beersaba', 536) in the south where Palestine borders on Egypt.

540–653 Satan looks down on the interior universe (–561), then plunges down in flight till he reaches the orb of the Sun, where he alights (–588). The scene is described (–612). Satan catches sight of the angel Uriel from behind (–629), disguises himself as a 'stripling Cherub' (–644), and accosts him (–653).

A single sentence runs from 'As when . . .' (543) to 'beheld so faire' (554). There should be no full-stop at the end of line 551. The wonder that seizes Satan (552–3) at the sight of the universe – even though he is a being who has seen Heaven itself (552) – is like that which seizes the weary, travelled 'Scout' (543) when he reaches a hill-top to catch a sudden, unexpected view of a fine city in the dawning sunlight. Even so Satan's envy (553) at the lovely prospect is greater than his wonder. He is no longer a being capable of worship or pure, self-forgetful appreciation. Standing above the enveloping canopy of the night sky, he can survey the full stretch of the inner universe from east to west, Libra to Aries ('the fleecie star', 558), and from 'pole to pole' (560). (Surely Milton must have consciously intended the correspondence between Satan surveying the world as a whole from east to west, from north to south, 557–60, and God keeping the 'choice regard' of his watchful eye over Palestine, from north to south, 534–5.) He flies down through the smooth ('marble', 564) air, surrounded by what are stars when seen distantly, but 'other Worlds' when more nearly approached (565–6) – indeed reminiscent of the Islands of the Blessed ('happy Iles', 567) to which Greek mythology consigned the fortunate mortals selected to evade death. It is the 'golden Sun' that lures Satan, because its golden splendour is what most resembles the magnificence of Heaven. He makes his way towards it, but one could scarcely define the direction of his progress, 'up or down' (574), centripetal or centrifugal (575), here where the Sun, in his planetary lordship exalted and apart ('aloof', 577), sheds his light from a due distance, while the lesser stars, his subjects, keep up the orderly dance of those measured movements by which times and seasons are calculated. The sun, it should be noted, is not just the lordly monarch of the planetary system and the directing force of its movements (582–3), for his 'magnetic beam' also sends out a nourishing warmth that penetrates 'each inward part' (584) of the system with a pervasive unseen potency ('vertue', 586).

In landing, Satan becomes a 'spot' (588) on the solar surface such as no astronomer has yet seen through his telescope ('Optic Tube', 590). Thus he defaces the sovereign source of light and warmth. The brightness of the surface exceeds that of any earthly metal or stone because it is not the brightness of a single steady consistency, rather an all-pervasive inner radiance (593–4), like the glow of heated iron, shining through various precious substances, metallic and mineral. The precious stones listed in exemplification appropriately recall again both the jewelled imagery of the New Jerusalem of Revelation and the jewels of the priestly breastplate of Aaron (Exodus XXVIII. 17–20) associated with the tabernacle of the Old Covenant (598). Finally an allusion to the philosophers' stone (600) of medieval alchemy completes a little circuit of allusions, which has given the sun's magnificence a corresponsive symbolic flavour of grandeur at its summit in vast spheres of religious, historic, and cosmic universality.

The theory that it is the sun whose influence produces gold in the earth (see below, 608 ff.), as the Moon produces silver, Mercury quicksilver, or Saturn lead, makes the excursion here into the subject of alchemy relevant and logical. The alchemists' desire to find the secret of transmuting baser metals into gold has its philosophical and practical implications at a time when the sovereignty of gold among material substances represents at a crude level the sovereignty of man in the animate world, of the sun in the cosmos, of reason in the human microcosm, of God in the totality of things. Milton presses home the vanity of the alchemists' efforts as being more impossible of realization than attempts to 'bind/Volatile *Hermes*', that is quicksilver (Mercury), or to call up Proteus (604), the old man of the sea who would transform himself into any shape to evade capture.

It is not surprising, the poet adds, that here is found an exhalation savouring of tincture of gold, and rivers flowing with liquid gold, when the sun is such a master of alchemy ('Arch-chimic Sun', 609) that its touch can produce in our own environment, at this immense distance, and in the dark earth, so many precious things. The devil gazes undazzled in the shadeless light such as the sun sheds on the equator at its midday zenith (613–17). (There is no 'obstacle' here to cause a shadow, 615, and no opaque body on the equator could cast a slanting shadow if the sun were directly above it, 618–19.) The clarity of the air sharpens Satan's sight ('visual ray', 620) and extends its range, so that he soon sees the back of the angel whom St John saw ('And I saw an angel standing in the sun.' Revelation xix. 17). He wears a golden crown ('tiar', 625) and his bright ('illustrious', 627) hair waves round the shoulders feathered ('fledge', 627) with wings. He seems to be employed on some important duty ('charge', 628) or deeply preoccupied. Satan is pleased because he now sees hope of learning which way to get to the Garden of Eden.

First he decides ('casts', 634) to disguise his true appearance which otherwise might get him into danger or difficulty. So he assumes the shape of a 'stripling Cherub'* with the celestial smile of youth in his face. The completeness and effectiveness of the transformation recall the sudden Spenserian transformations of Archimago and his like. His dress ('habit', 643) is girt up ('succinct', 643) for quick action.

The angel hears him approaching and turns to reveal himself as the archangel Uriel, one of 'the seven angels which stood before God' (Revelation viii. 2) and one of 'those seven' who 'are the eyes of the Lord, which run to and from through the whole earth' (Zechariah iv. 10).

654–742 *Pretending a great desire to gaze in admiration on God's newly created race, Satan asks Uriel the way (–680). Uriel is deceived by Satan's hypocrisy (–693), expresses his delight in the wonder of the new creation (–721), and points to the Earth, the Moon, and the Garden of Eden (–735). Satan flies to the Earth (–742).*

Satan addresses Uriel as one of the seven archangels privileged to stand near God's throne and carry his first-hand directions ('authentic will/Interpreter', 656–7) to where the lesser angels gather to hear them ('thy embassie attend', 658), and assumes that Uriel has a similar special authority

---

* The apparently pathetic 'blind stripling' of Joyce's *Ulysses* receives directions from Bloom on his way to tune up the instrument of betrayal (*Ulysses* 231). It is with a shock that we later learn his true character from the curse he mouths (*Ulysses* 322).

for keeping a watchful eye on God's behalf on the new creation. He pretends that an 'Unspeakable desire' to marvel at the new 'works', and especially the favoured new being, man, has brought him here. He asks which of the 'shining Orbs' man inhabits or whether he is not restricted to one alone – for Milton allows for the possibility of interplanetary travel by men as well as angels (667–70). Satan's pretended motive is to admire God's works and thus 'in him' (man) and all things (675) worship God who has so justly and wisely cleared Heaven of rebels and created this new race to 'repair that loss' (678).

Satan's deception passes undetected ('unperceivd', 681) because only God can see through hypocrisy. This is logical for, as Milton explains, though men and angels have wisdom which would be capable of detecting it, they also have a genuineness and trust that keep suspicion at bay (686–9). Thus, though Uriel is the 'sharpest sighted Spirit of all in Heav'n' (691), his very integrity ('uprightness', 693) enables him to be taken in by the 'fraudulent Impostor' (692), and he warmly praises Satan's desire to 'know/The works of God' (694–5) and 'thereby to glorifie' the Creator. Milton, we can be sure, is making a significant point here in thus distinguishing the two very different motives for exploring God's works, and at the same time showing how the two motives may be overtly indistinguishable at first sight in the eyes even of the wise and good. The moralist might add that the tragic destiny of a civilization and a culture gone astray is here foreseen, indeed forecast. You cannot trustfully open the door freely to honest enquiring knowledge and understanding without at the same time opening it to calculated plans to exploit and corrupt.

Thus Uriel bursts out in praise of the wonder of God's works (702), the delight of knowing them, and the deep mystery both of their multiplicity and of their origin (706–8). For Uriel himself saw how at God's first creative word there came the potential substance of the universe ('worlds material mould', 709) gathered and delimited out of the formless chaos of infinitude (708–11). At the 'second bidding' light appeared and order emerged, distributing and disposing both the four 'cumbrous' elements (earth, water, air and fire) and the etheral 'quintessence' of the upper heavens with the innumerable, animated ('spirited', 717) revolving stars. 'The rest' (721), that is to say what is left of the ethereal quintessence after the making of the stellar system, forms the outer wall of the Universe (721).

Uriel points to the 'Globe' (722) which is the Earth. The light shining from it, he observes, is the light reflected back from the orb of the sun on which they now stand, and its unseen further side ('th'other Hemisphere', 725) would therefore be in complete darkness were it not for the 'neighbouring Moon' (726) to which he also points. Uriel instructs Satan on the day–night sequence, on the monthly cycle of the moon (728–9) with its threefold ('triform', 730) phasing (crescent, full and waning), and on the 'borrowed' (730) character of the light that the face of the moon thus sheds on the Earth. Finally Uriel points to Paradise, the home of Adam. The contrast is hinted at between Satan's free exploration and Uriel's resumption of duty ('Thy way thou canst not miss, me mine requires', 735). In parting, Satan gives to Uriel that due obeisance which is never neglected in the reverently observed hierarchical manners of Heaven. He leaves the sun's orbit ('Ecliptic', 740) and is now so heartened with the hope of success (740) that he dives steeply and swiftly, executing many an angelic cart-wheel or loop, and does not rest till he alights on Niphates (the 'Assyrian mount' of IV. 126).

Book IV

The poet wishes man could be so forewarned of the approaching danger as to escape the fatal trap ('mortal snare', 8). He feels the need for some such 'loud voice' (Revelation XII. 10) as St John heard in his vision of Heaven, proclaiming the day of salvation, the kingdom of God and the power of Christ, and declaring that 'the accuser of our brethren is cast down.... Woe to the inhabiters of the earth ... for the devil is come down unto you, having great wrath, because he knoweth that he hath but a short time' (Revelation XII. 10–12). The reference to the final consummation of human and earthly history, planted here at the very beginning of it all, enables the reader to share Milton's sweeping grasp of time's totality, and to sense the significance of the present journey whose effects will reverberate so far. If the full horror of the evil is thus pressed home, the advance irony of its inevitable failure is pressed too. Satan's 'rage' (9), and the duplicity of the sequence which makes him first 'Tempter', then 'Accuser of mankind' (10) surely de-glamorize him adequately for the balanced reader not to be taken in by the hollow emotionalism soon to flow.

Satan has as yet no success ('speed', 13) to rejoice in. At this preliminary stage his action ('attempt', 15) against mankind is like a cannon ('devilish Engine', 17) whose recoil may injure the man who fires it before ever its fire strikes the foe. The poet has impressed on us the enormity of what Satan is about to do: we are not surprised that 'horror and doubt' (18) stir up that hell which is now his own inner condition. The inmost thought ('conscience', 23), which even in the most corrupted being must still *know* the difference between good and evil – for otherwise he would no longer be a person responsible but a machine inculpable – wakens that desperate realization of the true character of what he is, what he is about, and what terrible evil and suffering he is initiating (–26). With his first glimpse of 'pleasant' (28) Eden he turns a grieved eye on Heaven and on the sunlight.

The outburst that follows (32 ff.) is as artistically appropriate as the poet's initial outburst above (1–8). The one gave a sweeping glance at man's future destiny, pre-setting the Garden of Eden story in the context of the vast and ultimately saving events to follow. The other takes a sharper backward glance at the birth and development of that spiritual evil which is now at large to corrupt the new creation. Satan's outburst is triggered off by the sight of the sun, which he hates because of its godlike 'Dominion' over the new world (33–4), and because he hates the light (37) – as the former angel of Light, now reminded of what he was before pride and ambition brought him low (40). In thus casting his mind back to his former condition, Satan recovers the unfallen Luciferian sense of proportion sufficiently to admit that God gave him his own 'bright eminence' and did nothing to deserve or provoke rebellion, since he demanded no hard return service, but only the easy return ('recompence', 47) of praise and thanks for what had been freely given. This 'good' turned to evil ('prov'd ill', 48) in Satan. Being so highly blessed, he wanted to be superior to all 'subjection' ('sdeind' – *disdained*, 50), to take in one moment the step which would pay off ('quit', 51) the debt of being eternally grateful. It is the burden of being eternally indebted, always paying yet always owing ('still paying, still to ow', 53) that he rejected. He did not understand the true character of the creature's indebtedness to the Creator, whereby the repayment in praise and gratitude is part of a dance-like mutual relationship in which the movements of giving, gratitude, discharge, and grateful acceptance of continuing obligation, succeed each other in a pattern of interchange which is burdenless and free (55–7). Milton's didactic generalization is a powerful one.

It is difficult to take seriously Satan's pretended wish that he had been made an 'inferior Angel' (59) so that 'unbounded hope' would not have tempted him with ambition. This train of thought is a subtle move back towards putting that blame on God which he has just accepted as his own (42). The thought does not mature. Satan sees that he might have joined a rebellion as a lesser angel, by the same process by which he came to lead one as an eminent angel (62–3). Other angels withstood temptation, and he had the same defences of 'free Will and Power' (66) as they had. Logically he has arrived at the conclusion that he has no one and nothing to accuse except 'Heavns free Love equally dealt to all' (68). The tortuous intellectual sequence that Satan derives from this logical pronouncement represents the disintegrating irrationality of evil, as its perversions ravage the foundations of intelligence and inner stability. He curses that divine love whose consequential operations his own perversity has engineered to the end that love and hate seem to produce the same kind of misery in his condition (69–70); but immediately afterwards correctively curses himself for freely choosing, against God's will, what he now justly regrets.

Satan has thus accurately expressed despair (74). He has accurately voiced the inner condition of Hell (75), revealing what it means to be sucked into its devouring depths: for his own mind and feelings are devouring themselves before our eyes and ears. A last melodramatic gesture in the direction of that 'Repentance' and 'Pardon' (80) on which he has already turned his back, now follows. It is a ritual gesture only. Not only is the way closed by his own pride: he has also staked his leadership of the other devils on the boast that he 'could subdue/Th'Omnipotent' (85–6). The admission that, even while the devils see him exalted ('advancd', 90) on the throne of Hell, he is inwardly tormented with misery and thus paying dearly for the falsity of his claim (87), seems once more to stake a claim for sympathy in a wilfully chosen self-doom. And indeed he concedes that, could he repent and by an act of divine grace (94) be restored, the restoration would but breed a renewal of ambition and show his repentant 'submission' to be a sham ('feignd', 96). That he should assume God capable of being duped by a sham repentance is indicative of the intermittent incapacity to sustain even the logic of illogical evil. Next moment he foresees that the 'ease' of a restoration to Heaven would quickly cause a recantation of empty promises made under the compulsion of pain (97). There can never be a 'true reconcilement' (98) after a hatred so deep. In short, this hypothetical excursion into the way of penitence would buy only a 'short intermission' and then a 'heavier fall'. God knows all this, Satan grants (103), so that to postulate a forgiving act by God is as unreal as to postulate a request for pardon by himself. The elaborate excursion into labyrithine might-have-beens seems to have been a waste of mental energy: but surely the twists and tergiversations of argument have accurately represented the incestuous intellectual activity of egotism. A last note of self-pity is sounded as he notes God's 'new delight/Mankind' (106–7), made to replace ('in stead', 105) him and his followers, and then bids farewell to hope, fear and remorse, and claims 'Evil' for his 'Good' (110).

The outward facial contortions accompanying the tortured inner sequence of argument and feeling, create havoc with the 'borrow'd visage' of the youthful cherub which he assumed in order to deceive Uriel (III. 634–44), and thus shows up his false disguise ('betraid/Him counterfet', 117). Heavenly minds do not experience the foul moods reflected in his features. Remembering this, Satan, the 'Artificer of fraud' (121) composes his features. But Uriel has taken note of the degree of disfigurement and violence in feature and gesture, which is not proper to a blessed spirit ('of happie sort', 128). Satan is unaware that he has been observed.

131–287 Satan comes to Eden and to the Garden of Paradise, which is described in detail (–171). He cannot gain access through the thick undergrowth, and he leaps over the wall (–193). He sits on the Tree of Life and surveys the extent of Paradise. The Garden is described, in particular the Tree of Life and the Tree of Knowledge (–222), the river that irrigates the Garden (–246) and other delights of the place (–287).

The Garden of Paradise is a circular area of table-land surrounded by a tangled, overgrown wall of thicket and greenery, which protects it (132–7). Outside, the ground falls away in a steep slope, covered with trees and shrubs. Though the wall overtops these trees (142–3), there is an inner circle of trees overtopping the wall. These are laden with richly coloured fruits, showing more colourfully in the sunlight than a sunset or a rainbow (150–1). As Satan approaches, the pure air meets him and the breezes ('gales', 156) carry rich scents like those which are carried out to sea from the east coast of Africa. The allusion to the smell of burnt fish (168), by which Raphael drove off the devil Asmodeus from Sara, the wife of Tobias, son of Tobit, is notable because Milton alludes to the same story again (v. 221–3 and vi. 365) and has relevant correspondences in mind (see pp. 129 and 156). The story comes from the apocryphal Book of Tobit. It is told dramatically in James Bridie's *Tobias and the Angel*.

Satan struggles up the steep, uncultivated ('savage', 172) hill, but the tangle of shrubs and bushes, which forms the wall at the top, defies penetration on foot (176–7). The only gate is on the further, eastern side. Satan does not care for an opening that offers fitting or lawful ('due', 180) entry: he leaps the wall. So doing, he is likened to a wolf leaping into a sheepfold or a thief climbing in at a window. Correspondences between sheepfold, Church, and Heaven, are commonplace in Christian imagery (cf. 193 and *Lycidas* 115 ff.). The irony of using the Tree of Immortality as a vantage point for spying ('prospect', 200), while 'devising Death/To them who liv'd' is for Milton a neat instance of how the good things God gives are perverted to 'meanest use' or total abuse (204). Satan sits 'like a Cormorant'.

The Paradise now open to Satan's eyes is a little compressed summary of the whole wealth of Nature – and indeed more than that, for it is 'A Heaven on Earth' (208). In Genesis II. 8, we learn how the 'Lord God planted a garden eastward in Eden' (209–10) and Milton suggests locations in Syria and Mesopotamia (210–14) on the basis of references in Ezekiel (XLVII. 15 ff.) and 2 Kings (XIX. 12). From Genesis II. 9 ('And out of the ground made the Lord God to grow every tree that is pleasant to the sight, and good for food; the tree of life also in the midst of the garden, and the tree of knowledge of good and evil') develops the expanded version (214–22); and the account of the river, which in Genesis 'went out of Eden to water the garden; and from thence it was parted, and became into four heads' (Genesis II. 10), is the basis for Milton's river, which takes a subterranean course under the 'shaggie hill' (224) of the garden. (Satan is to effect his entry through this passage in IX. 72–6: see p. 209.) A fountain rises up from this river to refresh and irrigate the garden 'with many a rill' (229). The rills reunite to join the main stream as it issues again into the daylight and then divides (233) into the four rivers of Genesis (II. 11–14). The implication that 'Art' (236) – that is, poetry – can scarcely do justice to the beauty of the blue waters ('Saphire Fount', 236: cf. II. 1050 and see p. 63) of the spring, from which the brooks meander in bewildering twists and turns ('mazie error', 239) under the overhanging ('pendant', 239) foliage, establishes a contrast between Art and the perfection here of natural beauty, which is further stressed in Milton's description of the flowers, where the controlled fastidiousness and fancifulness of laid-out flowerbeds is contrasted with the sheer overflowing plentifulness of natural vegetation ('Nature boon/Powrd forth profuse', 242–3). (The same contrast is made in Spenser's idealized Garden of Adonis, *Faerie Queene* III. vi. 34, 36, 44.) The abundance of growth is found both in the 'open field', which gets the full sunlight, and in the thickly shadowed ('imbround', 246) bowers. In short, though the emphasis has been upon 'Nature' (242) in respect of profusion, it is apparently an idealized perfection that we encounter in other respects. The 'happy rural seat' (cf. 1. 5) of varied appearance ('view', 247) sounds like an estate in which cultivatedness is important. The romantic dichotomy between Nature tamed and Nature free is not yet with us. Indeed here is a place, and here only, where stories told of golden fruit, such as the apples in the legendary garden of the Hesperides, are realized. The image of the shining, polished ('burnisht', 249) golden fruit hanging there, lovely and desirable ('amiable', 250), may be regarded as a symbolic one. Remembering the significance of the tempting apple in both Christian myth and Classical story, we ought not to miss Milton's emphasis upon Paradise as the only place where the natural is idealized without losing its naturalness, and poetry correspondingly made real. Milton presses his point firmly. If the fruit 'burnisht with Golden Rinde' (249) looks too good to be true, we are told that it has a 'delicious taste' (251). The thornless rose to follow in line 256 provides another instance of Milton's balancing of ideal and real. Meantime the description of glades ('Lawns', 252), downland, flocks and hillocks, which are interspersed between the streams, leads to an image of the 'lap' of a well-watered (irriguous', 255) valley, which indicates that traditional correspondences between the garden of the world and the garden of the human body (the female body notably) are feeding English poetry long before the unbalance of Freudianism comes along to vulgarize this vein of symbolism. The 'mantling Vine' here laying forth her purple grape (258-9) is soon to be paralleled in the natural curls ('wanton ringlets', 306) of Eve's hair, which are like the tendrils of the vine (307). The vocabulary from 254-68 is notably alive with words, which thus give the garden the flavour of a living body ('Layes forth . . . gently creeps', 259; 'murmuring', 260; 'fringed . . . crownd', 262; 'breathing', 265; 'trembling', 266) until the whole scene is fully animated in the procession of Pan, the god of all nature, the

Graces and the dancing Hours. Another blend of incompatibles is delightfully realized, for the dance of the Hours symbolizes the orderly succession of the seasons, but here they lead on 'Eternal Spring' (268).

Four famous places are listed as being unable to compete in beauty with Paradise. They are Enna (269) in Sicily, from where Pluto ('Dis', 270) carried off Proserpina to the Underworld; Daphne on the river Orontes (273) near Antioch, a park ('sweet Grove', 272) sacred to Apollo; Nysa (275), a Mediterranean island near Tunis, where the Libyan king Ammon (277) hid his son (by Amalthea) Bacchus (279) so as to protect him from his wife Rhea (279) (Bacchus's name *Dionysus* derives from 'Nysa'); and Mount Amara (281) in Abyssinia, where the royal princes were held in seclusion for their protection (Dr Johnson calls the place 'Amhara' in *Rasselas*). Milton has perhaps selected his places for their respective associations with danger from the Underworld (Enna), delight (Daphne), and guarded seclusion from possible danger (Nysa and Amara). The allusion to Proserpina and Pluto (269-71) is to be developed in further correspondences later on (cf. IX. 395-6: and see commentary on IX. 432, p. 220).

288-392 *Satan sees Adam and Eve, whose beauty and innocence are described (-318). They pass by and go to eat and rest by the side of a stream (-340). Around them play the animals of Eden (-350). Evening falls (-357). Satan bursts out in envy of them, and declares his determination to undo them (-392).*

In the first description of Adam and Eve, Milton's emphasis is upon their superiority to all other creatures in this new world and to their sovereign lordship over it (290). 'Far nobler' in 'shape' than any of the animals, they are 'erect' (the word is repeated, 288-9: see VII. 506-9, where the animals are 'prone', man 'erect' and 'upright'). Their superiority in form and lordship marks their special status as reflecting the 'image' of their maker. The Miltonic theology gives us a 'Godlike' man and woman (289) whose 'Honour' and 'Majestie' are inherently natural ('native', 289) to them. The only hint here of a puritanical rigorousness comes in the repeated adjective 'severe' (293-4), but even this word seems to be employed to preserve a balance. The strictness and purity of their 'sanctitude' (293) is neither a crampingly servile nor an assertive and authoritarian strain in them, rather a guard and guarantee of the essentially free and son-like (not subject-like) relationship with their maker (293-4). Milton underlines the point (295). It is from the divinely reflective characteristics in man that man's true authority derives.

Too much has been made of the relationship between the sexes formulated in lines 295-9. Milton's connotative use of the word 'equal' requires him to say that 'both' are 'not equal', which shows that the usage is nearer to our usage of *identical*. Indeed he seems to be saying little more than that the two differ; he being formed (i.e. fashioned) for reflection and bold physical action, she for less strenuous and more graceful pursuits. Since the two of them are naked, this observation is quite naturally the first differentiation to be called forth. That he was formed for God singly and directly ('only', 299) and she 'for God in him' is firstly a fact about their physical origin: its implications for their psychology and relationship have yet to be made clear.

Milton has a sense of the unity of humanity, which transcends sexual differentiation and which has to be weighed against possible charges of anti-feminism, especially in respect of *Paradise Lost*. What the man displays pre-eminently and what the woman displays pre-eminently are after all equally *human* characteristics (Joyce goes to great lengths to make the same point in *Ulysses*). If the man's broad forehead ('large Front', 300) and bold uplifted glance ('Eye sublime', 300) express the assurance that man exercises in his 'rule' over the world he inhabits (300-1), is it not true that the woman's very style of self-presentation expresses a corresponding vein of 'subjection' – *not* servile, but demandingly responsive to an approach that is sympathetic (308)? These are *both* aspects of man's humanity. Man (i.e. *both sexes*) is both subject/son in relation to God and ruler (*both sexes*) over his world. Man (both sexes again) as ruler derives his authority from his 'filial' (both sexes) relationship to God: his freedom is his willing obedience. Milton has hammered this doctrine into our minds several times, and indeed has just repeated it, speaking of *man and woman together* in lines 289–95. Man and woman have nobility, erectness, honour, majesty, are Lords of all and reflect the divine image of their Maker in '*their* [not *his*] looks Divine' (291). Now Milton turns to take a closer look at the two naked bodies, observes (to the horror of some twentieth-century critics) that they seem to differ in some respects, and notes that the outer differences seem to correspond to the respective balancing emphases upon man as ruler and man as subject, which he has already explained. Anyone who finds this observation hard to stomach must surely be blind to the human form and to the character of poetic and theological symbolism.

The network of theological symbols and correspondences that underlies so much perceptive and discerning Christian literature establishes the human soul as feminine in relation to God's masculinity. Milton is but giving his own twist to the parallelism that drives Eliot to use a female Chorus in *Murder in the Cathedral*. If man is the king by symbolic tradition, woman is the garden, the very body of his world. That differentiation hangs over the imagery of this first introduction to Adam, with his breadth of shoulder and manliness of bearing (301–2) and to Eve with her untamed curls ('wanton ringlets', 306) like the tendrils of the vine. The garden and the family (or the home), like the city or the kingdom, may all be symbolically related to the New Jerusalem. That woman is man's garden, his city, his kingdom, and the very embodiment, in her Beatrician status, of that New Jerusalem in which he is to find eternal bliss – these are aspects of Christian symbolism which in other ages educated people have thought it superfluous to explain. Even the very mode of woman's sexual yielding to man (310–11) has that character of dance-like interchange, withdrawing and conceding, movement for movement, which we noted in relation to the creature's indebtedness to the Creator in our comment on IV. 55–7 (see pp. 93–4).

Man's shame of his sexual organs (both sexes), a guilty and unchaste ('dishonest', 313) shame, is unknown in the innocence of Eden. Only later is the 'native Honour' of line 289, a natural endowment of man in his naked dignity, transformed into the dishonourable honour, the product of sin, whereby the natural is 'clad' (see line 289 again) in the unnatural showiness of fine clothes and decorations. Thus the 'simplicitie' (318) of Adam and Eve in their innocence carries its social as well as its moral implications. In the age of Restoration finery and permissiveness it was scarcely necessary to press the point.

Adam and Eve pass 'hand in hand' (321: the phrase is to gather symbolic weight later, cf. IV. 689 and XII. 648; also 'handed', IV. 739), the 'goodliest' man and the 'fairest' woman. They sit down by a stream, having done just enough gardening to make them appreciate the cool breeze and the rest, and to give them an appetite. Nature is indeed at their service, for the easily bent ('compliant', 332) boughs that bear fruit can be grasped by a side reach even from a reclining position (332–3). Thus all natural things around them have a built-in usefulness and a ready-made adaptability, which, as frustrated man well knows, the world of our fallen daily experience almost always lacks. The bank, which is so beautifully ornamented ('damaskt', 334) with flowers, turns out to be 'soft' and 'downie' to recline on in the nude. This is an innocent child's Paradise indeed. For fallen man such a bank would prove a positive hoard of hidden things that scratch and bite. Surely Milton's sense of humour is never more gentle and alert than here. Likewise, having chewed the heart out of a fruit, they can use its skin to scoop up a drink of water from the stream (335–6). They can even mingle delights now so incompatible for fallen man as eating what sound like sticky oranges, indulging in tender conversation ('gentle purpose', 337) and love-play ('dalliance', 338). Meanwhile the animals, which have since become wild beasts to be hunted, are romping together, the lion jumping playfully ('Sporting . . . rampd', 343), not pouncing in hostility, and dandling the kid in its paws. Among the gambolling creatures the elephant recognizes its fittedness to do comic turns with its unwieldiness and its flexible trunk ('Lithe Proboscis', 347). Only the serpent seems to be outside the cheerful paradisal circus. Winding ('insinuating', 348) its sly way, it weaves a knotty tangle ('Gordian twine', 348) with its intertwined length ('breaded train', 349) and thereby, unnoticed, shows its potentiality for trickery. Other creatures, cattle it seems, are either down on their haunches, well stuffed with grass ('pasture', 351) and just gazing, or chewing their last cud of the day before sleeping ('Bedward ruminating', 352), for the sun is now low in the sky ('Declind', 353) and hurrying in its downward run ('prone career', 353) to the Atlantic islands in the west. Conversely, to balance this downward weighting, the stars of evening now rise in the upward-moving 'Scale of Heaven' (354).

Satan notes that Adam and Eve are not pure spiritual beings like the angels, but have a physical nature ('mould', 360) appropriate to their earth. Nevertheless they are 'little inferior' to the angels ('For thou hast made him a little lower than the angels . . .' Psalm VIII. 5) and so vitally reflect the image of their Maker and the 'grace' of his handiwork that Satan's mind is filled with wonder and he senses that he 'could love' them. The reminder of the essential Lucifer, created by God, is an impressive one, theologically and emotionally. But its incidence serves only to make Satan's intensified zeal to destroy them more negative. Indeed Satan wallows verbally in the fact that the greater the joy they now taste the deeper will be their coming 'woe' by contrast. As for the degree of their present happiness, he regards its continuance as 'ill secur'd' (guaranteed) and their present heaven an inadequately defended one ('Ill fenc't', 372). As the argument moves here there are all the superficial noises of a balanced sequence of parallels, contrasts, correspondences, and antitheses. The repetitions are hammered out – 'delight', 'woe', 'woe', 'joy'; 'happie . . . Happie'; 'Heav'n . . . Heav'n'; 'foe . . . foe'; 'pittie . . . unpittied'.

Yet the substance of the argument is at loggerheads with the
form. Satan's argument is a non-argument, his mood
virtually a non-mood. Posture seems to cancel out posture
before it has time to clarify itself. Claiming not to be the
foe of Adam and Eve by design (372–3), rather one capable
of pitying their 'forlorn' condition, though he himself is
unpitied (this sounds like a parenthetical *More-merciful-than-
thou*, directed at God, but if it is, it is immediately cancelled
out by what follows), he then asserts (lapsing into what
sounds like sarcasm) that he is seeking an alliance ('League',
375) with them, a bond of mutual amity so firm and close
that they must in future live together, sharing a common
dwelling. The dwelling he offers is, he concedes, perhaps less
palatable to human senses than 'this fair Paradise' (379), but
it is of God's making and Adam must accept it as such. As
the phrases roll out – 'he gave it me/Which I as freely give'
(380–1) – we recognize the familiar note of Satanic parody,
insanely malicious and humourless. The unfolding of Hell's
widest gates, formally to receive these two to share its
hospitality, represents, by the very use of the word *entertain*
(382), an irony of grand ceremonial proportions. The sending forth of kings to welcome them makes the future reception sound even more like a stage in a royal progress. The
spaciousness of Hell, over against the manifest cosiness of
Paradise (383–4), is a further irony in the satanic advertise-
ment. The posture of the estate agent gives way to that of
the apologetic host as Satan adds: that the dwelling I offer is
not better than it is, for this you must blame ('Thank', 386)
God, who drives ('puts', 386) me, loath as I am, thus to
revenge myself on you who have done me no wrong for the
wrong he has done to me. The final afterthought is a piece
of hypocrisy political in flavour and magnitude. I feel personal sympathy for you, in your 'harmless innocence' (388),
but demands of 'public reason' compel me to do what
otherwise I should hate to do. The give-away phrase is 'with
revenge enlarg'd' (390), for the cause Satan serves is not an
impersonal quasi-national one 'enlarg'd' by revenge, but an
individualistic one rooted in personal lust for revenge.

393-491 *Satan comes down from the tree to get a closer view of his human victims (-410). Adam speaks to Eve of God's goodness in giving them so much (-419) and restricting them so little (-439). Eve agrees (-448), and tells how she first woke to life (-452), first saw her own features reflected in water (-469), first was led to the sight of Adam (-480), heard his call, and responded to it (-491).*

The Devil's claim that his action is forced on him by 'necessitie' is the familiar excuse of tyrants, Milton notes. Satan comes down among the four-legged animals and assumes the shape first of one, then of another, as best suits his need to get a closer view, so that he can pick up ('mark', 400) what there is to be learned of their situation ('state', 400) from what Adam and Eve say or do. First he is a lion, then like a tiger who has seen two fawns playing and keeps changing his position till he finds the best one from which to pounce on them. He is 'all eare to heare' (410) when Adam turns to speak to Eve.

Adam addresses Eve as the sharer ('partner', 411) in his joys and the dearest element ('part', 411) in them. His topic of conversation is God's unbounded goodness and generosity (414-15), the most natural thing of all to talk about in Adam's situation. So Adam himself makes clear. They have been raised from dust to happiness though they have earned nothing and can make no repayment, because God needs nothing and asks nothing (cf. the Satanic attitude to such indebtedness, IV. 52-7), except that they should keep the one prohibition against tasting of the Tree of Knowledge. God has made death the penalty for breaking this prohibition, which is the single token of their relationship of obedience to him, and balances the vast evidence all around them of their authority and rule over the world and the creatures that inhabit ('possess', 431) it. Adam sees no negativity in a prohibition that is counterbalanced by 'Free leave so large to all things else'.

Though feminists might wish to quibble over the opening of Eve's speech, what she says in initially addressing Adam goes little further than to balance his own praise of her as

'partner' and 'part' of his joys. That she was formed 'for' him
and 'from' him and flesh of his flesh is not disputable. That
she was so made in response to Adam's plea for a partner
makes it undeniable that she exists to that purpose ('end',
442). Without Adam there could have been no such purpose
to serve. Eve's recognition of this and her consequent
recognition of Adam as her 'Guide' and 'head' have no
doubt a Pauline flavour (see 1 Corinthians XI. 3 – 'The head
of every man is Christ; and the head of the woman is the
man; and the head of Christ is God'). Eve now claims to
have the 'happier lot' of the two of them in having the
greatly superior one ('Preeminent by such odds', 447) to
delight in. This is the balancing expression of courtesy and
love to Adam's assurance that she is 'dearer' herself than the
entire abundance of good things around them (412). The
return of praise for praise, claim for claim, in competitive
mutual admiration is psychologically appropriate and sharp.
If the universal masculine tendency is to say 'You are the
most wonderful of all things', is it not the universal feminine
tendency to say 'How lucky I am to have such a wonderful
person as you to admire'? Such interchanges, pressed into
the idiom of unfallen sexuality surely produce exactly what
we have here.

Milton is consciously exploring the psychology of unfallen
womanhood. Eve describes her first awakening to consciousness (449–52). The murmuring sound of waters drew her till
she came to a smooth lake. To her inexperienced thought
and eye it looked like 'another Skie'. As she bent down to
look at it closely, she saw opposite a shape in the water
bending to look at her. She 'started back' (462) at the sight
of what was her own reflection, and of course the reflection
'started back' too (463). She took pleasure in what she saw,
and might have remained there, fixed in the delightful
activity of exchanging identical looks of sympathy and love:
but a voice warned her that she was looking at herself (468)
and called her to follow to where no reflection awaits
('shadow staies', 470) her coming, but a substantial being
whose image she is; one whom she shall enjoy as her own

'inseparablie' and to whom she shall bear multitudes of beings like herself.

Thus woman's first sight of herself, in her state of innocence, is a great and natural delight: and the reason for drawing her away from the pleasure of staring at herself is not a question of vanity – the issue just does not arise; rather it is because there is no future, no fulfilment, in staring at yourself, however beautiful; you will only pine 'with vain desire' (466). What the divine voice calls her to is a substance instead of a shadow, a being who can be embraced (471) and sexually enjoyed. When Eve actually sees Adam, whilst conceding that he is indeed handsome and 'tall' (477), her first reaction is that nevertheless he is not *quite* so delightful as the image she saw in the water ('less winning soft, less amiablie milde', 479). She is right, of course. Unfallen woman's good sense and good taste, disentangled from later vanity, and here *antedating* sexual experience, are finely presented.

So innocent, inexperienced Eve's reaction to the first sight of man is to turn back with a frank feminine preference for what can be seen in the mirror (480). It is Adam's cry that calls her back, the cry of his claim upon her (of whom she is bone of his bone, flesh of his flesh – Genesis ii. 23), and of his need for her, an inseparable comfort ('individual solace', 486), a 'part' of his very soul, indeed his 'other half' (488). With that the hands of the two of them are first joined. Eve yields. And *after* the yielding the woman's judgement on man is different. She now sees that 'beauty' (woman's beauty, of course) 'is excelled by manly grace/And wisdom' (490-1). Woman is still unfallen and innocent. But she is no longer inexperienced.

492-588 *Adam and Eve embrace and Satan turns aside in envy (–504). He contrasts their bliss with his torments (–513), then declares his plan to exploit the prohibition imposed on them (–527). First he will seek around for further information (–538). Meantime at the gate of Paradise the angel Gabriel sits with a guard around him (–554). Uriel joins him (–560) and warns him of the escaped evil spirit he has seen (–575). Gabriel is determined to find out who, if anyone, is about (–588).*

As they recline in their naked half-embrace, Eve looks up at Adam with a glance of blameless ('unreprov'd', i.e. not to be reproved, 493) wifely attraction, and he in turn smiles down (this is surely what 'with superior Love' amounts to, 499) on her as Jupiter, the sky god, shines down on Juno, when he impregnates ('impregns', 500) the clouds – so that they burst into rain that brings flowers to life on earth. The linking of Adam and Eve, first man and first woman, with the universal figures of ancient myth and the fruitful seasonal life of nature is interesting. The Devil has only envy and the malicious leer of jealousy with which to react to the wholesome delight and the implicit universal fruitfulness.

That Milton intends to keep us aware of the correspondence between the paradise of natural fruitfulness and the paradise of human and sexual fruitfulness is clear from Satan's outburst against the torment of seeing the two of them 'Imparadis't' (506) in an embrace. The 'Eden' (507) they enjoy is both a place and a condition (a mutual relationship), as Satan's Hell is likewise (see IV. 75). The contrast is pressed here. Hell is a place of unfulfilled individual longing (508–12) (cf. 'pines' here, 511, and 'pin'd' in IV. 466: it is the relationship with Adam that saves Eve from a lifetime of pining).

There is one consolation for Satan. He has heard from their own lips of the divine prohibition against eating from the forbidden tree called the Tree of Knowledge. Satan does not understand, or affects not to understand, why knowledge should be forbidden. He finds the prohibition 'suspicious' and 'reasonless' (516). So does the reader, if it is put like that. But we must be careful. Milton is not a fool. Satan's *non sequiturs* move swiftly from the bare fact that a tree is 'call'd' (514) 'of knowledge' to the theory that we are dealing with a God who imposes an irrational ban on knowledge in general out of 'envie' (517), and who makes willing acceptance of 'Ignorance' (519) the test of human 'obedience' and 'faith' (520). Devil's talk indeed, but 'fair foundation' (521) on which to build the very 'ruin' (downfall) of mankind.

Within a few moments the Devil has elaborated a scheme of human destruction so plausibly worded that we are tempted to 'fall' for his trickery. The exploitation of loaded words and emotive connotations turns God's one prohibition into 'Envious commands, invented with design/To keep them low whom knowledge might exalt'. *Envious* has become an accepted qualification; *invented* and *design* imply a mean and malignant purpose. We have to read the Devil's words as closely as we read those of contemporary persuaders. The Devil however has put his cards on the table – 'I will excite thir minds . . .' (522) – so we ought to know where we stand.

Thus, determined to play upon the human aspiration to be 'equal with Gods' (angels, 526), so that they break God's prohibition and suffer death, he moves away to search around for some possible 'wandring Spirit of Heav'n' (531) who may be able to tell him more. He has been made over-confident by his assumed success in taking Uriel in (III. 681 ff.).

Meantime the setting sun is directly confronting ('with right aspect', 541) the eastern gate of Paradise (seen from within, of course). The gate is a massive white rock towering up to the clouds. On the outside the rock has a single winding 'ascent/Accessible from Earth' (545–6), at the top of which is the entrance. The rest of the rock face is craggy and unclimbable (547). Between the 'rockie Pillars' (549) formed by the entrance sits the angel Gabriel. Gabriel, one of the archangels and second only to Michael (VI. 44–6), is associated in the Old Testament with bringing divine comfort to men (see Daniel VIII. 15 ff. and IX. 21 ff.). He is especially appropriate as the guard of Eden, because St Luke names him as the angel of the Annunciation who brought to the Virgin Mary the news that she was to conceive our Lord (Luke I. 26 ff.). That the angel who watched over the Adam of the old creation before the Fall should be the one who is to announce the coming birth of the new Adam in whom mankind is to be saved is apt. (There are parallels yet to come between the old Eve and the new Eve – the Virgin Mary – which will fill out the relevant fabric of correspondences.) Though the 'unarmed' young angels around Gabriel are exercising themselves in what seems to be off-duty time, their arms are near to hand.

It is a brilliant scene, with horizontal evening sunshine flaming on the alabaster gateway and the jewelled armour of the guard; and Uriel comes gliding on the level sunlight like a comet that sweeps across ('thwarts', 557) the night sky.

It would appear from Uriel's first words that the sequence of angelic duties is determined by lot, and that on this basis Gabriel now keeps guard over the entrance to Paradise (561–3). Uriel explains frankly that the spirit he met (Satan) seemed very keen ('zealous', 565) to learn more of God's works, and especially of man. He gave the spirit directions ('describ'd his way', 567), as he was in a hurry ('Bent all on speed', 568), and took note of his flight through the air ('Aerie Gate', 568); but when Satan landed on 'the Mount' (569 – Mount Niphates, III. 742), and then indulged his angry passions, Uriel marked his disfigurement and ferocity (see IV. 127–9) and thus here tells how 'looks/Alien from Heav'n' (570–1) betrayed his identity as one of the fallen angels.

Gabriel recognizes that Uriel's duties in the bright sphere of the Sun enable him to see far and wide, but assures him that none can pass his guard ('vigilance', 580) except recognizable spirits from Heaven, and none such has come since noon today. But he cannot deny that a spirit 'of other sort' (582) might have illicitly jumped over the surrounding earthworks ('earthie bounds', 583) of Paradise. If so, and he is still lurking within, Gabriel insists that he will know of it by dawn.

589–688 *Uriel returns to the sphere of the Sun (–597). Evening falls over Paradise (–609). Adam calls Eve to rest (–622), observing what gardening must be done tomorrow (–633). Eve agrees (–638), declaring her delight in Paradise (–649) and in Adam (–656). She asks why moon and stars shine when all else sleeps (–658). Adam explains (–676), adding that they are surrounded by unseen beings (–688).*

Uriel returns to the sphere of the sun. When he came, the sunbeam on which he glided was horizontal, but now the sun has fallen lower in the west, below the horizon ('Beneath th'Azores', 592), so that Uriel's return by sunbeam is a downward flight. Milton leaves open the question whether the sun ('prime Orb', 592) has actually rolled with such unbelievable speed on a daily course (592–4) or whether the earth, rolling ('volubil', 594) less far to the east, has moved its position over against the sun. Milton thus allows for the more recent Copernican theory, though he has generally adjusted his narrative to the Ptolemaic cosmology. He returns to the Copernican version in Raphael's account of the movement of the earth in Book VIII (128 ff.). Milton is clearly dissastisfied with definitions of movement and position in pre-relativity thinking (recall how dimensional oversimplifications, 'up or down', were out-dimensioned in III. 574 ff.).

The lordship and majesty of the sun are reflected in the divinely sovereign and liturgical 'Purple and Gold' (596) of the 'Clouds' attendant on his 'Throne' (597). On Earth, as evening takes over, things are clad in the more 'sober Liverie' of twilight gray. This is a vital universe, animated at all levels, and reflecting both the order and splendour of Heaven. Even 'Silence' (600 and 604) is a living presence, moving over the ground in the company of 'Twilight' and taking dignified pleasure in the slinking to rest of beast and bird. That the firmament glows 'With living Saphirs' (605) reminds us that Heaven's towers and battlements were 'Of living Saphire' (II. 1050; see p. 63; and cf. IV. 236); and the stars are a 'Host' (606) like the angels. The image of the City is stamped out in the fabric of the natural unfallen world where now by night, under the manifest queenship of the moon, man and woman are about to add in their own way to the animated pattern of hierarchical beauty.

It is a dancing universe of measured movements and orderly cycles. Labour balances rest as day balances night. And work is not yet a curse but a delight. The animals 'Rove idle unimploid' (617), but the daily purposeful activity ordained ('Appointed', 619) for his body and mind gives evidence of man's superior worth ('Dignity', 619) and the continuing concern ('regard', 620) of Heaven for all that he does. The other animals 'unactive range' because God is less interested in what they are doing from moment to moment (621–2). Adam points the need to work early next morning on the arbours and alleyways where trimming is called for. The overgrowths draw attention to the inadequate cultivation ('mock our scant manuring', 628). The need for more hands is already being felt (629). The hint is delicately placed. Fallen blossoms and gums that disfigure and roughen the walks call out for removal ('Ask riddance', 632); but first Nature and night call them to rest.

Eve, at this evening hour, 'with perfect beauty adornd' (634) is happy to let Adam, her source of being ('Author', 635: see p. 53) and the director of their labours ('Disposer', 635) decide these things for her. The pattern of obediences relating God to man and man to woman (and the Father to the Son: see Filial 'obedience', III. 269) is but the obverse of that 'First Disobedience' (I. 1), angelic and human, by which all harmonious relationships are disintegrated. It takes in matters so small as tomorrow's gardening and tonight's love-making. The woman gains both delight and credit for her due femininity (638). Woman's joy in a man is of a kind that shuts out awareness of those things on the basis of which directions are issued and activities organized.

Eve hymns the beauties of their world, the song ('charm', 642) of birds at dawn, and the round of natural delights till 'silent Night' (647). We remember that 'Silence was pleas'd' with the interruption of the 'wakeful Nightingale' (IV. 602), and 'silent Night/With this her solemn Bird' (reiterated, 647–8, 654–5) is Eve's repeated joy. The repetitive, incantatory rhythms and phrases build up an atmosphere of semi-liturgical beauty and dignity, the word 'solemn' (648 and

655) adding its ritualistic flavour. The celebrated passage
(641–56) is a kind of evening office in whose final versicle
Eve makes her admission that nothing of what she delights
in, without Adam, would be sweet. We need to foresee, at
this point, what is to depend upon her later decision to
forego Adam's company for a time (IX. 214 ff.). Milton
draws the two occasions together by his customary method:
cf. 'and require/More hands then ours to lop their wanton
growth' (IV. 628–9) and 'till more hands ... Lop ... wanton
growth' (IX. 207–11).

There is a neat transition from Eve's thought that without Adam she could not enjoy what is about her to the
question why stars should shine when there is no one awake
to appreciate them. Later Satan, in the serpent, wants to
know from Eve why her beauty should be wasted on
insensitive animals and a human audience of one (IX. 539–46:
see pp. 223–4).

Adam, the ancestor of all of us ('our general Ancestor',
659) can fitly call Eve 'Daughter of God and Man' (cf. IX.
291) because of the way she was born. Moreover she thus
has a status in some respects corresponding to that of the
Son who will reign both God and man, 'Son both of God
and Man' (III. 316). Unless the significance of these parallels
is fully weighed, we shall fail to do justice to the poem. As
Eve's relationship to Adam in Paradise images the Son's
relationship to the Father in Heaven, so Sin's relationship to
Satan parodies that same relationship in Hell. If Hell is the
parody of Heaven, Paradise is its image. There is an image
in man and woman of the divine consubstantiality of Father
and Son. The full glory of Godhead is Fatherhood and Sonship in unity: the full glory of humanity is manhood and
womanhood in unity. If there seems to be a relationship of
sovereignty and obedience between man and woman, it is
no more remarkable than that between Father and Son.

Adam explains that the stars have their due courses to
fulfil so that 'total darkness' shall not by night regain control
of a universe whose very origin was heralded by a *fiat lux*.
Life in Nature and all things is dependent on light. The stars

not only preserve that light, they also, by the emanation of an appropriate ('kindly', 668) heat, infuse a 'stellar vertue' into all forms of life on Earth (671–2). This infusion operates in many different ways by processes of fomenting, warming, tempering or nourishing (669–70). The efficacy of these processes is such that things growing on Earth are rendered more susceptible to the finishing touch which the 'more potent Ray' (673) of the sun brings to bear on them. So even if the stars at night were unseen, their shining would not be in vain.

But it would be a mistake to assume that if there were no man and woman there would be any lack of beings either to watch the sky or to praise God. He and she, waking or sleeping, are surrounded by numberless spiritual beings, ceaselessly watching God's works and praising him. Eve and he have often caught the sound of celestial voices. The picture Adam gives is of companies ('bands', 684) of angels keeping watch or making their rounds by night (685), joining in full chorus, and with instrumental accompaniment (686–7), to mark off the watches ('divide the night', 688) and lift human thoughts heavenwards.

689–775 *Adam and Eve go to their bower* (–708), *the scene of their first act of love* (–719). *They say an evening prayer together* (–739), *then enter, lie down and make love* (–749). *The poet sings a hymn to 'wedded Love'* (–770). *Adam and Eve sleep* (–775).

Adam and Eve walk 'hand in hand' (cf. IV. 321 and IX. 385–6: see p. 216) to their bower of bliss, a place specially designed for them by God when he made everything for their use and enjoyment (691–2). The thick protective roof is made of intertwined laurel and myrtle; bushes and shrubs, interlaced with irises, roses and jesamine, form the walls; and there is a carpet of flowers to lie on, colourful as a richly inlaid mosaic (692–703). The 'awe' (705) in which man is held by the animals keeps out birds, insects, worms and so on. The 'sacred' and secluded privacy of the place is stressed (706); they come here 'alone', and here in the withdrawn secrecy ('close recess', 708) Eve first prepared their marriage bed. It is a paradise within Paradise, over which 'heav'nly Quires' sang the marriage song ('Hymenaean', 711) on the day when the nuptial ('genial' – Latin *genialis*, 712) angel brought in to Adam the naked bride.

Classical parallels enrich the picture. Of the place, Milton notes that there is nothing imagined in Greek or Latin poetry or story to match it (705–8). Of Eve, the bride divinely given to man, Milton declares her more beautiful than Pandora. When Prometheus stole the original ('authentic', 719) fire from heaven, Zeus used Pandora to revenge the theft. Pandora was endowed by the gods 'with all their gifts' (715), but Zeus also gave her a box containing all evils for the torment of mankind. Hermes led her to Prometheus who wisely rejected her, but his brother Epimetheus, 'the unwiser son' (716; their father was the Titan, *Japhet*, 717), married her, opened the box and let loose its afflictions on humanity. Pandora's status as the first woman and her fatal role in bringing distress to mankind bring classical equivalents to bear on the figure of Eve, thus reinforcing the universality of Christian myth. The overtones of cosmic ambition, uprising and vengeance, involving primal man and divinity, which the Promethean story carries, are similarly apt and corroborative. The ensnaring of mankind (717–18) is the tragic outcome ('sad event', 716) common to both stories (cf. IX. 392).

Adam and Eve stand and worship. They praise God, giver of the night, the day, their nuptial love ('crown of all' their bliss, 728). Paradise, with its abundant delights, is too big for the two of them, its over-abundance of fruits requires more beings to enjoy them ('wants Partakers', 730–1). But God has promised them a fruitfulness to match that of the garden, a race of men to fill the earth, who will be united with their first ancestors in praising God's goodness at waking and sleeping. After prayer they do not perform any other rites, but go into the bower still 'Handed' (739). Freed ('eas'd', 739) from the troublesome necessity to undress, they immediately lie down together, and the poet assumes (for he would not have us so intrusive on their privacy as to see it for ourselves) that Eve yields to Adam in the act of love (741–3). Milton defends the purity of unashamed sex and attacks as 'Hypocrites' (744) those who imply that it is impure. God's command to man, 'male and female', was to 'be fruitful, and multiply' (Genesis 1. 27–8), and if the Creator's command is to increase, the order to 'abstain' (748) can issue only from man's 'Destroyer' (749), the Devil (cf. x. 987–9).

The poet sings a hymn in praise of 'wedded Love', the act in which mystery and legality are blended (750). It is the one thing in Paradise exclusively the private right ('sole proprietie', 751) of Adam and Eve. It is the means whereby free-ranging lust is driven from the human to the animal world. Loving relationships and all interlinking family affections are, on the basis of this mystery-in-legality, grounded in reason and the virtues (754–7). It is over the act of love even now being performed by Adam and Eve that the poet pronounces his universal benediction. The act is not out of keeping with the 'holiest place' (759). We are at the heart of the garden, the paradise within Paradise, which we have already defined as the image of the City, and the act is the 'Perpetual Fountain of Domestic sweets' (760) – continuing source of the home's delightfulness. The bed on which the act is performed has its undefiled chastity permanently guaranteed by the practice of saints and patriarchs. This is the place for genuine love. Milton's image of the 'golden shafts' (763) derives from the legend that Cupid used gold-tipped arrows to arouse love and lead-tipped arrows to repel it. The lamp of fidelity ('constant Lamp', 764) is lit over the bed of marriage.

Milton draws a sharp contrast between married love and the loose relationships of permissive London society – the endearments of the prostitute bought for cash, the 'loveless' and 'joyless' coitions of casual connections. The liaisons and dissolute revelries of the court are offensive to Milton (767–8), and so is the romanticization of extra-marital passion in such conventions as that of the lover, 'starv'd' with cold, serenading his mistress by night (769–70). The contrast to such shallow artificialities is here before us in the naked, embracing pair, 'lull'd by nightingales' (771) and showered by roses. Let them sleep on in their happiness. It would be happiest of all if they could continue to want no happier state than this and could have the wisdom to want to know no more.

776–876 *Gabriel orders angelic patrols to keep watch on the northern and southern borders of the garden (–787) and a third, under Ithuriel and Zephon, to search the garden itself for a possible infernal intruder (–796). They find Satan at Eve's ear in the form of a toad, trying to poison her dreams (–809). At their touch Satan's disguise leaves him (–819), and the astonished angels demand to know who he is (–826). Satan assumes that he is recognizable (–833). Zephon rebukes him. One devil is like another (–843). With charge and countercharge Satan is led before Gabriel, who recognizes him (–876).*

Since the earth is a sphere, and smaller than the sun, the side of the earth which is facing away from the sun (the hemisphere which is having its night-time) will have its darkness in the form of a black cone of shadow pointing outwards from the earth to the vault of Heaven. At midnight the point of the cone would be in the meridian. The 'shaddowie Cone' (776) of night would therefore have measured half this climb up the sky by nine o'clock. At this point the cherubim come out and stand ready to undertake their night watches. Gabriel despatches a band under Uzziel, half to patrol the southern border and half to patrol the northern, the two halves to meet at the western extremity of the garden (782–4). In a magnificent image we see the two bands curl out like a split flame, half 'wheeling' shieldwards (to the left), half swordwards (to the right). Gabriel orders Ithuriel and Zephon to search the garden itself and especially the region of the bower where Adam and Eve are now probably sleeping without thought ('secure', 791) of danger. Gabriel explains how someone came this evening from the sunset ('sun's decline', 792) and spoke of seeing an infernal spirit of Hell coming in this direction ('Hitherward bent', 794), no doubt with some evil plan in hand. If they find him, they are to seize him and bring him back.

Ithuriel and Zephon go straight to the bower and find Satan at Eve's ear, 'squat like a toad' (800), trying by his devilish skill to make contact with her faculty of 'Fancie' and thus to fabricate fantastic and illusory dreams, or to inject such poison into the vapours ('spirits', 805) emanating from the blood ('Like gentle breath from Rivers pure', 806, in the case of unfallen woman) that they produce moody and discontented thoughts, vain hopes and purposes, disproportionate desires inflated with the lofty pretensions that give birth to pride (–809). (For a full explanation of the mechanics of dreaming, see v. 100–21, where Adam comments on Eve's dream.)

Touched lightly by Ithuriel's spear, Satan (such is the force of heavenly tempered steel) perforce resumes his own shape. The sudden transformation is like the sparking-off of a pile of gunpowder just waiting to be put into a barrel ('Tun', 816). The savour of dirt ('smuttie', 817), smell and danger is appropriate, and the sudden up-leaping of flame from 'graine' (817) matches the emergence of fiend from toad (Luciferian fiend, of course). The two angels start back in astonishment. Asked which of the devils he is, Satan is at first scornful of the angels' ignorance, which suggests that they themselves are small fry in Heaven (830–1). Zephon, however, has a nasty shock for Satan. He reminds him that his appearance is not what it was in Heaven. Whatever brightness and glory he had when he was 'upright and pure' departed from him, and he now carries about with him the marks of his sin and of his 'place of doom' (the outer marks of Hell on the features match the now persistent character and flavour of Hell in the Satanic mind). The contrast is pressed. The gravity and severity of the rebuke, blended with the 'youthful beautie' (845), make for a union of gracefulness and power that one would not expect to find at the earthly level. Milton has an eye for the transcendence of Earth's incompatibilities in Heaven's transfigured harmonies, as he has for the distortion of Earth's incompatibilities into

Hell's disfigured perversities. In the relation of ideal to image and to counterfeit, the unity-in-triplicity of Milton's isolated concepts of Heaven, Earth, and Hell (with their respective inhabitants) is worked out in every book of *Paradise Lost*. Thus the Devil stands 'abasht' (846), *feeling* 'how awful goodness is', *seeing* how lovely virtue is and, not surprisingly, *pining* his loss. It is a moment of momentous realization for Devil and reader alike: suddenly to find yourself unrecognizable through the visible impairment of the 'lustre' which made you what you were. He only *seems* (850) 'undaunted'. He tries to rescue his dignity and superiority by back-chat. 'If I've got to fight ('contend', 851), it's more appropriate to match myself against the best of yours, the being who sends others on errands, not those who are sent, or indeed the whole lot together. More glory that way.' The epigrammatic swagger is empty. Satan has no choice. 'Your fear of defending yourself here and now', says Zephon, 'will save us the trouble of testing what the least cherub can do on his own when he is up against a being utterly weakened by wickedness' (854–6). The sting is in the tail.

Ithuriel and Zephon lead Satan, champing angrily, like a 'proud Steed reind', to the western end of the garden where the two patrols have met for further orders, after having each made their half-circuit of the border (857–64). Gabriel sees them coming and does not so much *recognize* the former Lucifer as conjecture his identity from his princely bearing ('Regal port', 869), his 'faded splendour' (870), his gait and his outward ferocity. This must be 'the Prince of Hell' (871) and, if so, he is unlikely to go away without a struggle. Coming up, Ithuriel and Zephon explain where they found him and what he was doing.

877–1015 *Gabriel challenges Satan on what he is up to (–884) and Satan replies scornfully (–901). Gabriel answers mockery with mockery (–916), then asks Satan why he has come alone (–923). Satan says that he is spying out the new world with a view to settling there (–940) and mocks Gabriel's unadventurous angelic fidelity*

(–945). Gabriel rebukes Satan's dishonesty (–949), disloyalty (–956), and hypocrisy (–961), then despatches him with a severe warning against any return (–967). Satan answers with a threat (–976). The two prepare to fight (–990), but the sudden appearance in Heaven of the divine scales checks Gabriel (–1005). He points to them: Satan sees and flees (–1015).

Gabriel challenges Satan. Why has he broken through the restrictions imposed on him for his transgressions and come to interfere with the rightful performance of duty ('charge', 879) by others who demonstrate ('approve', 880) their disapproval of transgression but have the power and right to question what he is doing here? Satan expresses contempt. In Heaven Gabriel had the reputation ('th'esteeme', 886) for being wise, and Satan considered ('held', 887) him to be so. This question he has asked raises a 'doubt' about his supposed wisdom (887–8). Is there anyone who likes his punishment and would not get away from Hell if he had the chance? Gabriel would do the same himself, and take the risk of getting as far away as possible from pain to wherever there might be a hope of replacing 'Torment with ease' (893) and cancelling out grief with delight ('recompence/ Dole with delight', 893–4). That is what Satan is about. He foresees that the explanation may not satisfy Gabriel ('To thee no reason', 895), since Gabriel has experience only of good, not of evil, and will therefore naturally urge in reply ('object', 896) that it is God's will that imprisoned them in Hell. God's will is not an answer to any question for a fallen angel – only for an unfallen one. If God wants them to remain in imprisonment ('durance', 899) he should lock the iron gates more firmly. So much for your questions, Satan concludes. He admits that he was found in Paradise as described.

Gabriel's reply contains its ironies. So heaven lost a great judge of wisdom, did it (904), when Satan fell through his own foolishness? And now here he is again (906), very seriously wondering whether he can regard as wise those who want to know what bravado has induced him to escape here illicitly from imprisonment (–908), but convinced that it is very wise indeed to run away from pain and punishment! Milton's emphasis is on Satan's total lack of wisdom, self-knowledge, and rationality – and the corresponding disintegration of intellect and personality whereby he continues to address others in the name of those same values, and to judge them by the criteria of those same values. At this point Gabriel's tone changes (912): Continue to indulge this presumptuous pretence of being in a position to make judgements ('So judge thou still, presumptuous', 912) until your escape provokes divine anger to send you packing back to Hell, with this wisdom of yours which seems to amount to little more than the obvious elementary understanding that there is no punishment to match that which you ask for when you provoke the anger of God (912–16). Further basic flaws in Satan's plausible pseudo-coherence are brought to light in Gabriel's final questions. Why have you come on your own? Is the pain of the other devils less than yours; something less obviously to be fled from? Or are you not so tough as the others in putting up with it? (917–20). Lastly the discrepancy between Satan's claim to courage and his action in being the 'first in flight from pain' (921) is noted, and another discrepancy, too, for Satan scornfully insisted that any sensible being would get away from Hell as quickly as possible (887–90), yet presumably can scarcely have cited 'this cause of flight' (922) to the abandoned devils whom he left behind.

Gabriel has tied Satan up in knots, but Satan blunders into further inconsistencies. He reminds Gabriel what a brave showing he put up in the war in Heaven, and insults him gratuitously by adding that without the backing of the artillery fire from the divine thunder his own 'spear' would not have been 'dreaded' (929). Then he is foolish enough to denigrate Gabriel's argument as ill-thought-out ('words at random', 930) and as evidence of his own inexperience of what the role of a 'faithful Leader' (933) must be when he has made tough but unsuccessful attacks. He must not risk everything on a dangerous enterprise till he has tried out the venture himself. This is Satan's excuse – a quite different one, of course, from that already given (888 ff.). He is engaged on a pilot mission to spy out the 'new created World' of which there has been a rumour in Hell ('Fame is not silent', 938). The purpose is for the devils to settle on Earth, even though for possession of it they are compelled ('put', 941) to try their strength once more against God's fine ('gay', 942) legions, more fitted for the 'easier business' of heavenly hymn singing, bowing and scraping, than for battle. (N.B. 'practis'd distances to cringe' – presumably to walk backwards and bowing from the royal throne over the appropriate distance.)

The lucid sharpness of Gabriel's reply – the acute epigrammatic economy of his reasoning – is irresistible. The reader comes face to face with the Good of the Intellect, the sheer beauty of it, in contrast to the evasive incohesiveness of Satan, as he clutches at successively incompatible postures of verbal defence. Exposing the inconsistencies (947–9), Gabriel fastens then on Satan's absurd reference to the duties of a 'faithful Leader' (933). The name of faithfulness is desecrated ('profan'd', 951) if it is used of loyalty to a 'crew' of devils by one who has broken his allegiance to God himself. Equally it is hypocrisy for Satan to pose as the guardian ('Patron', 958) of liberty, when he himself fawned in servility before God while at the same time plotting to dispossess him (957–61). Finally Gabriel bursts into a wrathful dismissal of Satan ('arreede' – advise, 962), threatening him with chains if he appears again within the sacred borders ('hallowd limits', 964) of Paradise.

It will be time enough to talk of chains when I am your captive, Satan retorts, mocking Gabriel's guard duties on the borders of Paradise ('limitarie' duties, 971), his duties as one of those cherubim on whose wings God rides ('Hee – the Son – on the wings of a Cherub rode sublime', vi. 771), and the duty given to cherubim of drawing God's chariot, a duty which makes them 'Us'd to the yoak' (975). The mockery now touches the entire 'Angelic Squadron', which fans out round Satan like a two-horned crescent moon, hemming him in with their spears at the ready over their shoulders ('ported Spears', 980). Comparison is made with a field of waving corn suddenly swayed by the wind so that the worried ('careful', 983) ploughman stands wondering apprehensively ('doubting', 983) whether the hoped-for sheaves may prove to be so much chaff when the time comes. Satan stands his ground, enormously expanded ('dilated', 986) in stature by gathering his strength. The threatened tumult ('commotion', 992) might have involved not only Paradise, but the vault ('cope', 992) of Heaven, or brought all the elements to destruction ('rack', 994).

But God intervenes, revealing the golden scales, which still hang in the sky as the sign of the Zodiac, Libra. In these God measured the weight of the hanging ('pendulous', 1000) Earth and the counterbalancing weight of air at the Creation, and now he weighs ('ponders', 1001) in them the results of historic action. Thus here the consequence ('sequel', 1003) of going away is measured against that of fighting, and the consequence of fighting is so negative for Satan as to weigh nothing: it flies up and kicks the 'beam' (the crosspiece from which the scales hang, 1004).

Gabriel points the moral. They know each other's strength. It is not their own, but given to them by God, so there is no point in boasting of it. Satan can do no more than God allows, nor can he himself, though in fact he has twice his usual strength so that he could tread Satan in the dust, as the scales, in which Satan can 'read' his own fortune ('Lot', 1011), testify. Satan recognizes that it is his scale which has gone up. Like Belshazzar, he has been 'weighed in the balance' and 'found wanting' (Daniel v. 27). He flees.

Book V

1–94 Next morning Adam wakes to find Eve still sleeping (–17). He rouses her and she wakes, startled (–27). She has had her first bad dream (–35) in which she was invited by what seemed to be Adam's voice to walk out and enjoy the delights of the night (–47). She rose, as if at Adam's call, and went seeking him, and came to the Tree of Knowledge (–53). Here she saw what looked like a heavenly spirit, who ate of the tree (–65), praised it (–73), and invited Eve to do the same (–84). She accepted and flew aloft with the spirit till he vanished, and she awoke (–94).

Adam wakes early, as usual ('so customd', 3), for he enjoys the light sleep which comes from a good digestion. The 'vapours' rising within him are temperate and soothing ('bland', 5) and therefore do not cause heavy or restless sleep. The mere ('only', 5) sound of leaves stirring with the dawn wind ('Aurora', 6) and of steaming streams is enough to waken him and clear his head (disperse the vapours). He is all the more surprised to find Eve still sleeping, with ruffled hair and flushed cheek, as though restless. His whisper to her to awake (echoing the Song of Solomon: see p. 221) is gentle as the breath of the west wind on flowers – and ought to have roused her as lightly as the voices of Nature roused him, but she awakes 'with startl'd' eye (26).

The sight of Adam's face and of the morning brings immense relief. She has dreamed, not – as often before – of the day's events, past or to come, but of harm ('offence', 34) and trouble. The voice at her ear that praised the beauty of the night overpraised it. It called the shadowy moonlight on the face of things 'more pleasing' than the light of the sun (42). The hint is of a world seen under darkness that is more interesting and exciting than when seen under light. That Satan's voice declares the beauty of night 'in vain' (43) if no human beings are awake to see it directly contradicts what Adam has already told Eve in answer to her own question (IV. 659–88). But the point has scarcely been made by Satan before he reverses it. The starry sky becomes now a mass of watching eyes intent on seeing Eve. First she is needed to appreciate the beauty in the 'face of things' (43): then she is needed so that 'all things' can gaze with joy and ravishment on her beauty (44–7). When, led by the deceptive voice and seeking Adam, she comes to the tree of prohibited ('interdicted', 52) knowledge, it looks to her 'Fancie' (the faculty which is active in dreams when other faculties are inoperative, 53) more beautiful than 'by day'. We are moving conceptually now, under Satan's influence, where things are more beautiful in the darkness than in the light, in the dream than in the reality.

Satan has appeared in Eve's dream (see lines 54–5) in the disguise by which even Uriel was taken in (cf. III. 636 ff.), though in fact he is actually 'squat like a toad' (IV. 800). He addresses the tree as overladen ('surcharg'd', 58) with fruit, and affects surprise that neither angel ('God', 60) nor man tastes it. Is it that knowledge is not valued? Or is it that envy, or some other restriction ('reserve', 61), has laid a prohibition on tasting it? The oblique introduction of an unmentioned *persona* who envies and restricts, by use of the appropriate abstract nouns, is characteristic of Satan's technique of persuasion. Forbid who will, here is an 'offerd good', which could not have been put here for any other reason than to be taken. The Satanic *non sequitur* by which the last clause of the utterance logically cancels out the first is familiar.

Taking and tasting, Satan finds the fruit not only sweet of itself but much more sweet for being taken in these circumstances. It is forbidden, apparently, as being only fit for angels, when it could in fact make angels of men. And why not? What is good increases by being shared: the 'Author' of it is not damaged but more honoured by its wider diffusion. Now that the argument has changed the implicit *persona* from a disobeyed being to an honoured

being, he assumes shape and is given a name, 'Author' (73).
Eve is urged to eat on the grounds that she will thereby
become a 'Goddess', no longer confined to Earth, but able
to move in the air and even to 'ascend to Heav'n' by her own
entitlement ('merit', 80). In the dream it is finally the
irresistible smell of the fruit that so stimulates (quickens,
85) the appetite that she tastes. Next moment she is flying
with the spirit, marvelling at her exalted transformation.
Equally suddenly she is alone. Then she falls asleep in her
dream. Now she is delighted to find the whole thing a
dream.

95–208 *Adam does not like what he hears* (–100). *He explains the
nature of dreams* (–113) *and the possible origin of this one* (–119).
He cheers her (–135). *They go out, see the sunrise* (–143), *and make
their morning act of worship* (–152). *Their hymn praises God for
his works and calls upon them to declare his wonder* (–208).

Adam addresses Eve as at once 'Best Image' of himself and
the 'dearer half', implying a relationship with a blend of
reflection and consubstantiality such as binds together
Father and Son in Heaven, Satan and Sin in Hell. Hence he
cannot but be troubled by the troubling of her thoughts.
The inexplicable ('uncouth', 98) dream would seem to spring
from evil, were it not that evil could not reside ('harbour',
99) in her. The theory of dreams now propounded by Adam
is based on standard medieval psychology. Reason is the
chief faculty of the soul. Fancy is the chief of the subordinate
faculties. The five senses feed in their impressions of the
external world. Fancy shapes these into images and Reason
combines or disentangles them into a coherence from which
judgements can be derived. These judgements constitute our
'knowledge or opinion' (108). When sleep comes and
'Nature rests' (109) Reason retires into a privacy and is out
of contact with the other faculties. While Reason is thus
absent, Fancy sometimes takes over her function in imitative
mimicry. But she then combines received sense impressions
in such a way as to produce, not a coherence, but an inco-
herence ('wilde work', 112) – words and deeds that are at

loggerheads in respect of meaning and chronology.* That is the sort of thing Adam detects in Eve's recorded dream, which seems to be compounded of fragments from last night's conversation and strange additional material. Nevertheless he reassures Eve that evil can move through the angelic or human mind without doing damage, provided that it is not approved of. He trusts that she would never in practice consent to do what in sleep she found so hateful. In telling her not to be disheartened and not to 'cloud' (122) her looks, which usually have a cheerfulness like the 'morning', he reasserts the preference for the clear unshadowed light of the day, a preference which Satan's perverted judgement subverted in favour of the darkness and the night (42–3). The 'choicest bosom'd smells' are 'Reservd from night' (128).

The mood of reproach and deference brings tears to Eve's eyes, but they are kissed away by Adam, and they come out into the open and see the dawn ('day-spring', 139). They worship and pray spontaneously. Unfallen man and woman, it is clear, have no need of fixed liturgy and repetitive, memorized prayers. They do not lack either the naturally varied verbal fluency or the fervent awareness of the holy, which will spontaneously produce a flow of eloquence, spoken or sung, and either in prose or rhythmic verse. These lines do not seem to constitute a comment on the best way for *fallen* man to worship (since there is an outpouring of extempore versifying such as we should find impracticable, to say the least) so much as a characterization of the state of paradisal innocence (144–52).

First the praise is of God, whose wonder is shown forth in his works. Reminiscences of the psalms occur and the imitation of the *Benedicite* is unmistakable. Thus Adam calls upon the angels, 'Sons of light' (160) who circle God's throne rejoicing in endless day, and on all creatures on Earth, to declare God's goodness (160–5). Then he calls upon

* What the other faculties get up to when separated from Reason is, of course, parallel to what Eve does when separated from Adam later on.

the morning star to praise him at the dawn (166–70), upon the sun as 'Eye and Soule' of the world to praise him in the morning, at noon and in the evening (171–4), upon the moon and the planets that move in 'mystic Dance' (178) and make the music of the spheres, to praise him who brought light out of darkness (175–9). The elements (earth, water, air, fire), moving in their endless cycle of fourfold permutations, are called to ring some new praise of their maker (180–4). Likewise Adam calls upon the 'Mists and Exhalations' (185), the winds (192), the waving pines and plants, fountains and singing brooks, the birds of the air (197), the fishes of the sea, walking beasts and creeping things, the morning and the evening, to join them in the universal act of praise.

209–307 Adam and Eve go to their morning work (–219). God sees them with compassion and calls upon Raphael (–223). He sends Raphael to warn Adam of the approaching danger (–245). Raphael flies to the gate of Heaven (–254) where he looks down on the Earth (–266). He flies down (–274) to the eastern gate of Paradise, where he is greeted by the angel guard (–290). He passes through them to where Adam sees him from the door of his bower (–307).

Calmed in mind by prayer, Adam and Eve go to their morning work. It is highly significant work. The 'overwoodie' (213) fruit trees have 'reached too far' their overindulged ('pamperd', 214) boughs and their 'fruitless' embraces have to be checked. In just such control of nature's appetitiveness is man properly employed: but of course it is the over-reaching of Eve's arms in natural appetitiveness which is soon to prove fatal. Similarly Adam and Eve quite properly train the 'marriageable arms' (217) of the vine around the elm. But the disciplining of this intertwining in marriage is not matched in the later events of their own day. (Elm is to vine as Adam is to Eve and as Father is to Son. We recall how the golden tresses of Eve waved in wanton ringlets as 'the Vine curles her tendrils, which impli'd/ Subjection, but requir'd with gentle sway', IV. 305–8.)

God calls Raphael, remembered here as the guardian help

of Tobias (cf. IV. 168 and VI. 365: see p. 96 and especially p. 156) who also had to deal with a wife whose nights were disturbed by demonic visitation. He sees Satan at work 'to ruin all mankind' (228) and wishes Raphael to go to Adam, when he is resting at noon, and to turn conversation in such a way that he may impress upon him the character of his 'happie state' (234) – that his happiness is at his own disposal, not an imposed but a free condition, subject to his own will which, being itself free, is not a fixed and unchangeable will. He must be wary of erring ('swerve', 238) through overestimating how 'secure' he is. Raphael is to explain exactly what danger awaits him and from whom it derives. He must understand that he will be assailed, not 'by violence', but 'by deceit and lies'. Adam must be told all this to ensure that he does not break his obedience wilfully and then claim to have been taken by surprise and quite unprepared for the test (–245).

The Father has now completed in abundant detail ('fulfilld', 246) the structure of justice undergirding Adam's freedom. The magnificent orderliness of life in Heaven is once more exemplified as the angelic quires divide to give a swift direct passage for Raphael's departing flight. And animate action is perfectly matched in the controlled inanimate environment. For the self-opening gate of Heaven, as devised ('fram'd', 256) by the 'sov'ran Architect', likewise gives swift passage (Milton would have been no enemy of modern technology, provided that the guiding mind kept a grip on it). From the gate there is neither cloud nor star to obstruct his view of the earth. For, however small, corresponding to ('Not unconform to', 259) other globes at this distance, the earth and Paradise can be seen by the angelic eyes. Galileo's telescope gives a less reliable ('assur'd', 262) view of the moon's surface (263) than Raphael has of the Earth's. The second comparison, of Delos first sighted from among the encircling Aegean islands known as the *Cyclades* (264), associates the 'garden of God' (260) with the ancient world's island and shrine sacred to Apollo, where solemn festivals drew people from many lands. The speedy, 'prone' and 'steddie' (268) flight of Raphael contrasts sharply with the stumbling, erratic journey of Satan to the Earth. His wing winnows the yielding ('buxom', 270) air like a living ('quick', 269) fan. When he reaches the soaring level of eagles, he looks, to the birds, like the *Phoenix*, the unique bird with magnificently coloured plumage. (The new-born Phoenix, bred of the worm from the marrow in the crumbled bones of its unique predecessor, collects those bones and carries them off for burial in the 'Bright Temple' at Thebes.)

Raphael unfolds his six wings (cf. Isaiah VI. 2): the royally ornamented shoulder wings that can cloak his breast, the golden middle wings girding his waist, which can wrap around his loins and thighs, and the sky-coloured heel-wings. Immediately his seraphic status is apparent. It is like a sudden self-revelation by the divine *Hermes* ('Maia's son', 285), the graceful messenger of the gods employed on such missions as that by which he recalls Aeneas from Dido and Carthage to further his destined duty in Italy (*Aeneid* IV. 222 ff.). The angel guard stand in due deference. Raphael passes through the outer regions of the Garden, where there is a wild abundance of natural growth, where Nature in her youthful primitive abandon has revelled in unregulated productivity. The 'enormous bliss' (297) resulting is an ecstasy to the senses as Milton's riotous verbal richness (292–3) indicates. Unfallen Nature can be allowed her romp where no evil has yet taken hold; but the wantonness of nature is one thing and the control that rational man brings to bear on it is another, as Milton's contrasting emphasis on Adam's work as a gardener makes clear (v. 212–19).

It is noon. The image of the sun beating down to warm earth's 'inmost womb' (302) maintains the correspondence between the body of the earth and the human body already implicit. Adam is sheltering in the door of his bower, Eve at work within, preparing lunch.

308–403 *Adam calls Eve to see the approaching angel and asks her to make ready a meal for him (–320). Eve agrees (–330). She gathers food and prepares it (–349) while Adam receives the guest (–360) with a courteous speech (–370). Raphael responds (–377) and they go in to be received by Eve (–387). Raphael greets Eve (–391). They sit, and Adam bids Raphael eat (–403).*

Adam's first sighting of the approaching angel is voiced with a rhetorical splendour and a rhythmic dignity which is interestingly echoed in the description of Dalila's approach in *Samson Agonistes* (cf. 'Comes this way moving', 310, and 'Comes this way sailing', *Samson Agonistes*, 713). He bids Eve hurry to prepare a generous meal fit for a heavenly visitor. To give liberally to liberal givers, and 'large bestow/From large bestowd' (318) is of course to imitate the dancing interchange of divine love in the life of Heaven as well as to match Nature's fertile bounty which increases 'by disburd'ning' (319). One must draw such parallels as these in order to bring out the full significance in modes of address like 'Adam, earths hallowd mould,/Of God inspir'd' (321-2), which stresses Eve's awareness of Adam as earthy substance indwelt by the divine spirit. Eve does not need to keep a large hoard ('store', 322) of food when there is a plentiful supply ('store' again, 322) at all seasons of the year available in the garden. The only fruits she has to gather in advance are those which by careful 'storing' (324) gain in nourishing firmness by the loss of superfluous moisture. But she will hasten to gather such choice fresh food as will persuade the angel that God has 'dispenst his bounties' (330) on Earth as in Heaven.

Eve goes off in businesslike ('dispatchful', 331) fashion, her mind intently planning the forthcoming meal in detail. The selection of appropriate foods must answer the demands of 'delicacie' (333), and the arrangement of courses, individually and in sequence, must be such that there are no 'inelegant' (335) incompatibilities offered together and no crude succession from one course to the next; only the easiest and most natural transition ('kindliest change', 336). She has the fruits of all lands at her disposal. (Milton's reference to *Alcinous*, King of Phaeacia, introduces the host who in

Homer's *Odyssey* lavishes hospitality on Odysseus. It is his daughter, Nausicaa, who finds the storm-tossed hero on the sea-shore. She is the prototype of Gerty MacDowell in Joyce's *Ulysses*: cf. IX. 441 and see p. 221.) 'Earth all-bearing Mother' (338) yields of her store as generously as Eve, all-bearing Mother, yields of hers, first gathering, then heaping on the board 'with unsparing hand' (344). For drink she prepares harmless grape-juice and other fresh fruit juices. She concocts ('tempers', 347) sweet creams and there is no lack of clean vessels to hold them. She strews the ground with rose petals and the leaves of shrubs (not burnt for the purpose of fumigation, but in their natural scented condition, 349).

Meanwhile Adam walks out to receive his guest, and the dignity of unfallen man is such that no train or ceremony is needed to enhance it; it resides in himself, in his own complete perfection, and far surpasses the 'tedious pomp' (354) of ceremony, retinue and livery now used by royalty to impress the crowd. Adam is not overawed ('awd', 358) in the angelic presence but is duly deferential ('with submiss approach', 359). He can confidently address the visitor as 'Native of Heaven' (361) for no place other than Heaven could 'contain' so glorious a figure. He can also speak with the assurance of a sovereign in possession of his own 'spacious ground' (367). As such he invites Raphael to rest in their bower and share their meal.

In reply Raphael concedes that this is the very purpose he has come for, and observes that Adam is fitly endowed in person and by possession to entertain 'Spirits of Heav'n' frequently ('oft', 374). The 'oft' is interesting. It points to a vigorous future social life as between men and angels unfortunately prevented by the Fall. It seems odd, however, that Raphael should speak of having 'these mid-hours' (376) of the day 'at will' (377), as though they were leisure hours, off-duty time, when he is in fact carrying out God's commission. One may doubt whether Milton thought out clearly what constitutes the angelic working day.

They enter the arbour, decked with flowers and fragrant

with their scent. Eve, however, is naked ('Undeckt', 380).
Like Adam who needs no retinue to advance his dignity
(351–3), she carries her own perfection in herself, 'more
lovely fair' (380 – echo of *Othello*) than any of the three
goddesses, Juno (Hera), Minerva (Athene) and Venus
(Aphrodite) who contested for the title of supreme beauty
and were judged on Mount *Ida* (382) by Paris. (Since this
contest arose out of the competition for the apple of discord
thrown into the gathering of the gods, and since it set in
motion the events recorded in Homer's epics, it is plain that
Milton is touching here a theme of correspondingly universal weight to that which attaches to the theme of Eve's
apple.) The angel Raphael's first word to her is 'Haile' (385).
It anticipates the angel Gabriel's greeting ('salutation', 386)
to the Virgin Mary when he comes to announce to her that
she is to be the mother of the divine Son (Luke 1 28). The
Virgin Mary, as mother of the new man in whom all shall be
saved, is parallel to Eve, the mother of fallen man. The 'old
Adam' within us, the manhood that has fallen, is replaced
by the Christ of the new creation. The Virgin Mary is thus
the 'second Eve' (387). Addressing Eve as 'Mother of
Mankind', Raphael speaks immediately of the fruitfulness of
her womb as matching the fruitfulness of the garden
(388–91). They sit at table ('rais'd of grassie terf', 391). Adam,
offering of their food, which is God's gift and therefore
wholly delightful, nevertheless meets the demands of eti-
quette by making the host's due apology for the quality of
what he is offering, allowing that perhaps what is right for
man may be 'unsavourie' (401) to 'spiritual natures' (402).
(Note that at this moment of fruitful harmony the seasons
'*Spring and Autumn*' dance 'hand in hand', 395. After the Fall
there is to be a change to the cyclic sequence: cf. x. 668 ff.
and see pp. 258–9.)

404–505 *Raphael explains that angels need to eat as men do
(–413), indeed that all created things take nourishment (–433), and
they have their meal (–450). Adam asks for more information about
the relationship between earthly and heavenly things (–467). Raphael*

describes the unity underlying the correspondence between the different forms and degrees of life (–505).

Raphael's reply is directly instructive. Because man is in part a spiritual being, the food which suits him is also satisfying to angels who are wholly spiritual. The angel, as a pure intellectual being, needs food just as man does as a rational being. The key to the thinking here is that while rational man contains within his being the corporeal faculties (the five senses and the involuntary processes of digestion, nutrition, and so on), so the 'intelligential' (408) angels contain within their being these same human rational and corporeal faculties. The higher being is not higher by virtue of any exclusion, but by virtue of greater inclusiveness. The theory is logical: for indeed if the angels were not conceived in this way, it would be difficult to justify their ability to assume shapes visible to human eyes and to communicate with them. Raphael extends the correspondences. All created things need to be 'sustain and fed' (415). At the basic physical level the elements feed one another. The sea eats at the earth; the air draws up moisture and vapour from the earth and the sea; the air nourishes the fires (stars and planets) of Heaven. Looking at the surface of the moon, one can see patches, which are in fact vapours not yet assimilated (a seventeenth-century theory to account for the moon spots visible through the new telescopes, 419–20). Similarly the moon exhales vapours that feed 'higher Orbes' (422). Highest of all, the sun, imparting light to all, in turn draws up exhaled moisture from all that he warms. This is the sun's compensatory nourishment ('alimental recompence', 424), which balances its own outpouring of health-giving heat and light. Thus we encounter another aspect of the cosmic dance of giving and receiving which is threaded through the patterned life of all being and is consummately represented at the centre of Heaven in the relationship of Father to Son (imaged between Adam and Eve in Paradise, parodied in Hell). Raphael finishes his first statement here by noting the superiority of the 'natural' environment of Heaven (trees laden with ambrosial fruit, nectar-bearing vines, etc., 426–30), yet there is a variety and multiplicity of 'new delights' (431) in Eden, which make its fruits comparably delectable to angels. In short, he has no inclination to be fastidious ('nice', 433) in tackling Eve's excellent meal.

With that they fall to. And the angelic eating is not a mere appearance ('nor ... seemingly', 434) as theological explanations ('gloss', 435) often suggest. Raphael eats eagerly to satisfy a real appetite. There is within him that same assimilative process whereby digestive heat converts what is received into non-corporeal substance: and any overflow is easily exhaled ('what redounds, transpires', 438). This is not surprising, when you consider that the practical scientist ('Empiric Alchimist', 440) considers it possible to turn crude dross into gold by means of coal-fire. Naked Eve serves the food and keeps the cups full. If ever there might have been an excuse for the 'Sons of God' (447) to fall in love with the daughters of men (see Genesis VI. 2, and cf. pp. 281–3), it would have been at sight of such beauty and innocence as this; but here in Paradise, before the Fall, 'Love unlibidinous' reigns (449).

After the meal it suddenly occurs to Adam that he should not let pass the opportunity ('occasion', 453) offered by this conversation ('Conference', 454) to learn about these heavenly beings who are so superior to human beings. His approach to Raphael is a cautious one. He thanks Raphael for the honour bestowed in that he has condescended ('voutsaf't', 463) to come under his 'lowly roof' and eat earthly food as though it were on a par with heavenly food. Yet surely there can be no comparison between the two.

Raphael explains the uniform pattern of hierarchical relationships whereby all things proceed from God and return to him, provided they are not perverted ('deprav'd from good', 471), for they are all completely good as created, and are made from a common basic essence ('matter', 472), which is endued with various kinds of substantial form and (in the case of animate things) of life. This substantial content is more refined, 'spirituous' and pure, as the thing is higher placed in the scale of creation, and therefore nearer to God in its placing or its directional tendency (476), for in their various respective spheres of operation things have an inner movement working up from corporeal to spiritual. Thus from the crude root springs the 'lighter' (480) green stalk, from the stalk the more refined leaves, and finally the more delicate flower, giving off a scent, which is itself the least corporeal, most 'spirituous' aspect of the little whole. Flowers and fruits belong to that vegetable category of things that nourish man. When man consumes them, they are assimilated by digestion, and then by being vapourized into 'vital spirits' move up the scale from vegetable being to animal being within the little world of man himself. This illustrates the aspiring movement from inanimate form to vegetable, to animal, to intellectual, whereby first life and growth, then sense and feeling, then fancy and understanding are added. In the human being the highest faculty is reason with its twin categories, discursive and intuitive. The discursive reason is more proper to man, the intuitive reason more proper to angels.

It should be no surprise, then, that Raphael can within his own being convert the matter of human nourishment to nourishment proper to angelhood. The time may come when conversely men may be able to 'participate' (494) with angels in this respect, feeding on angelic food and finding it neither inappropriate for human assimilation nor too insubstantial for the human appetite. Indeed, perhaps in this way men may eventually eat themselves into angelhood, so that human bodies turn to pure spirit and live the life of winged angels or perhaps dwell at will either in the earthly or in the heavenly Paradise. (All this is later to be parodied in Satan's persuasion of Eve selfishly and disobediently to eat herself out of humanity into divinity, ix. 705 ff.) That is, of course, Raphael concludes, if you prove 'obedient' (501) and firmly retain the entire love of the God whose progeny you are. For the meantime they are to enjoy to the full whatever happiness their condition in Paradise makes them capable of. They are not yet capable of anything 'more' (505).

506–560 *Adam questions how man could possibly be disobedient to God (–518). Raphael explains the gift of free will to men and to angels, and mentions the angelic Fall (–543). Adam wants to hear more of the Fall (–560).*

Adam is grateful for this instruction about the way to develop in knowledge (508–9). Raphael has laid before him the hierarchical character of the natural order (509–10) and shown how man, by taking full account ('In contemplation', 511) of this, may by degrees rise to angelhood. (It is important that human aspiration to angelhood is not in itself evil. Indeed Raphael has here planted the seed of it in Adam's mind, 496 ff.) But Adam cannot conceive how he and Eve could possibly disobey their Maker, who has given them the maximum happiness they could desire.

Raphael's reply is crisp. Adam's initial happiness is God's gift (520). The continuance of that happiness will be dependent on Adam himself – that is, on his obedience. He must 'stand' (522) firm in obedience. God made you perfect, but not immutable, Raphael insists. He made you good, but gave you free will. You are not the slave of fate. God wants 'voluntarie service' (529) from us, not compulsory service. Indeed, Raphael argues, compulsory service would not be service. The notion of a heart responding to God under the compulsion of destiny is untenable. Free will is the only kind of will there is. No choice, no will. Finally Raphael explains that angelic happiness depends on the same obedience as human happiness. He adds that some angels have already fallen from Heaven to Hell through disobedience.

The allusion to man overhearing celestial music, now linking with Adam's delight in angelic discourse, has already been used in connection with Adam's corresponding 'instruction' of Eve (IV. 680 ff.). We are hearing the harmony of obedience. Adam is firm in his mind that he and Eve could never forget to love and obey their Maker. And though what Raphael has said of events in Heaven might perturb him with 'doubt' (554), even more it stimulates his desire to hear a full account ('relation', 556) of it.

561–672 *Raphael agrees to tell the story* (–576). *It begins before Creation when God calls the hosts of Heaven together* (–599), *declares the Son head of the heavenly hosts and at one with himself in authority* (–615). *The angels sing, dance* (–627), *feast* (–641); *then go to their rest* (–657); *all except Satan who is envious of the Son* (–672).

Raphael defines the forthcoming narration as a 'High matter' (563), a 'Sad task' and a 'hard' one (564). The three-fold difficulty is that of describing invisible exploits of spirits so as to make them intelligible to human beings whose understanding is dependent on 'sense' experience (565); that of recounting without pitiful anguish ('remorse', 566) the fall ('ruin' 567) of so many glorious beings; and that of unfolding the secrets of another world, which perhaps cannot lawfully be revealed. The last reservation is to be waived ('dispenc't', 571) on Adam's behalf; and as for the problem of communicating what is out of the reach of human conceiving, he will describe things spiritual by analogous reference to things 'corporal' (573). This method may be especially justifiable in that earthly things perhaps image heavenly things more closely than man recognizes. (Milton gives us plenty of food for thought here.)

Thus we reach the beginning of the story of *Paradise Lost*.

Raphael takes us back to when 'this world was not'. It is necessary therefore to explain that, even in eternity, time, applied to movement and action ('motion', 581), measures all continuing things in terms of past, present, and future. Thus we get over the first hurdle. Events in eternity may be expressed in chronological terms. One day all the angelic hierarchies are summoned before the throne of God. It is a magnificent gathering, with thousands and thousands of ensigns, flags and banners ('Gonfalons', 589) streaming in the air. The heraldry here emblazoned is not just a matter of signs denoting hierarchical degrees and distinctions, for some of the signs are sacred records chronicling outstanding 'acts of Zeale and Love' (593–4). The thousands stand, circle within circle, around the throne, the Father and the Son at the mid-point, like the centre of a blazing volcano whose top is invisibly lost in its brightness (594–9).

Milton has been at pains to indicate the analogous character of finite utterance when used of things eternal: it would therefore be foolish to press the question – What, expressed dogmatically, would be the exact theological equivalent of the imaginative narrative poetically represented here? It is the poet's privilege not to have to answer that question. As a poet he chose to write poetry. And, as often in his richest passages relating to Heaven, borrowings from the Bible are important. Here he takes the psalmist's words 'Yet have I set my king upon my holy hill of Zion. I will declare the decree: the Lord hath said unto me, Thou art my Son; this day have I begotten thee' (Psalm II. 6–7) and weaves other recollected phrases with them into a pattern of praise in which the persona of Milton is wholly submerged under words of worship familiar to Christians.

The Son's lordship over all the hosts of Heaven is established. It is the Father's deputed ('Vice-regent', 609) lordship. It is the Father's lordship in action. It is the Father's lordship made manifest. Under this lordship the hosts of Heaven are bidden to remain firm in a unity that is indivisible ('individual', 610). To disobey the Son is to disobey the Father and to break the unity of Heaven. Anyone who in fact breaks it will be cast out from the presence of God and the beatific vision into a gulf of darkness, the place irrevocably ordained for him for ever.

That the hosts of Heaven should spend their festal ('solem', 618) days in song and dance is highly appropriate. In our progress through the poem we become increasingly aware that the 'Mystical dance' (620) of Heaven is indeed the pattern of all harmonious movement and interchange in the life of the universe and its inhabitants. The nearest resemblance to this dance of Heaven is the dance of the stars, the complex cycles of movements, not strictly circular ('Eccentric', 623), intertwining one with another, yet most regular when they appear, superficially, to be least regular. Music blends with movement. The relationship of Father to Son is also one of patterned interchange. So, too, is that of Adam to Eve. The reader will be well advised to weigh often Milton's strong hint about 'Earth . . . the shadow of Heav'n and things therein/Each to other like, more than on earth is thought' (see 574–6 above).

In Heaven morning and evening are not necessities but chosen delights. (The parenthesis, 628–9, is noteworthy.) There is change because the inhabitants of Heaven enjoy change. Time is not a dimension imposed and inescapable; but temporal variation is a delectable indulgence. The heavenly banquet has an overflowing richness which the abundance of nature images in Paradise. And all enjoy the fruit of 'delicious Vines, the growth of Heav'n' (635). Neither in feast nor in fellowship is there possibility of satiety where excess lies beyond the range of 'full measure' (639).

There is no blackness in Heaven's night, only a pleasing twilight (645), which brings a fragrance (cf. 'ambrosial', 642) and dewiness that induce rest. The angel hosts disperse and settle down like a great army in an immense far-flung array of tents and pavilions, except for those who maintain the unceasing liturgy of praise around God's throne. Against this background Satan (whose former name in Heaven is 'blotted out', I. 361–2) alone is awake for a purpose other than that of worship ('but not so wak'd/Satan', 657–8). His envy is stirred against the Son. The proclamation of his anointed kingship is intolerable to Satan's pride: he imagines himself down-graded, and that is the origin of his malice and disdain. He decides to defect with all his legions. He wakens his 'next subordinate' (671), presumably the angel to be known in Hell as 'Beelzibub' (cf. II. 299–300), and confides in him.

673–771 Satan orders a sudden withdrawal of his legions from the present muster (–693). The order is conveyed to the commanders, and they obey (–710). God sees what is happening (–718) and suggests that the Son take action (–732). The Son agrees (–742).

The rebels assemble and move north (-756). Satan goes to his estate (-766) and gathers them together (-771).

Satan draws his 'dear' companion's attention to the latest divine decree. A confidential interchange of conspiratorial thinking has bound the two of them in the past, when awake, and sleep must not now be allowed to come between them (676-9). They face a 'new' situation, Satan pretends, 'new Laws ... impos'd' (679), which will justify new thinking ('new minds', 680) and new planning ('Counsels', 681) on their part. He gives the order to match the coming withdrawal of night's 'shadowie Cloud' (686) with a withdrawal of their forces (the symbolism is plain) 'Homeward' (688). The official pretence is that they are to prepare a reception for their 'king', the Messiah, who is to make a triumphant progress through all the hierarchies.

As Satan has mingled innuendoes and misrepresentations with his false commands, so Beelzibub conveys what is supposed to be a divine order, wrapping it about with ambiguities and 'jealousies' (703) designed to probe ('sound', 703) or corrupt integrity. A parallel between disencumbering (see line 700) Heaven of the night and dismembering it of the rebels' dark presence is implicit (699-700). The legions obey the customary order ('wonted signal', 705) and the authority of their leader. So Lucifer moves off with a 'third part' of Heaven's host.

The Father's ever-watchful eye discerns the most hidden ('Abstrusest', 712) thoughts. From within the 'lamps of fire burning before the throne' (Revelation IV. 5) he sees the rebellion taking shape. ('Morning Starr', 708, and 'the sons of Morn', 716 : cf. Isaiah XIV. 12, 'How art thou fallen from heaven, O Lucifer, son of the morning!') The key to what the Father now says (719-32) is to be found in lines 718 and 736-7. The Father is 'smiling' (718) as he speaks because he is speaking sarcastically. The Son afterwards underlines the sarcasm, noting that it is *just* to *deride* foes of this kind and to *laugh* at their empty and useless ('vain ... vain') schemes. The Father can do so because he is impregnable and free from conceivable discomposure ('secure', 736). With this anticipatory glance forward we can detect the tone of what the Father says to the Son (719–32) and savour the Miltonic humour. 'Son, we'd better look after this omnipotence of ours, and make sure we can hold on to the rule we claim by tradition ('anciently', 723) as our own.' The humorous mockery of Satan's nonsensical pretentiousness reaches its peak in the Father's use of the word 'anciently'. The rebel is going to test the 'Power' (728) of the all-powerful and the 'right' (728) to rule of the eternal maker of all things. By the time we reach the word 'hazard' (729) we are listening to a divine belly-laugh, which must be the only thing that *could* rock the eternal throne. We must quickly gather together 'what force is left' (730, further irony) so that we do not get pushed off our throne while we are not looking ('unawares', 731). This utterance comes from where 'th'Eternal eye' (711) keeps ceaseless watch on all things. The Son, we have noted, enjoys the joke at the expense of the Devil. Indeed the rebels' 'hate' (738) will add lustre ('Illustrates', 739) to his authority. A note of divine delight can be detected in the prospect of exercising righteous power to destroy ('quell', 740) pride, so that the rebels learn by experience how skilful ('dextrous', 741) the Son can be in action. There is an implicit compound correspondence and contrast here such as frequently marks the consubstantial fullness and variety, plenitude and richness, of the divine relationship. To the Father, omnipotent and omniscient, the rebellion is fit matter for laughter. To the Son, active and manifest, it is 'Matter of Glory' (738).

Meantime Satan's vast following, numberless as stars of night, or stars of morning, as pearls of dew on leaves of flowers at dusk or dawn, have sped through the mighty hierarchical dominions ('Regencies', 748) whose immensity would dwarf the earth proportionately as the earth dwarfs Adam's Garden. They come within the boundaries ('limits', 755) of the north, home, Satan hastening to his princely estate ('seat', 756), high on a hill, a 'Mount/Rais'd on a Mount' (757–8). Later, laying claim to ('affecting', 763) equality with God, Lucifer is to parody the Father's declaration of the Son's authority (600 ff.) and his anointing on the 'holy hill' (604) by calling his rival seat the 'Mountain of the Congregation' (766: cf. Isaiah XIV. 13, 'I will sit also upon the mount of the congregation, in the sides of the north' – the verse following the quotation above cited in reference to lines 708 and 716). The host is mustered under the official claim that there must be consultation about a fit 'reception' for the Son, due to make a royal progress there.

772–907 *Satan addresses his followers on the indignity of servitude to the Son's royal authority (–802). Abdiel rises in anger (–808), rebukes Satan for the presumption (–825), ingratitude (–831) and absurdity of his arrogant pretence (–845); and calls him to ask for pardon (–848). Satan denies angelic indebtedness to God for their creation (–863). He claims independence and equality (–871). His followers murmur approval (–876). Abdiel foresees the coming Fall and the penalty that will have to be paid for disobedience (–895). Then he leaves them (–907).*

Satan's initial implication is that the fine titles by which he addresses the angels have become titles without reality, since the Son has now monopolized all power to himself and as 'King anointed' has obliterated ('eclipst', 776) their own authority. It is only for the Son's sake that they have had to make this hasty, uncomfortable night march and meeting – in order, that is, to plan new ways of honouring the royal Son who is coming to receive the formal homage they have not yet accorded him ('knee-tribute yet unpaid', 782); and indeed a cheap, undignified deference ('prostration vile', 782), bad enough when it has to be shown to the Father, unendurable when it has to be shown equally to a second person now declared to be 'his image' (784).

Suppose wiser thinking were to exalt ('erect', 785) their minds above this level of servitude. Satan appeals to their dignity as heavenly beings 'possess before/By none', not equal in rank, but equal in the common freedom they share. This equality in freedom extends to *all* heavenly beings, God included, and differentiations in rank – or 'in power and splendor' (796) – must not over-rule it (792–7). On the basis of such reasoning, Satan argues that no one has the right to promulgate laws for them: they do not err without law. Certainly there could be no legal proclamation of a lordship requiring from them acts of adoration that would make nonsense of their own authoritative titles.

Abdiel, one of the seraphim, here interrupts (his name means 'Servant of God). The seraphic flame of his zeal is 'oppos'd' (808) to the flow of Satanic 'fury'. He condemns Satan's argument for its blasphemy, dishonesty, and presumption (809). It is the last thing to be expected from one who has been given so high a rank in Heaven, that he should condemn the giving of sovereign authority to the Son. As for the argument from equality, how can Satan dispute the subtleties of liberty with the God who himself made the angelic beings in accordance with his own wish and defined the limits of ('circumscrib'd', 825) their being? By experience they know how good God is and how watchfully attentive ('provident', 828) he is to their own good and their own dignity. He has never been concerned to reduce their happiness and dignity, only to exalt it and increase their close fellowship 'under one Head' (830). And suppose, Abdiel adds, we grant your argument that it is unjust that among equals any should reign as monarchs, could you, however 'great & glorious' (833), consider yourself – or indeed all angels rolled into one – as being equal to the begotten Son by whom all things, even yourself and all the other 'Spirits of Heav'n' (837) were made? The sovereign rule given to the Son has not reduced ('obscur'd', 841) their hierarchical glory and authority but rendered it 'more illustrious' (842), since, by being declared their head, the Son has become *one of them* ('One of our number', 843). In this status, just as the laws he gives are now their laws (they partake in the giving of them), so the honour they do to him is honour done to themselves, because he is one of themselves (they partake in the receiving of it). The reducing (see 843) of Godhead to the angelic level, and the consequent upgrading of angelhood, have an implicit correspondence with the reducing of

Godhead to the human level in the Incarnation, and the consequent upgrading of manhood in the Ascension.

Abdiel's fervour wins no support, being judged out of place, or peculiar to himself and ill considered (850–1). Satan's confidence is increased. He mocks as 'strange' and 'new' (855) the doctrine that the angels were created, and by the 'secondarie hands' of the Son. He has now, of course, slid through half-truth and misrepresentation to direct falsehood. 'Secondarie' (854), implying subordination of Son to Father, is not an appropriate word: 'by task transferd' (854), implying separation of Son from Father, is not an appropriate phrase (literary criticism of *Paradise Lost* has begun its work within the poem itself!). But they have their emotive effect and Satan now demands proof of the doctrine of their creation. Who saw the creation? Who remembers his creation? 'We know no time when we were not as now' (859) – and from this naïve declaration he slides into use of the self-flattering notion that angels are 'self-begot, self-rais'd' (860) by their own life-giving ('quickening', 861) power in the due cyclic course of destiny.

Satan's argument has now erected falsehoods in place of the acts and truths of God. Against them he has arrayed counterfalsehoods. Thus, by appealing to the angels' love of their 'native Heav'n' (863) and their just delight in their own dignity and power (864), and by presupposing divine deprivations and encroachments calculated to damage them, he has distorted potentially righteous fervours and loyalties into resentments and rebellious angers. He is in a position to throw out a challenge and a taunt for Abdiel to convey to God himself, and to hear only the murmur of applause from the rest of his audience.

Abdiel recognizes the challenge as denoting an alienation from God and a consequent damnation, a fall involving all the satanic crew in whom the contagion of treachery and deceit has spread its poison. There need be no more argument about keeping or not keeping the laws of Heaven, or escaping the allegedly burdensome rule ('yoke', 882) of the Messiah. Such 'indulgent' laws will no longer be on offer to them (884). Other decrees will have irrevocably come into operation. They have rejected the golden sceptre. The 'Iron Rod' will bruise and break them. Abdiel will flee from their doomed ('devoted', 890) tents for fear the imminent divine wrath, breaking suddenly into flame about them, fails to distinguish him from the company he is in. For they will soon learn to their sorrow who created them by finding out who can discreate them (see p. 78).

With a moving tribute to the fidelity, constancy and unshakeable love of the departing Abdiel, the book closes.

Book VI

Abdiel travels through the night over the open terrain ('Champain', 2) of Heaven. Milton explains how the pleasing alternation ('Grateful vicissitude', 8) of light and darkness operates in Heaven. There is a *Box and Cox* system whereby the two lodge in turns in the same cave, light coming out at one door while obedient ('Obsequious', 10) darkness goes in at the other. So the poet can speak of the Morn arrayed in that 'Gold' (13) which is now established as the pre-eminent heavenly colour. Abdiel sees the blaze and flame of arms and armour reflecting the light. The forces are embattled already, war duly prepared ('procinct', 19 – Latin, *procingere*, to gird up), his hot news cold. The powers receive him with especial acclamation and the Miltonic verse ('that one . . . yet one/Returnd not lost', 23–5) reverberates with echoes of the lost sheep found and the one repentant sinner who causes such joy in Heaven (Luke xv. 7). He is led to the Mount and God's commendation of him is again rich in biblical echoes (e.g. 'well done', 29 and Matthew xxv. 21), which universalize Abdiel's loyalty didactically in terms of human behaviour. He has fought the good fight (2 Timothy IV. 7), singly defended the truth, opposing to the rebel swords the mightier weapon of the word, and so doing has born 'reproach' (Psalm LXIX. 7) worse to bear than violence.

His only concern ('care', 35) has been to stand commended ('approv'd', 36) in the sight of God. There remains for him now to effect the 'easier conquest' of the foe in battle, to return in the glory of victory to those he had to depart from under the lash of their scorn. They reject the rule of Reason and the sovereignty of the Son: they have chosen the rule of force, by which they will be defeated. God commands Michael and Gabriel to lead to battle 'invincible' (47 – the word is stressed) forces, equal in number to those of the rebels, and drive them out from bliss to their 'place of punishment' (53).

As the voice of divine commendation 'milde' (28) gives place to the voice of divine 'wrauth awak't' (59), the 'Golden Cloud' (28) gives place to the 'Clouds' of rolling smoke (56–7) and the darting, struggling ('reluctant', 58) flames. At the sound of trumpets the powers militant assemble in squared formation, irresistible in their unity, and then move on in silence to the sound of instrumental music. The combination of discipline (the formation and the silence) and inspirational music is noteworthy. Nothing that stands in their way breaks their formation – neither the impeding obstacle of a hill ('obvious Hill', 69), nor the restricting ('streit'ning', 70) valley, nor a stream. None of these cuts into ('divides', 70) their formation because their agile ('nimble', 73) march is high above ground level through the unresisting ('passive', 72) air. The comparison of their movement to the flight of birds of every breed ('total kind', 73) who came in formation to receive their names from Adam serves to remind us that we are still listening to Raphael's narration to Adam (73–6), and of course it corroborates the continuing correspondence between the orderliness of Heaven and the orderliness of Eden. But the contrast in magnitude between the heavenly and the earthly is immediately afterwards noted too.

A distant glimmer on the northern horizon of a stretched-out region skirted ('skirt to skirt', 80) with fire gives the first sighting of the foe (cf. 'thy skirts', III. 380). As they draw nearer, we see the bristling array of packed spears throwing up numberless 'beams' (82) of reflected light. Shields are decorated with arrogant emblems of rebellion ('boastful Argument portraid', 84). Satan's force is hastening on with wild speed ('furious expedition', 86), much in contrast to the swift but steady and disciplined march of the loyalists. They cherish the wild irrational hope of taking the 'Mount of God' (88) by surprise and replacing God by Satan in a sudden *coup*: but their plan proves foolish and futile ('fond and vain', 90) at this mid-way meeting. It is a strange experience, Raphael adds in parenthesis, when angel meets fellow-angel in the fierce encounter ('hosting', 93) of battle, after being accustomed to joining in the united fellowship of joyful and loving celebrations. It was an experience, of course, sadly familiar to the seventeenth-century mind in the Civil War. But the onset of battle soon puts an end to such reflections.

Satan, the mock-God, the 'Apostate' (100), the 'Idol of Majestie Divine' (101), sits in pantomimic exaltation in his sun-bright chariot. The burlesque charades of divinity have begun, the mock-up of things heavenly, which is to be realized ultimately in the vast discreational parody that is Hell. He alights. Between the two armies remains but a frighteningly narrow intervening space ('interval', 105). Host and host, eyeball to eyeball, extend in long and hideous confrontation. As Satan advances haughtily on the rough cutting-edge of the battle to come, Abdiel finds his towering arrogance insupportable. It is the spurious lingering 'resemblance of the Highest' (114), where fidelity is gone, which irks him. May it not be that strength will fail in this being in whom virtue has failed, and that the appearance of invincibility will prove to be false? He has tested Satan's mind and found it false. Trusting in God, he will now test his strength ('puissance', 119). It would be just that he, the victor in 'debate of Truth' (122), should also be victor in arms, brutish though it is when the cause of Reason has to descend to contest of force with force in order to retain its supremacy. So minded, Abdiel steps forward and meets Satan half way. The face-to-face confrontation angers him

more, and without fear or anxiety ('securely', 130) he
defies him.

131–261 *Abdiel rebukes the absurd pride of Satan in thinking he
could overcome God in a surprise move (–142). He himself is no
longer a solitary loyalist (–148). Satan welcomes Abdiel's opposition
and mocks the servility of the loyalists (–170). In reply Abdiel
distinguishes between the free service of Heaven and the servitude of
Hell (–188), then strikes Satan (–193) who recoils (–198), to the
anger and joy of the two sides (–202). The signal is given and the
battle joined (–219). Its ferocity and magnitude are pictured (–245).
Satan fights his way to a confrontation with Michael (–261).*

Abdiel rightly has the first chance to answer Satan's late
mockery (v. 853–71 and v. 903–4) with counter-mockery,
and to drive home the arrogant unreason of thinking to
catch off guard the God omnipotent who could have raised
up a never-ending series of armies (137–8) to defeat him, or
indeed with one blow of the divine right arm have obliterated
him and his followers. Then he contrasts his own solitary
stand for loyalty when last they met and the present situation. There was then no crowd of loyalists visible to Satan's
eyes. Abdiel was the odd one out, apparently the erroneously
dissenting individual. The cause ('sect', 147) he stood for is
now visible in the fullness of its strength. The lesson, that
a minority of one should not be lightly written off as
necessarily wrong, is hammered out by Milton (147–8).

Bad for you, but sweet revenge for me, Satan replies, that
you should receive your due reward. The topsy-turvy satanic
mind labels Abdiel 'seditious Angel' (152) who opposed a
'third part of the Gods, in Synod met/Thir Deities to assert'
(156–7). He shall now receive the first taste ('assay', 153) of
the satanic 'right hand' (154: the parody of divinity continues), as his was the first 'tongue/Inspir'd with contradiction' (154–5). The satanic idiom explores the vocabulary of
theology with ever-defiling irony. The strength of the rebels,
who can allow 'Omnipotence to none' (159), is dependent on
what 'they feel' (157) within them. It is well, Satan concludes, that you come before your associates to challenge

me; for what happens to you ('thy success', 161) will reveal
to others the destruction they will let themselves in for. In
this 'pause between' (162 – before the blow falls), for fear
you might boast that your words have not been answered
(163), let me tell you this: I thought liberty was a *sine qua non*
to the souls in Heaven; but now I see that most of them
have become lazy, servile and self-indulgent, accustomed to
the familiar round of 'Feast and Song' (167). These are the
beings you have armed to defend the cause of servility
against that of freedom – a band of heavenly choir-boys. The
performance of the two sides today will prove it.

Abdiel replies. The apostate is now wandering remotely
from the path of Truth. It is unjust to depreciate ('deprav'st',
174) service by labelling it '*Servitude*' (175) when the service
is what God or the true order of Nature ordains. One has
a double duty to serve the ruler who has the double qualification of divine authority and natural endowment of superiority to his subjects. Conversely servitude consists in giving
service to the 'unwise' (179) or the unjustified rebel, as do
Satan's own followers now. For Satan is not free but enslaved to himself, and has the impudence ('leudly', 182) to
mock ('upbraid') the due service ('ministring', 182) of the
loyalists. Reign in Hell: let me serve in Heaven, Abdiel
concludes, giving the audience a slogan for later use, earlier
in the poem (i. 263).

With that Abdiel strikes the first blow of the battle. It is
a blow too swift and sudden for sight, thought, or shield to
intercept its fall ('ruin', 193). Satan recoils ten paces, to
finish upheld by his spear on bended knee. It is like the over-
turning, by subterranean wind or sidelong flood, of a whole
mountainside of pines. There is rage on the one side, joy on
the other, the cry and desire of battle. Michael commands
the trumpet to sound, the loyalists shout '*Hosanna* to the
Highest' and the opposing ('adverse', 206) forces no longer
stand in confrontation, eye to eye ('at gaze', 205). The shock
of the hideous collision, the storm of noise and fury, is
unprecedented. Milton compresses his imagery of tumult –
clashing steel, grating chariots and twisted wheels – into a

hideous grind on the ground, while flaming volleys of darts provide an umbrella of fire overhead (209–15). As all Heaven resounded, so would the Earth, had it existed, have been shaken to its centre.

The violence is that of an encounter between millions of beings, any one of whom could seize and wield earth's elements as weapons. Indeed the tumult ('combustion', 225) of such immense resources in conflict might well have upset – though it could never have destroyed – the estate of Heaven itself. But God asserted his over-ruling power and 'limited' (229) the angelic 'might'. Though the numbers involved are such that each section of a legion is like a 'numerous Host' (231) and though the strength involved is such that each 'armed hand' matches a whole legion, yet when brought to battle they are so led that every individual warrior seems like a commander-in-chief, having full cognizance of what is happening over the field of battle as a whole, and knowing exactly ('expert', 233) when to advance, when to stand, when to 'turn the sway' (234), when to fan out into more open formation, when to come to closer grips (229–36). There is no thought of flight or retreat or cowardly act. Each warrior relies on himself as though the issue ('moment', 239) of victory depended on himself alone. Moreover the conflict rages both on the ground and in the air. This is warfare idealized – as we should expect of angelic contestants.

The balance is evenly maintained for a long time. Then Satan, who has manifested 'Prodigious power' and found no match in the conflict as he ranges through the fighting seraphim, at last catches sight of the sword of Michael in action. Its double-handed sweeps are felling whole squadrons at a time (250–3). Satan hurries to check ('withstand', 253) this destruction by interposing the gigantic rock-like circle of his vast adamantine shield. As he approaches, Michael ceases from his 'warlike toile' (257) with the sweeping sword. He is glad, thinking that now there is the prospect of bringing the civil war in Heaven to an end. He foresees Satan brought to heel or dragged off in chains, and sternly rebukes him.

262–405   Michael rebukes Satan as the Author of evil (–271) and orders him to take his followers to Hell (–280). Satan retorts that they will win – or turn Heaven into Hell (–295). Michael and Satan fight (–320). Michael's sword wounds Satan (–334), and he is carried back to his chariot (–343) where he quickly recovers (–353). Elsewhere in the field Gabriel wounds Moloch (–362); Uriel, Raphael, and Abdiel vanquish other rebels (–372). The poet chooses not to name other contestants (–385). The day ends with the rebels demoralized and in disorder (–397), and the loyalists firm in resistance and in spirit (–405).

Michael addresses Satan as the 'Author of evil' (262). We recall that the angels called the Father 'Author of all being' (III. 374), that Eve called Adam 'My Author' (IV. 635), and that Sin called Satan 'my Author' (II. 864). The key word again links the Father–Son, Adam–Eve and Satan–Sin relationships into the general pattern of the heavenly, the earthly (its image) and the hellish (its perversion or parody). Before Satan's revolt evil was 'unknown' and 'Unnam'd' (262–3) in Heaven. His crime has corrupted thousands 'once upright'. Let him quickly take his 'crew' (277) off to Hell, where they can manufacture disorders ('broiles', 277), before the avenging sword strikes.

Satan mocks Michael for trying to achieve with the 'wind' (282) of threatening talk what he has not been able to achieve with deeds. Have you, he demands, put the least of my followers to flight (notice the sharp biblical parody in 'least of these' – Matthew xxv. 40) or felled one of them (only to see him rise 'Unvanquisht', 286), that you should hope to find it easier to negotiate ('transact', 286) patronizingly ('imperious', 287) with me, and chase me out with threats (287–8)? Do not be so mistaken as to imagine ('erre not', 288) that such will be the upshot of the strife which you call evil, but which to us is glorious. We mean either to win it or turn Heaven itself into the Hell you chatter about in your fairy stories ('fablest', 292). We mean to live here free – if not to reign. I do not flee from the maximum strength you can summon up – and throw the so-called

Almighty's in to help you as well. I have sought this encounter.

The two take up their positions ('addrest', 296) for the indescribable ('unspeakable', 297) fight. The poet, even if he had an angelic gift of utterance, could not give an adequate account of this contest: there are not among the outstanding ('conspicuous', 299) things on Earth the things one could use as comparisons to lift the human imagination to the level at which it could comprehend events of this god-like magnitude. For indeed Michael and Satan are like gods themselves in their stance and immensity. Their swords sweep circles of fire in the air as they tune up for action, their shields are two blazing, confronted suns. The anticipatory suspense is terrifying, and where the throng around them has been thick, it thins away rapidly. A spacious empty area is left around them, for it is dangerous to be near enough to feel even the disturbance of the air ('wind', 309: cf. *Hamlet* II. ii. 472) caused by a collision as violent as this.

In the attempt to make a comparison, even though it is far too small a thing to set beside the angelic contest, Milton turns to the conflict of planets, when they are opposed to each other in mutual antipathy through occupying diametrically opposite positions in the heavens. Placed so, their respective rays of influence collide and compete, giving off, as a result, a 'noxious efficacie' (see x. 659–60), which is shed upon the earth instead of the pure influence of either planet. This positioning presents an 'aspect maligne' (313) to human beings. Raphael conceives of a breaking up of the cosmic 'concord' sustaining the natural order, such that war springs up among the constellations, and opposed planets rush towards each other and meet in fierce combat in mid sky. The cosmic derangement sets the spheres 'jarring', throwing the vast moving fabric of the universe into confusion. (The careful reader will agree that T. S. Eliot probably had this passage in mind when he pictured the 'constellated wars' of *East Coker* II. 60.)

Each of the two contestants has the same tactical idea, to strike one initial blow of such force that it might decide the

issue ('determine', 318) once and for all, leaving no need for
any 'repeate' (318). So the two uplifted swords sweep down
together. Michael's sword, from the 'Armorie of God' (321),
is so tempered that its edge is irresistible: meeting the
descending sword of Satan in mid-stroke, it cuts it in two.
Quickly Michael re-wheels it in a contrary direction (326)
against Satan himself, cutting deeply into his right side. This
is Satan's first experience of pain. He writhes convulsively,
for the piercing ('griding', 329) sword goes through him and
leaves a gaping ('discontinuous', 329) wound. However, the
ethereal substance of which angels are framed does not,
when it is cut, take as long to heal as human flesh. (It is 'not
long divisible', 331.) The wound closes, and the heavenly
fluid ('Nectarous humour', 332), which issues from the gash
like blood, stains his armour. There is a general dash ('was
run', 335) to his aid from all sides by angels. Some interpose
themselves to ward off any further attack, while others carry
Satan back to his chariot. There he chafes in pain, resentment
and shame (340), having learned that he is 'not matchless' as
a warrior, and having to digest Michael's humbling rebuke so
far out of key with his confident boast of equality with God.

But he is soon healed. Raphael explains the technicalities:
the frail human being can be fatally wounded by damage to
any one of several parts of his body: not so the angel, whose
vitality is so all-pervasive that only annihilation can put an
end to his being. The incorporeal 'texture' (348) of the angel
is invulnerable as the 'fluid Aire'. (The Ghost in *Hamlet* is
'as the air, invulnerable', I. i. 145.) The diffusion of faculties
whereby the angelic heart or head, eye or ear, is not corporeally localized and damageable represents a highly logical
concept of angelhood in relation to manhood (350-1). So,
too, does the freedom of the angel to opt at any moment for
a frame corporeally identifiable, if not corporeally limited
(351-3).* These two notions represent a concept of angelhood which is extra-dimensionally superior to humanity. It
suggests interesting analogies very much in line with what
we are now in the post-relativity era learning about the

---

* 'condense or rare' (353): cf. 'dense or rare' (II. 948), and see pp. 58-9.

limitations of our own scales of observation, modes of awareness, and dimensional constrictedness.

Raphael now takes a few glances at other points of the battlefield where deeds worthy of record (that 'deservd/ Memorial', 354–5) are done. Moloch (see I. 392–405 and II. 43–105) has defied Gabriel, threatened to drag him bound to his chariot wheels, and blasphemed God himself. In return Gabriel has cut him down the middle to the waist (361) so that he flees bellowing with pain previously unknown ('uncouth', 362). Meantime Uriel has dealt with Adramelec (the idol for whom the 'Sepharvites burnt their children in fire', 2 Kings XVII. 31), and Raphael, appropriately, with *Asmadai*, the devil he encounters in the Book of Tobit and drives off from the tormented bride of Tobias (Milton has referred to the story previously, IV. 168 and V. 221–2: see pp. 96 and 129). These two rebels (ranked as 'Thrones', 366), who think too much of themselves to be anything less than Gods, have to accommodate themselves, as they flee mangled with wounds, to a 'meaner' (367) estimate of their status. The three rebels here cut down – Moloch, Adramelec and Asmodeus – are especially associated with destruction of the human family, of the joys and fruits of marriage; for children are sacrificed to Moloch and Adramelec, while Asmodeus is the intruder who comes between Sara the bride and the consummation of her marriage.

Raphael chooses not to extend his list of heroic deeds on the battle field. There is no need to immortalize ('Eternize', 374) on Earth the names of good angels who are contented enough with their fame in Heaven. As for the rebels, though they can compare with the loyalists in strength and in warlike achievements and zeal, the judgement ('doome', 378) passed on them wiped out their names from the history of Heaven (379) and they deserve to be forgotten. Warlike strength, if its exercise is separated from the cause of truth and justice, does not call for praise but disgrace ('ignominie', 383). Even though it is accompanied by the aspiration to 'glory', it is an empty glory – the vain and self-contradictory pursuit of a famous name by doing infamous deeds.

Many of the mightiest rebels have been put out of action ('quelld', 386). Their line of battle has been cut into at many points and the disorder of rout sets in (386–8). The ground is strewn with the shattered debris of battle. Those rebels who are still on foot withdraw out of sheer weariness through the weakened host, which is now scarcely offering resistance (391–3), or else, overcome with panic and pain for the first time, flee ignominiously. Such are the fruits of disobedience. On the other side the impregnable ('inviolable', 398) loyalists advance in one unbroken four-square formation (399). They are invulnerable, their force impenetrable, by virtue of their innocence of sin and disobedience. They cannot be wearied in fight, and they are not susceptible ('unobnoxious', 404) to pain or wound. If the gravity of the morality seems here overweighted, we must remember that we are listening to Raphael, doing his very best to warn Adam and discourage disobedience. In view of what is to follow, it cannot be said that the implicit advice is either redundant or over-stressed.

406–523 *Night brings a pause in the fighting, but Satan calls a council of war (–417). He sums up the military situation (–436) and suggests that new weapons might turn the scale (–445). Nisroc argues that their novel experience of pain is making the contest an unequal and intolerable one (–468). Satan urges the manufacture of engines and explosives (–495). The devils are heartened (–506). They work through the night on the new machines (–523).*

Night, bringing on ('inducing', 407) darkness, imposes a pleasing ('grateful', 407) truce. Michael and his angels, having won the day ('prevalent' – being superior, 411), camp on the field that has been fought over ('foughten', 410). Guards and watch-fires surround them. Satan's force, dislodged (415) from the field, has disappeared into the darkness. There is no rest for Satan's leaders: he calls them to a council. He addresses them as 'Companions', now tested in battle and therefore sure by experience that they cannot be beaten. They are therefore worthy, not just of liberty – this would be now too modest an ambition ("Too mean pretense', 421) – but of 'Dominion, Glorie', etc. (422), on which they set a much higher value ('more affect', 421) – for they have today resisted, in a struggle that has gone neither way ('doubtful fight', 423), the 'powerfullest' force God could send against them, a force he must have judged adequate to subdue them, which has not done so. (In fact, of course, they do not know themselves invincible: the day has suggested otherwise: it was not 'doubtful' for them by nightfall, but disastrous: God has not committed his full strength, but a limited force whose capacities he further limited.) Satan concedes that they have endured some 'disadvantage' (431) and the novelty of pain: but their first experience of pain showed that they could scorn it (432), since they have proved unable to be fatally wounded. Quickly healing wounds are a minor problem and the solution of it ought to be comparably easy. Perhaps stronger ('more valid', 438) and more violent weapons might next time give them the advantage that would tip the scales sufficiently to defeat the enemy or to cancel out that slight advantage he has gained so far in what is strictly still a contest between equals (438–42).

Nisroc is the next to speak, and his name brings potent associations to bear on the situation. Not only was he a vulture-god of Assyrian sculpture, but it was in his temple at Nineveh that Sennacherib, king of Assyria, was worshipping when his own sons murdered him. And Sennacherib had just returned to Nineveh after the disastrous conclusion to his invasion of Palestine. The saving of the city of Jerusalem and of the holy Mount (of Zion) from his destructive army is the relevant and crucial parallel. ('Therefore thus saith the Lord concerning the King of Assyria, He shall not come into this city. . . . For I will defend this city. . . . And it came to pass that night, that the angel of the Lord went out, and smote in the camp of the Assyrians an hundred fourscore and five thousand: and when they arose early in the morning behold, they were all dead corpses. So Sennacherib king of Assyria departed, and went and returned, and dwelt at Nineveh. And it came to pass, as he was worshipping in the house of Nisroch his god, that Adrammelech and Sharezer his sons smote him with the sword . . .' 2 Kings XIX. 32, 34–7.) Nisroc here, like his servant Sennacherib, is 'escap't from cruel fight . . . his riv'n armes to havoc hewn' (448–9).

Nisroc finds it an unequal contest, 'to fight in paine' (454) against an enemy who cannot suffer wounds. What is the use of matchless valour if you are overcome with pain which can weaken ('makes remiss', 458) the strongest arm? One can put up with loss of pleasure and exist contentedly, but pain is the 'worst of evils' (462–3) and too much of it overcomes all power of endurance ('patience', 464). Anyone, Nisroc concludes, who can invent means by which we can really damage ('offend', 465) our as yet unwounded enemy, or give us defences comparable to his invulnerability, will in my opinion ('to mee', 467) deserve everything we owe in payment for deliverance.

Satan's look is contrivedly steady ('compos'd', 469). The emphasis of feeling is now where he wants it to be. He has what purports to be an immediate answer to the problem of pain now worrying them. He has already invented the very thing they are quite rightly urging as vital to the outcome of their struggle ('main to our success', 471). Superficial survey of the surface of Heaven, he says, notes its richness of growth and glitter. Deep in the ground underneath all this are hidden dark raw foam and froth which, when touched and 'temperd' by the ray of Heaven, send up the beautiful shoots that open in the surrounding light. Satan's plan is to deal with these materials in their dark pre-natal condition (482), so that what is latently a potential up-flowering of fruit and gem shall be abortively perverted into a kind of gunpowder. The firing of this explosive in infernal cannons is described. The blast will hurl 'implements of mischief' (488) to shatter whatever stands in its way ('Adverse', 490). Satan concludes with a rousing claim that the application of strength and forethought ('counsel', 494) together can save them from worry or despair.

The rebel leaders are heartened. They marvel at the

invention. It seems so obvious, once discovered, that everyone wonders why he didn't think of it first. Yet they know it is one of those things which most 'would have thought impossible' had it not been discovered. Raphael takes the opportunity to warn Adam of the possibility that some mischievous member of the human race may unfortunately devise comparable machinery in the future.

The rebels quickly get to work: they dig up the chemical foam which, when mixed, baked and dried ('concocted and adusted', 514), forms a black powder that is then stored away. Mineral sources are tapped for the manufacture of cannons and balls. Matches ('incentive reed', 519) are also made. The rebels finish their secret work quietly.

524–679 *Next morning the loyalists send out scouts (–536) and Zophiel reports the fresh approach of the rebels (–546). The loyalists advance to meet them (–555) and Satan, at their head, makes an ambiguous and ironical offer of parley (–567). The rebels' ranks open to disclose the new cannon (–580), which they immediately fire (–591), and thus overwhelm and drive back the loyalists (–607). Satan rejoices scoffingly (–619). Belial echoes him (–627) and others join in the derision (–634). The loyalists throw away their impeding arms, then tear up hills and rocks and woods, and hurl them at the engines (–658) and the rebels, burying them (–661). The rebels take similar action (–670), whereupon God addresses the Son (–679).*

The morning ('matin', 526) trumpet calls the loyalists to arms. Scouts are despatched to scour the surrounding terrain and discover where the foe has taken refuge or whither he has fled, and, if he is intent on fighting again, whether he is moving or stationary ('in alt', 532). They soon meet him, drawing slowly near in firm formation (532–4). Zophiel flies back and calls the loyalists to prepare for battle. They need not fear that the foe has fled. They will be saved the trouble of a 'long pursuit' (538). The rebels are returning in thick formation with an appearance of grim determination and confidence ('Sad resolution and secure', 541). He recommends them to fit armour and helmets tightly and to grasp shields firmly, whether at shoulder-level or head-level ('eevn or high', 544). He is expecting a shower of fire-tipped arrows (546). The loyalists move on in battle array, free of their baggage and carriage (548). Soon they meet the massive body of rebels lumbering ponderously forward, dragging ('Training', 553) their 'devilish Enginrie', which is enclosed ('impal'd', 553) on every side with packed troops to conceal 'the fraud'.

There is a brief, static, face-to-face confrontation ('interview', 555); then we learn why Raphael has used the word 'fraud' (555). Satan comes forward and sarcastically indulges the thinly veiled pretence of a mock parley. The ironic ambiguities are crude. He will show his foes how he seeks peace and a settlement ('composure', 560). His foes may well like to stand in readiness to receive what he has to offer 'with open breast' (560), and see whether they like his 'overture' (i.e. approach/introductory bombardment) and not turn back from it 'perverse' (negatively/in reverse). He calls Heaven to witness that they will discharge (fulfil/explode) their contribution freely. Then he directs those who stand 'appointed' (instructed/equipped) to 'briefly touch' (quickly explain/quickly apply the fuse to) what they are putting forward ('propound', 567) and loudly too, so that all may hear.

Immediately the front ranks fan out and the new engines are revealed. Raphael carefully describes what they looked like to the eyes of angelic innocence – rows of hollow pillars mounted on wheels, with horrible orifices at the front promising a 'hollow truce' (578). So much for the ambiguities of Satan, whom Raphael quickly out-puns (the Devil is not allowed to emerge as the unchallenged arch-punster). A seraph stands at the back of each cannon with a taper ('Reed', 579) in his hand ready to fire the cannon. (The reiteration of the words 'stood', 579, 580, 581, and 'Reed', 579, 582, and the phrase 'and in his hand a Reed', together provide parodic echoes of Revelation and Isaiah appropriate to Milton's presentation of Satan as a mock-up divinity and the diabolical as a parasitical burlesque of the divine.) Through Raphael's eyes we see the loyalists held in suspense, bemused ('amus'd',

581) in thought, till the rebels apply their tapers with exact
('nicest', 584) touch to the narrow vent at the back of the
cannon. The explosion is a deep-throated belch. It fills the
air with a thundering blast as of burst and torn bowels and
entrails, while the devilish vomit ('glut', 589) is disgorged
from the overfed mouths of the cannon. The rain of metal
hail and thunderbolts, directed ('Level'd', 591) on the loyalists, smites so wildly that none of those who are hit can keep
their footing. They fall by thousands, rolling on top of one
another. The situation is all the worse because of their heavy
armour. Unarmed they would have more easily exploited the
advantage native and proper to them as spirits – taking swift
evasive action by quick self-diminution or removal ('con-
traction or remove', 597). Instead there is a scatter and a
rout. No tactical contrary or evasive move is open to them.
It would not have helped to loosen their packed lines
('serried files', 599). If they dashed forward, there would be
a second repulse, a doubly ugly ('indecent', 601) overthrow,
which would subject them to more derision from their foes;
because a second line of seraphim stands ready behind the
first to fire ('displode', 605) a second row of cannon.

Satan mocks their plight sarcastically. And if he gained
a sneaking admiration from us for his ironical patter when
he introduced the cannon like a conjurer (558-67), he loses
it all now by repeating the same jokes, not only trying to
make his audience laugh at the identical puns twice over, but
even underlining them (610–3). He is not an entertainer after
all: he is a bore. He makes the worst blunders of the tedious
amateur japester. What *is* new in the mockery is a heavy-
handed addition to the already overworked vein of ambi-
guity. He derides the loyalists for having responded to his
terms of parley by hurriedly changing their minds, flying off
the handle, and falling into strange vagaries as if they wanted
to dance – though their movements represented a rather
eccentric ('extravagant', 616) mode of dancing. Perhaps this
is just their joy at hearing peace terms offered. May be, if the
proposals were repeated, they would be compelled to reach
a quick decision.

Belial takes on the role of flatterer by imitation. Another clutter of puns is unloaded – about the 'weight' (621) and 'hard contents' (622) of the terms just sent to the loyalists, about the way they were 'urg'd home' with great 'force' (622) and therefore 'stumbl'd' (perplexed/knocked down, 624) many of them. The climax is a riot of indigestible quibbling. Anyone who receives terms like that has to 'understand' (and under-stand) them well 'from head to foot' (beginning to end/keeping his footing). Terms like those show up, if they are not 'understood' (withstood in a standing position) foes who can't remain 'upright' (627).

Such is the rebels' arrogance, as they scoff in jocular mood ('pleasant veine', 628), imagining that they have invented a thunder to match and outclass the divine thunder. But anger stirs the loyalists to quick thinking and quick action. They throw away their arms and dart to the hills with the flashing speed of lightning. They rip up firmly planted ('seated', 644) hills, rocks, lakes and woods, and carry them in their hands. There is terror among the rebels as they see whole mountains carried, bottoms upward, and then hurled down on top of the triple row of cannon. Their confidence as well as their cannonry is buried deep under 'the weight of Mountains' (652). Then they are themselves assaulted. Bulky ('Main', 654) headlands are flung into the air, shadowing the hosts beneath, and come crashing down on the heads of the rebels. Whole legions are crushed underneath, the more damagingly because their weighty armour bruises their enclosed ('pent', 657) 'substance', and torments with unalleviable ('implacable', 658) pain. There is long and grievous groaning and struggling before they can wriggle ('wind', 659) free of this entombment, for though they are in origin spirits of 'purest light', the texture of their composition has already become more crude ('gross', 661) through their sinfulness.

A symbolic vein threads its way through the narrative here. It is appropriate that the products of the raw materials abortively dug up from underground should be re-buried under the rocks and soil of torn-up hills: it is appropriate that what was manufactured by devilish abuse of natural resources should be shattered by this angelic recourse to the safeguarding solidity of natural resources torn up by the roots and re-planted on top of the wreckage: it is fitting that engines devised for the destruction and capture of the holy Mount at the heart of Heaven should thus be submerged under the weight of mountain and hill (652). The loosening of hills from their 'foundations' (643), the reiteration of the word 'Hills' (639, 644, 663, 664) as well as of the word 'Mountains' – these are things which bring many echoes of the psalms and other parts of the Old Testament with them.

The rebels – ever parasitical in their thinking – respond by also tearing up hills and using them as artillery. Hills collide with hills in mid-air, and under the dreadful hurling-about ('jaculation dire', 665) of hills they are virtually fighting 'under ground' (666). But Heaven is not to be allowed to go to rack and ruin. The Almighty Father 'secure' as ever 'where he sits' (in spite of all the rebels' intentions, inventions, claims and taunts), has weighed all these eventualities in totality (673) and in advance, and has already decided ('advis'd') to permit what has happened. The fulfilment of his great purpose will emerge from it all; the honouring of his Anointed Son, the manifestation of the power conferred upon him. Thus the Father turns to the participator in his sovereignty ('Th'Assessor of his Throne', 679).

680–800 The Father addresses the Son. Two days of evenly balanced warfare have been permitted (–698). On the third the Son is to end it by taking the full might of the Father into action and driving the rebels out (–718). The Son receives the Father's full authority to himself (–722) and replies, expressing the joy and glory of obedience to the divine will (–745). On the third day the Son sets out in the divine chariot with a vast force (–772). Michael and his host receive them with joy (–787). The rebels, obstinately perverse and envious, prepare for renewed battle (–800).

The Father addresses the Son as the one who projects into recognizability the radiant but unfaceable glory, makes visible in his features what the invisible Godhead is, makes evident in his action what the inconceivable divine purpose is (680–4). The two days of indecisive battle are accounted for. Michael and Satan were equal in their creation. It is true that sin has damaged ('impaird', 691) Satan's strength, but the damage has been done imperceptibly ('Insensibly', 692) as yet, because God is delaying ('suspend', 692) the judgement upon him ('doom', 692). Without interference there would be a continuance of fighting, a never-ending stalemate. War has achieved all that can be achieved by war: it has produced a wild and dangerous disorder.

God explains that he has allowed things to go so far ('thus farr/Have sufferd', 700–1) that the Son may have the glory of ending it. He has ordained the third day as the Son's (the parallels with the crucifixion and the resurrection are obvious). He has made available such abundant 'Vertue and Grace' in the Son that his matchless power will be plain to everyone, and he has so overseen the 'perverse Commotion' (706) as to make it a means of manifesting how worthy the Son is to be in possession of 'all things', how deserving of his right to be the anointed king. Thus the Son is sent into battle with echoes of the psalms reproducing an Old Testament flavour of dedicated monarchical militancy (cf. 714 with Psalm XLV. 3: 'Gird thy sword upon thy thigh, O most mighty . . .').

The inexpressible Godhead of the Father is fully expressed in the co-inherent Son through the interchange of divine radiance (719–21). And now Godhead answers Godhead through the voice of the filial co-inherence (722).

In the words of the Son the voice of the New Testament is as prominent as the voice of the Old Testament in the words of the Father above. If it is the Father's delight to glorify the Son, the Son considers that to find the Father well pleased with him (cf. Matthew XVII. 5) is what glorifies, exalts and delights him most (the prayer of Christ in John XVII – e.g. 1 and 5 – is plainly much in Milton's mind). The fulfilment of the Father's will in himself is the fulfilment of the Son's bliss. The Son, assuming the gift of 'Scepter and Power" looks forward to an end when the Father will be

'All in All' and himself eternally dwelling in the Father, not, as now, in distinction from the creatures God has made, but in himself bringing all whom the Father loves into the same co-inherent relationship of unity and plenitude (730–3). Meantime, faced with rebellion and the ugliness of evil, the Son can show forth the Father's detestation as surely as he can express his mildness (735). He will quickly rid Heaven of the rebels. Then the blessed ones will sing God's praise about the throne in sincerity of heart (744), no longer contaminated ('unmixt', 742) by the 'impure' hypocrites (who worshipped with feigned praise).

The chariot in which the Son rides out is a Miltonic version of the visionary vehicle in Ezekiel 1. One wheel is axled loosely ('undrawn', 751) within another, and each wheel is indwelt ('instinct', 752) with spiritual being ('for the spirit of the living creature was in the wheels', Ezekiel 1. 20), but they are drawn ('convoyd', 752) by four winged 'Cherubic shapes' (753), each of whom has four faces (in Ezekiel those of man, lion, ox and eagle, Ezekiel 1. 10). The cherubic bodies, their wings, and the wheels themselves are all set with jewelled eyes, 'as with Starrs' (754); and flames race forward between them. Above them the chariot-platform is a 'chrystal Firmament' – their sky a floor for the divine throne. The vehicle gives us a sharp symbolic representation of the Son's lordship over the heavenly realm of angel and spirit, over the created universe of firmament and star, and the living creatures, man and beast. The Son is riding into battle enthroned on a moving miniature universe, a compound vehicular Heaven and Earth. Moreover the blend of human, animal, and angelic in the shapes of the Cherubic beings who draw the throne denotes a harmony and unity among the living creatures fashioned by Godhead and subject to the Son. One should also note that the fruitful commixture of spirit and machinery in action (in the whole) signifies a positive linkage in direct contradiction to the perverse diabolical exploitation of cannonry and explosive in the second day's battle. The 'careering Fires' (756) are especially interesting in this connection. The whole contrast deserves detailed attention. As hills, rocks, waters and woods finally and fitly buried underneath the diabolical machinery (VI. 644–5 and 652); here the angelic machinery sustains from beneath and carries in triumph a starlit firmament, the footstool of God. The second day ended with the tearing to bits of the natural, living fabric within which creaturely life lives: the third day begins with the Son enthroned on a miniature living cosmos reconstituted in the perfect harmony of obedience.

The Son's heavenly armour ('Panoplie', 760) is fashioned of the mysterious, shining 'Urim' (761: see Exodus XXVIII. 30) – probably jewels inside the breastplate of judgement, which was part of the high priest's garment known as the 'ephod'. The divine workmanship (761) mentioned here in close association with this symbol of Jewish worship, with all the sacred secrets of temple rites and ritual, enriches what is already a packed miniature of gathered universalities. One could linger long on lines such as these. Suffice it to add that the smoke and darting ('bickering', 766) flame that roll around, a fierce outpouring ('Effusion', 765) from one who keeps his threefold thunder safely 'stor'd' (764), is again in direct contrast to the 'triple row' of engines (650), 'triple-mounted', (572) whose 'flame' and 'smoak' obscured everything (585) and in whose 'Thunder' (606) the rebels were sure they had worsted the divine 'Thunder' (632). With every such contrast or correspondence the parodic and parasitical character of the diabolical is corroborated.

Thus, on his 'Saphir Throne' (758, 772), the Son approaches the battlefield, attended by his 'ten thousand thousand saints' (767: see Revelation V. 11) and his twenty thousand chariots (769–70: see Psalm LXVIII. 17). Though his shining chariot illuminates a vast area ('Illustrious farr and wide', 773), he is first seen by the loyalists. He comes this time to 'his own' (773), and 'his own' receive him with 'joy surpriz'd' (774). When he comes to Earth later as the Light shining in darkness (John I. 5, 7, 9) then 'He came unto his own, and his own received him not' (John I. 11). Michael quickly brings back ('reduc'd', 777) his army, spread out on either side (778), and hands them over to be part of the single body under the one divine head (779). Divine power prepares the way before him (780). (See Isaiah XL. 3, Matthew III. 3, and Mark I. 3; for each such quotation or echo confirms the implicit correspondence between the coming of the Son to battle against the powers of darkness here in Heaven, and his coming to Earth in the Incarnation to battle against the powers of darkness on Earth. Milton has just pressed home the parallel by emphasizing that the Son rides under the 'great Ensign of *Messiah*', 775.) He commands, the hills hear his voice and return obedient ('obsequious' 783) to their foundations (the biblical sources are numerous). The customary ('wonted', 783) face of Heaven is renewed, while hills and valleys smile again.

Obstinately and perversely the rebels stand out against this rejoicing. In stupid ('Insensate', 787) self-exclusion they rally for continued resistance, madly hatching out hope from a situation of despair. One can scarcely conceive of such perversity in heavenly beings, Raphael observes: but what 'Signs' are there that are powerful enough, what 'Wonders' great enough to move obdurate beings to repentance (790)? Raphael's foreshadowing of the parallel resistance the Son is to meet from his enemies on his later coming to Earth is again evident ('Except ye see signs and wonders, ye will not believe.' John IV. 48). The Son's glory, which ought to bring them to their senses (791), hardens them to greater envy and ambition. They re-form for battle. They will succeed or bring 'universal ruin' (797).

801–912 *The Son addresses the loyalists. He commands them to stand and rest. He alone will deal with the foe (–823). He rides out against them (–834). His thunders and his blazing chariot wear them down (–852). He herds them together and drives them out of Heaven (–866). Nine days they fall, till Hell receives and encloses them (–877). The Son rides back in triumph with the rejoicing loyalists to his Father's throne (–892). In conclusion Raphael points the moral of his story to Adam (–912).*

The Son commends the army for their faithful warfare. They have done their part by being fearless in the cause of righteousness. The punishment of the rebels is not their responsibility but God's. 'Vengeance is his' (808 – 'Vengeance is mine; I will repay, saith the Lord.' Romans XII. 19), or his appointed representative's. What is laid down ('ordain'd', 809) for this day's work is not going to involve a great number or multitude. *I* am the object of the rebels' indignation, the Son insists, of their scorn, envy and rage, because the Father has chosen to honour me. It is *their* wish to try their strength against mine. They judge everything in terms of power and are not ambitious to excel in other ways (821–2). I shall not grant them opposition on other grounds than they have chosen.

The terror and wrath of God are in the face of the Son as he rides out against evil. The cherubic shapes spread their adjacent wings, making an unbroken shadow ('shade contiguous', 828). The chariot rolls forward with the noise of an approaching torrential flood. The wheels blaze. The 'Empyrean' itself is shaken. The ten thousand thunders are let loose from his right hand and penetrate their 'Soules' with poison (837–8). They are stupefied ('astonisht', 838), their courage and resistance broken. They are ridden down, prostrate, and could wish rather that they might have the mountains again thrown on them as shelter from this wrath (842–3: see Revelation VI. 16 – 'And said to the mountains and rocks, Fall on us, and hide us from the face of him that sitteth on the throne, and from the wrath of the Lamb'). A hail of arrows falls from the cherubic shapes and the 'living Wheels' (846), all of which are decorated ('Distinct', 846, 847) with 'multitude of eyes' (847), each one shooting fire among the rebels. The rebels' strength is withered: they are drained of their accustomed ('wonted', 851) vigour. The Son has not brought 'half his strength' (853) into play: indeed he checks his thunder in mid-volley (854): he does not mean to destroy the rebels but to rid Heaven of them. So they are herded together, a frightened flock ('Goats', 857 – not sheep, of course) and driven right out through a gap, which opens in the wall of Heaven. Fearful as the prospect is of the wasteful deep before them, a worse horror drives them from behind (863–4). They throw themselves from the edge of Heaven, the eternal wrath burning at their backs.

Hell sees the heavenly beings falling ('ruining', 868) from Heaven and is itself resistant at the prospect of housing them. The account of Chaos burdened ('Incumberd', 874) with the magnitude of the confused fall is recorded by Anarch himself in Book II (993–8). Hell receives them and shuts them in (875). The breach in Heaven's wall repairs itself as readily as angelic wounds close up of their own healthy accord (878). The loyalists, who have watched the Son's acts in silence, now gather around him and accompany him, as he rides in majesty and triumph, with branching palms in their hands. So, as the Messiah is to ride in triumph into the holy city of Jerusalem, with palms about him, he now rides through mid Heaven, into 'the Courts/And Temple of his mightie Father' (889–90).

Raphael concludes. His story is not to be taken too literally for he has been 'measuring things in Heav'n by things on Earth' (893) in order to bring them within the range of Adam's comprehension. The whole story of the war in Heaven and the Fall of the Angels might well have been hidden from the human race, were it not needful for Adam to take warning from what has happened (894–5); for the same Satan who rebelled now envies the human 'state' (900) and is plotting to seduce Adam from obedience, so that, deprived of happiness, man may share his punishment of misery. The warning not to listen to Satan's temptations is reiterated. Adam is reminded to warn Eve ('Thy weaker', 909), too.

Book VII

Milton calls upon *Urania* as a persona with a 'Voice divine' (2) not as a figure from Classical mythology (5), for indeed his narration has already taken him well above the reach of any Classical flights of imagination (3–4). The *'Urania'* he calls is 'Heav'nlie borne' (7) before creation, the power of poetic insight, which always existed side by side with Wisdom in the presence of the Father. The insight has already taken him as a guest to Heaven, enabling him to breathe its air, and now, he trusts, will guide him safely back to earth (12–16). He does not want to suffer the fate of *Bellerophon* who tried to reach Heaven on the back of the flying horse *Pegasus* (cf. VII. 4 above), was thrown to the ground, roamed on the *Aleian* plain, went mad and died. Milton's express fear lest he likewise 'fall/Erroneous' (19–20) hints at the mental strain involved in his work and situation.

The half of his story yet to be told concerns events confined ('bound', 21) within the narrower limits of the visible finite world. Milton will have his feet on the ground. He will not be taken up ('rapt', 23) above the summit of the universe. He will be dealing with matters safer for the human poet to tackle, but there will be in his voice neither new stridency nor new timorousness, even though he has fallen on evil days, is conscious of malice against him, and suffers from darkness, danger, and loneliness (23–8). Milton suffered imprisonment for some months after the Restoration for his public defence of Charles's execution. He was fined and lost most of his money. These misfortunes, the total transformation of the social and political scene, and the burden of his blindness, are movingly evident here. The comfort brought by the poetic fluency which his inspiration provides night by night (in his sleep) or morning by morning, is also evident (28–30), and he hopes to find a sympathetic, if small, readership for his epic. Meantime, in what sounds like a tilt at the permissive Restoration social scene, he trusts that the noisy vulgarities of drunken party-goers will be kept at a distance. He likens them to the orgy-crazy women who tore Orpheus to pieces, silencing his 'Harp and Voice' (33–7). His own muse is a truly heavenly inspiration, not, like Orpheus' muse, a figure created by empty fancy: he prays that she will not fail him.

First he asks the muse to tell what followed after Raphael related the story of the war in Heaven in order to forewarn Adam, by example and precedent, against the perils of disobedience, and the consequences of ignoring God's one command, by touching the forbidden ('interdicted', 46) tree. Then he tells how attentively Adam, accompanied by Eve (50), listened to Raphael, how astonished and deeply reflective (52) to hear of things so unimaginable as the war in Heaven. The fact that evil so soon redounded on those who initiated it is a comfort to Adam. He is innocently desirous to learn more of things more immediately relevant to him (61–2), how and why the visible ('conspicuous', 63) world originated, and what happened before the time of his own consciousness. He is like a man whose thirst ('drouth', 66) is not fully satisfied, who is still eyeing the stream whose 'liquid murmur' stimulates further thirst.

Adam thanks Raphael for his narration and for bringing the timely forewarning of what, had they not known it, might have been a grave loss to them. The history is one which unaided human knowledge could not attain to (75). It has had to be 'reveal'd' to them by the 'Divine Interpreter' (72). We seem to be listening to our first father taking up a theological position in relation to religious truth on behalf of the human race in general. However that may be, Adam recognizes that he and Eve owe 'immortal thanks' to God and he receives the divine warning with solemn intention always to obey God's will – which is the very purpose ('end', 79) for which they have been made.

Since Raphael has deigned ('voutsaf't', 80) to make known things out of reach of earthly thought, which were important for them to know, and to do it in easily understood form for their instruction (81), Adam asks that Raphael will condescend further, coming down nearer to their own level to tell what is perhaps equally helpful for them to know, the history of the universe – the heavens, the stars, and the air around them. What cause induced the Creator to build and so quickly to complete ('how soon/Absolv'd', 93-4) this new work? As Adam asks the question that is to lead up to Raphael's account of Creation, the phrasing and the rhythm (90-1) firmly recall the opening of Book I (28-9), aptly preparing us for the contrast between the rational order of Creation and the irrational disorder of discreation. Adam stresses that they ask not out of curiosity to 'explore the secrets' (95) of God's empire, but because the more they know the more they can magnify God's works. (Our Great Parent is not just making primitive man's primal request on our behalf, but establishing a moral principle in relation to the character and purpose of the justifiable pursuit of human knowledge.)

The sun, Adam concludes, still has to ('wants to', 98) run much of its daily course, though it is now coming down the 'steep' (99) slope from the midday zenith. It is held hanging in suspense in the sky by Raphael's voice and will delay its progress further to hear Raphael tell of its own birth ('Generation', 102) and the birth of Nature from the invisible ('unapparent', 103) deep. Or if the evening star and the moon hurry on the approach of night in order to get quickly to where they themselves can listen to you ('to thy audience', 105), night will bring a silence appropriate to your continuing story, and sleep will keep awake ('watch', 106) out of desire to listen to you. Or if necessary, Adam concludes, we can ourselves keep sleep away till your story ends. The poetic devices may at first sight seem a little stilted here (98–108), but in fact the passage gives a very fitting picture of an expectant, attentive universe, hanging on the words of the angel, sun and moon, day and night harmoniously competing for the privilege of listening to the story of their origin – with the same respectful attentiveness as man and woman. All are equally desirous to be in at the 'audience' (105: one must picture a great lord and patron holding court).

Adam's request is granted by Raphael because he has made it with due 'caution' (111), that is, circumspection and tentativeness (see 94–7). Difficult as it is for seraph to voice or man to understand the 'Almightie works' (112), what Adam *can* grasp ('attain', 115), and what will both glorify the maker and make Adam happier ('inferr/Thee . . . happier', 116–17), shall not be kept back from Adam's hearing. God's 'commission' to Raphael has been that he should answer man's desire for knowledge 'within bounds' (120). Adam must be prepared to accept a limit to what man's curiosity ('inventions', 121) can compass. There is such a thing as incommunicable divine knowledge. Knowledge is like food. The human appetite for both has to be disciplined. You can make yourself sick by getting too much of either – and turn yourself into a cerebral or physical gas-bag (130).

131–223 Raphael's story begins. After Lucifer's fall the Father addresses the Son. He will create another world and a new race of beings (–161). The Son shall perform the work (–173). There is rejoicing in Heaven (–191). The Son rides out of Heaven into Chaos (–223).

The Father surveys the 'multitude' (138) of faithful angels who have returned with the victorious Son. At least, he says, Satan has 'fail'd' (139: i.e. failed and miscalculated) in thinking everybody as rebellious as himself and in hoping by their help to dispossess us and seize our inaccessible throne. Satan lured many into the fraudulent scheme ('fraud',

143) but there are plenty left to possess Heaven and perform the due services and rituals of God's 'high Temple' (148). But lest Satan should boost himself by boasting that he has 'dispeopl'd Heav'n' (151; Satan does claim to have 'emptied Heav'n', I. 633) and by foolishly imagining ('fondly deemd', 152) that he has thus damaged me, I will compensate for the loss – if *loss* be the right word to describe the removal of the 'self-lost' (the divine smile is evident here) – and create a new world and a new race. The race will stay in their world till they prove themselves under obedience and Earth be changed to Heaven, Heaven to Earth.

Critics have wasted ink in misunderstanding this passage (157–61). No argument can be drawn from it about theological doctrines applicable to fallen man. God is propounding a plan whereby innocent man may work his way to Heaven. As soon as man has fallen, the plan becomes obsolete and inapplicable. Neither Milton nor God is committed to any doctrine here which affects the human situation as we know it.

Meantime God tells the angels to relax. The creative work he himself performs is to be performed through his Son, his word, now to utter. His 'overshadowing Spirit and might' will be with the Son at the utterance. In the difficult lines 167–73 Milton skates carefully over the thin verbal ice, which is all that human understanding can supply in the way of support for a reasoned account of creation. Heaven and Earth are to be fashioned out of the boundless deep: but this does not mean that there is, until their fashioning, some region not yet within God's control, not yet subject to his omnipotence or even to his omnipresence. God himself fills infinitude; there is no spatial vacuity wholly external to, or outside the range of, his being. He is not a being limited by an outline that would circumscribe its scope in terms of extension or influence. But the goodness of God is free: he may act or not act; and in so far as his goodness is not everywhere wholly operative (which could be the basis only of an enslaved universe), and in so far as he is not at all times omnisciently, omnipotently – and therefore benevolently –

active (which again could be the basis only of an enslaved universe), to that extent God is one who withdraws or retires (170), voluntarily not putting forth his goodness (171). And this means that creation can be metaphorically represented in terms of a divine excursion into a region of apparent otherness, and in the utterance of a divine *fiat*, which apparently extends the empire of omnipotence.

God speaks, and it is done. But if human understanding ('earthly notion', 179) is to make anything of it, a good deal more needs to be said through the slow 'process of speech' (178). So Raphael describes the heavenly rejoicing that greets the Father's decree. Milton so phrases the liturgy of praise as to echo the angels' song at the birth of Christ in Bethlehem (e.g. 182–3; cf. Luke 11. 14 – 'Glory to God in the highest . . . good will towards men'). The fabric of biblical echoes here reinforces again the correspondence between the old creation and the new creation. The unmistakable indebtedness to Genesis 1 is everywhere evident in this book. The particular correspondence between the 'overshadowing Spirit' (165) and the spirit of God that moves upon the face of the waters to remove darkness from the face of the deep (Genesis 1. 2) is blended with a hint of the annunciatory angelic message to the Virgin Mary (Luke 1. 35, 'The Holy Ghost shall come upon thee, and the power of the Highest shall overshadow thee . . .'). The use of the word 'Word' (163 and 175) is here so plainly indebted to John 1 that parallel between Creation and Incarnation (John 1. 1: 'In the beginning was the Word . . .' and John 1. 14: 'And the Word was made flesh and dwelt among us . . .') is inescapable anyway. The solemn liturgy of praise (182–8) links psalm and gospel, and once more implicitly binds together the whole vast scheme of Creation and Redemption. (The invocation to the Holy Spirit, present at Creation, to illuminate the darkness of the poet's mind, involves the poet's own creative work in the same fabric of correspondences, 1. 19–23. He has his own place among the four Authors of *Paradise Lost*.)

The Son sets out, omnipotence, glory, kingship, wisdom and love made expressly apparent in his going. Indeed 'all his Father' shines in him as he prepares to utter the creative word. The symbolic accoutrements of the divine authority and power muster about him; the living ceremonial equipage of Heaven moves spontaneously into festal readiness; the everlasting ('during', 206) gates open wide; and the King of Glory moves, not in (as in Psalm XXIV. 7) but out. Line 212 ('dark, wasteful, wilde') seems to echo II. 961 ('Wide on the wasteful deep') and to press home the parallel between Satan's excursion into Chaos for the purpose of destroying the new race and the Son's excursion into Chaos for the purpose of creating it. ('Abyss' ends the resounding line 211, as it ends resoundingly II. 910, 956, 969.) As Satan stands and pauses at the gates of Hell on the brink of Chaos (II. 917 ff.), so the Son pauses at the gates of Heaven. The Almighty Word calls the troubled waves to silence (216; as he is later in Galilee to bid them be still), and rides forward with his angel train.

224–448 *The first five days of Creation. Heaven and Earth are made (–242: Genesis I. 1–5). Light is created (–252) and Heaven rejoices over the first day of Creation (–260). On the second day the firmament is made (–275: Genesis I. 6–8). On the third day God makes dry land (–287), the waters (–308), plants and trees (–338: Genesis I. 9–13). On the fourth day God makes the sun, the moon, and the stars (–386: Genesis I. 14–19). On the fifth day God makes fish and birds (–448: Genesis I. 20–3).*

The account of Creation is modelled on the first chapter of Genesis, but it is a verse in Proverbs (VIII. 27, 'When he prepared the heavens, I was there: when he set a compass upon the face of the depth.') that lies behind the account here of God first marking out the bounds of the universe (225–31). It is the 'hand' (224) and voice of the Son that accomplish this, but it is the 'Spirit of God' that outspreads 'brooding wings' over the encompassed but yet unformed matter, in order to impregnate it with potency and vitality and to drain off downwards the cold negativities 'Adverse to life'. By this means a basis is laid on which the differentiations and en-clusterings of our known material world are effected: the air is 'spun' and the Earth 'hung'. The brooding 'Spirit of God' (235) has been foreseen, thus active, at the beginning of Book I (I. 19–21). There is now, therefore, a rich garnering of correspondences as the Holy Spirit, the Dove of the New Testament, which descends on the new man, Christ (Luke III. 22), and which broods over the formless matter in the first creational act of God, is the same Spirit invoked by the poet to give shape and substance to the formless matter in the mind, of which the poem is to be made. Moreover the presence here of the Spirit in action where the Son has ridden out to act ought to be enough to save us from the interpretative perils attendant upon oversimplifying the distinction between the Persons of the Trinity.

God speaks the *fiat lux* and a pre-solar, feminine ('her', 245; 'shee', 248) radiance, ensphered in a tent-like cloud (248), sails through the gloom. Light is divided from darkness: Day and Night are named: and it is the sight of light emanating from darkness that sets the angels in Heaven rejoicing at the birthday of Heaven and Earth.

On the second day God makes the firmament (the vault of Heaven, to 'divide the waters from the waters', as it does in Genesis I. 6 as well as here, 262–3). Milton presents this notion so as to accommodate it to his cosmology. In order to understand what Milton is saying, the modern reader must conceive of the earth as being supported *from the outside*, not from its centre. The foundation is, as it were, above our heads. The earth is like an orange, held by its skin, not like an apple concentrated on its core. Thus the firmament, the skin of liquid air with its 'top' dressing – the sea – is spread around to the outermost ('uttermost', 266) 'convex', forming a 'firm and sure' (267) basis on which what is contained within it rests. This basis is also a 'partition' (267), for just as the earth is in this sense 'built on' the waters that surround it ('circumfluous', 270), so the universe ('World', 269) is contained within the waters of the ninth, crystalline sphere. The tenth sphere, the *primum mobile*, forms the shell to the whole, and it is this shell with its inner layer of waters that contains the universe and cuts it safely off from the 'fierce extreames' (272) of adjacent Chaos, which, if they were contiguously in contact with what is within, might infect and erode ('distemper', 273) the whole fabric. The modern reader will grasp the concepts here easily enough if he starts by separating the concept of 'underneath' from the concept of what supports a thing and gives it a sustaining foundation.

The image that opens Raphael's account of the third day of creation will help us. The earth is as yet a foetus ('Embryon immature', 277) wrapped about ('involv'd', 277) with waters as in the womb. It has yet to make its appearance. From this beginning a complete metaphorical correspondence between the creation of dry land and the birth of a child is elaborated. For the water, which at present flows over all the surface ('face', 278) of the earth, is not useless or inactive ('idle', 279). All the time it is both cushioning and shaping ('soft'ning', 280) the embryonic globe of future earth with a warm generative fluid ('prolific humour', 280). A process of conceptual fermentation thus saturates the embryonic substance with a fertilizing ('genial', 282) fluid, so that when God says 'let dry land appear' (284 and Genesis 1. 9) the birth occurs. The huge mountains begin to emerge, their 'broad bare backs' (286) upheaving, and inevitably also forming basins and hollow valleys between, each valley ('bottom', 289) now a 'capacious bed' (290) for waters – ocean bed, lake bed or river bed, of course. The waters break out in a joyful rush ('glad precipitance', 292) to fill these spaces. It is not a purely downward rush: floods can up-roll (cf. 291) if there is sufficient pressure behind them. Hence the moving crystal walls, like immensely magnified drops such as those which form spherically ('conglobing', 291) on dust, upright in seeming defiance of gravity. Water thus moves into occupancy in great liquid masses and ridges, wave rolling after wave, like a mustering army trooping to where the standard has been raised. Over ground, under ground, wherever there is a fit channel, the waters find their way with serpent-like windings ('Serpent errour', 302). Channels are easily worn in the muddy consistency ('washie Oose', 303) where the ground is not yet dry. The dry land is called earth; the waters gathered ('congregated', 308) in the major receptacles are called seas.

Then God calls plants and trees to birth – different from the earth and the water in that they are higher up the scale of Nature, because they have the property of 'yeilding Seed' (310) and 'yeilding Fruit' after their own 'kind' (of the same nature as themselves). This is a form of animate being 'Whose Seed is in herself' (312). The metaphor of the Earth as a new-born baby is continued. It is a female baby, the future 'Great Mother' (281) Earth, whose conception and foetal development we have attended. Now the body, 'bare' (313–14) and unsightly at first, is gradually adorned and clad with verdure of grass about her 'Face' (316). The perfume of coloured flowers makes gay and sweet her bosom. Milton adds the 'humble Shrub/And Bush' entangled ('implicit', 323) with 'frizl'd hair', and his vocabulary ('unadorned', 314; 'clustering Vine', 320) firmly recalls the first description of primal, new-created man and woman in Book IV ('Clustring . . . unadorned golden tresses . . . As the Vine curls her tendrils . . .', IV. 304–8).

The correspondence between the body of earth and the human body is immediately followed by the correspondence between Earth and Heaven (328–9). The primal earth is an ordered earth where 'stately Trees' rise as in a 'Dance' (324): it is a country 'seat' (329) fit for gods to inhabit. There is need neither of 'rain' (a 'dewie Mist', 333, serves instead) nor of tilling.

On the fourth day (Genesis 1. 14–19) God matches his work of the third day with precision. As he made a firmament to divide the universe spatially and establish an ordered positional system of locations, so he now places lights in the firmament to divide the new system on a temporal basis and establish an ordered fabric working in chronological sequence. Hence the emphasis on the word 'divide' (340, 352) – day from night, light from darkness, and on the sun's duty ('Office', 344) to 'rule by Day' (347), the moon's 'by Night alterne' (348). Hence, too, the emphasis on the function of the stars to 'rule the Day' (350) and

by fit alternation and permutation ('vicissitude', 351) to 'rule
the Night' (351) also. The lights of Heaven are seen as
providing a means of marking off and measuring seasons,
days and nights. This is not just a system of illumination but
a machinery of chronological demarcation and control. Indeed the sun, a sphere fashioned of ethereal substance
('mould', 356), at first contains no light ('unlightsom', 355).
Light has already been made and is parcelled neatly up in the
'cloudie Tabernacle' of 248, now a 'cloudie Shrine' (360).
God takes from this what he has in store and transplants it
(360), the bigger share into the sun (359), a 'porous' (361),
apparently sponge-like orb, which can suck in the light in
liquid form and firmly contain it (362). The sun is now a
great 'Palace' of light (363). It is also a reservoir of light, for
the stars come to it and draw off light for themselves in their
'gold'n Urns' (365). Even the 'Morning Planet' comes here
to gild his horns. The stars in this way acquire but a minute
quantity of light as their own special property ('peculiar',
368), but they augment it by gathering a further infusion
('tincture', 367) from what the sun gives off and by reflecting the sun's light (their own store of light serving as a
mirror). Thus, though remote from human eyes, they can
be seen.

The Sun, ruler of the day, arrayed ('Invested', 372) in
brightness, rises in the east cheerfully to run his daily course
(cf. Psalm XIX. 5, where it 'rejoiceth as a strong man to run
a race'). The dawn and the *Pleiades* (the constellation that,
rising in May, was associated with fertilizing showers of
spring) dance before him. Directly opposite is the Moon,
whose face is a mirror that reflects light borrowed from the
Sun. In that position ('aspect', 379) she needs no other light.
When Heaven's axle has revolved and it is night, she maintains her rule along with the thousands of stars which share
in the divided ('dividual', 382) light.

On the fifth day (Genesis 1. 20–3) we move further up the
scale of creation from the vegetable level of the third day's
work to the animal level. In between, on the fourth day, the
fundamental regulatory system of temporal measurement

was established, matching the regulatory system of spatial positioning established on the second day. We can now see that the total plan of the six days' work is: *Day 1*: The Boundary marked; matter formed out of Chaos, light out of darkness. *Day 2*: The foundations of Locality laid. *Day 3*: Land and water differentiated and vegetable life created. *Day 4*: The foundations of temporal measurement, seasonal and diurnal, established. *Day 5*: Animal life (in water and air) – fish and fowl created. *Day 6*: Animal life on earth at the bestial level, then at the rational human level, created.

The fifth day, then, sees the spawning of fish and the first emergence on earth of 'living Soule' (388). The birds fly with wings outspread ('Displayd', 390). They and the fish are ordered to 'be fruitful and multiply' (396 and Genesis 1. 22). That is the keynote of what follows – prolific and rapid multiplication in the teeming abundance of natural life ('spawn abundant', 388; 'plenteously . . . generated', 392–3; 'Frie innumerable', 400; 'Shoales', 400; 'Sculles', i.e. *shoals*, 402), and in variety and colourfulness, as glimpses of shoals and darting, shining skins are mingled with glances at pearly shells, lobsters and crabs in their 'jointed Armour' (409), arching ('bended', 410) dolphins, and great whales that spout and seem like moving lands (415: as the great whale was mistaken for an island in the story referred to in 1. 203–8).

Just as numerous is the hatching-out of bird life by the natural breaking ('kindly rupture', 419) of eggs, which lets out the callow young. Soon they acquire feathers and wings ('Penns', 421), soar up and show by their scream ('clang', 422) how they now scorn the ground. Some fly through the air ('Region', 425) separately ('loosly', 425), others, gathered together ('In common', 426), cut their way in figured formation ('rang'd in figure wedge thir way', 426), instinctively aware ('Intelligent', 427) of the change of seasons. The 'prudent Crane' is cited as an instance of the migratory bird (we came across Milton's interest in cranes in a previous allusion, 1. 576). As with the fish, so with the birds, Milton rounds off his account with a neat little variegated survey, taking in the tuneful nightingale, the soft-breasted ducks, the swan with arched neck, uplifting ('mantling', 439) her wings like a cloak about her, and rowing gracefully forward with her oar-like feet. These can leave the water ('Dank', 441) if they wish and tower upwards on firmly spread wings ('stiff Pennons', 441). The cock and the peacock – clarion voice and rainbow train – complete the picture.

449–640 *The sixth and seventh days of Creation. God makes the animals (–504). One thing remains to be made, a rational being (–518): so God makes man and woman (–530) and forbids them the one tree (–547). The work finished, the Son returns amid acclamation to Heaven (–581). On the seventh day God rests, and blesses the day (–594). The hosts of Heaven praise God and his works (–625) and sing the blessedness of man (–632). Raphael completes his story (–640).*

On the sixth day God says, 'Let the earth bring forth the living creature after his kind . . .' (Genesis 1. 24). The Earth opens her womb and full-grown animals rise up, some scattered singly ('rare and solitarie', 461), others 'in flocks'. The grassy clods calve and there is a lion, its hinder parts still trapped, pawing to get right out (463–4). The lynx ('Ounce', 466), the leopard ('Libbard', 467) and the tiger, like the mole, rise and throw the crumbled earth about them in hillocks. The rare ('scarse', 470) elephant (*'Behemoth'*, 471) heaves himself up from the 'mould'. Flocks of sheep spring up like plants. Amphibious creatures ('ambiguous between Sea and Land', 473), the hippopotamus ('River Horse', 474) and crocodile, get a mention; then Raphael moves on to insects and creeping or crawling things ('Worme', 476 – a generalized term: Satan the serpent is 'that false Worm', IX. 1068). In the case of the insects it is the delicacy of their fashioning and the richness of their colouring that is noted – their supple ('limber', 476) fan-like wings, their minute and finely constructed frames ('Lineaments exact', 477). The crawling things that take a winding path ('sinuous trace', 481) are not all Nature's miniatures ('Minims', 482): some serpentine creatures wind round into folds bodies of great length and bulk. Other creatures listed are the thrifty ant ('Parsimonious emmet', 485), recommended for its foresight in providing for the future and its readiness to co-operate in communal living, characteristics that make it perhaps a pattern for the just and equal society of the future (485–9), and the female bee, which (according to current thinking) is the worker bee that feeds the 'Husband Drone' on its delicious diet. The animal catalogue is completed with a reference to the subtlest beast, the serpent. Raphael stresses that in spite of its hugeness and its frightening appearance it is not harmful ('noxious', 498) to Adam, to whom all animals are in obedient subjection.

The heavens now shine with glory and revolve in their courses at the touch of the first-mover's hand. The earth smiles in the finished ('Consummate', 502) loveliness of her attire. The elements are abundantly inhabited by animal life. But the sixth day is not yet ended and one thing more is needed, the 'Master work', the 'end' for which everything else has been done (505–6). That is a creature who will not have face or belly downwards bent ('prone', 506) like the other animals, but, being endowed ('endu'd', 507) with the divine gift of reason, will be erect and upright in bearing, governing the others with calm face ('Front serene', 509), gifted with self-knowledge – and therefore both sufficiently exalted in his thought ('Magnanimous', 511) to be able to communicate ('correspond', 511) with heavenly beings, and aware too of God's goodness and generosity. Thus he will 'adore/And worship' the supreme God who gave him his lordship over 'all his works'. The emphases here are on the endowment of Reason, differentiating man from all other terrestrial creatures; on the upright stance, the outward sign of his supremacy; on the self-knowledge and the consequent delight in worship.

Thus Raphael recounts God's decision to make man in his own 'image' and 'similitude' (519–20) and to give him lordship over the earth. Adam is made from the dust of the ground and the breath of life is breathed into his nostrils (Genesis I. 26–30, and also Genesis II. 7). Raphael scarcely touches on the making of woman here, because he is talking to Adam who already knows all about that. He is content to recall God's command to Adam to be 'fruitful' and 'multiplie', and to keep his dominion over the animal world – a needful reminder in view of the way Satan is to use the serpent. For the rest, he draws attention to the beauty of the garden and the plentiful richness of its free provisions, then finally repeats the veto against the Tree, which, if tasted, brings about ('works', 543) knowledge of good and evil.

Raphael now tells how God surveys what he has made and sees that it is good (Genesis I. 31), desists from his work and returns to Heaven. The return is marked first by a massive outburst of music. Angel harps by the thousand fill the resounding air, and the heavens and constellations ring out: this is celestial music such as Adam himself recalled in his conversation with Eve before they moved, hand in hand, to the bower and bed of consummation (IV. 680-8). Hence Raphael's brief reminder (561). The divine procession ('Pomp', 564) goes up in triumph and, once more, Milton has recourse to Psalm XXIV (vv. 7 and 9) – as at the Son's setting out (VII. 205-6, 208) – when the call is made for the gates of Heaven to open. The emphatic threefold reiteration of the word *Open* at the beginning of lines 565, 566 and 569 ('Open . . . Open . . . Open, and henceforth oft') conveys that sense of the freedom of frequent intercourse between Heaven and Earth, which the unfallen status of man makes justifiable and delightful for God, man, and angels alike (569-73). The 'errands of supernal Grace' on which angels will be frequently sent from God to man will in this context be errands to unfallen man, and the expression does not therefore raise any questions about the doctrine of Grace as applicable to fallen man.

The Son leads the way through the blazing gates to the Father's house on the broad road whose dust is gold and whose pavement is stars. It is twilight in Eden as the Son reaches the holy Mount of Heaven and the ever firm and sure throne of Godhead, where he sits at the side of the Father. Such is the co-inherence, such the consubstantiality, that the Father who receives him has been invisibly with him throughout his excursion. Such is the advantage of omnipresence that the Father both went and stayed. The Father, too, therefore, Originator and End of all things, must be said now to rest from work, to bless and hallow the seventh day.

But a holy day is not a silent day. There is no rest for the heavenly orchestra, which includes harps, pipes, dulcimers, organs, and stringed instruments ('sounds on fret', 597 - sounds produced from an instrument with strings stretched over a fingerboard), and which accompanies choral work in harmony and counterpoint ('Choral', 599) or in unison. The hymn of praise that the angels sing is a sustained and joyous cantata on the glory of God and his works, which occupies thirty-two lines of text (601-32). The 'Six dayes acts' are sung, and the Son's return from them pronounced greater even than his triumphant return from conquest of the rebel angels, for 'to create/Is greater than created to destroy' (606-7). The undamageable, illimitable sovereignty of God is hymned in the recall of how the apostate angels with their vain plots ('Counsels', 610) were repulsed, when they thought to reduce God's power and the number of his worshipping subjects (612-13). Whoever seeks to lessen God's power will find in practice that what he does serves the very opposite purpose by revealing God's power all the more: for God uses evil in such a way as to bring more good out of it (613-16). The new-made world, 'another Heav'n' (617), is itself evidence of this. It is not far from the gate of Heaven. It is founded on the crystalline sphere (see p. 178 and cf. VII. 269-71). The new universe is for the most part ('almost', 620) immense in its spaciousness, containing numberless stars, each one potentially a future world to be inhabited. The angels concede that God alone knows the 'seasons' (623) of the stars and therefore whether they can cater for habitation. The 'nether Ocean' (624), which is wrapped around the earth, is the waters 'under the firmament' as described in VII. 263 ff. The cantata concludes with a proclamation of man's happiness in being made in the divine image, to dwell on the earth in worship, lordship, and self-multiplication.

Raphael has now adequately answered Adam's request to be told how the world and all the things that confront him began, and what happened before the time his memory can compass. All has been told so that posterity can learn it from Adam. If there is anything else that Adam wants to know, which is within the scope of human understanding, now is the time for him to ask.

Book VIII

1–178 *Adam thanks Raphael (–13), then questions him about the seeming disproportion between the vastness of the universe and the smallness of the earth (–38). Eve goes away to garden (–65). Raphael notes the limitations of human knowledge about the universe (–84). Proportion is not just a matter of relative size, but of relative quality, not explicable to man (–106). From his terrestrial viewpoint man has a limited understanding of cosmic speed and movement (–122). Raphael illustrates the nature of scientific knowledge by presenting the Copernican theory as an alternative hypothesis to the Ptolemaic cosmology (–158), then bids Adam be content with what he has and knows on earth (–178).*

Adam has found Raphael's voice so enchanting ('Charming', 2) that he is still transfixed in silence after Raphael has ceased to speak. Then, starting as though newly awakened, he thanks the angel that he has so amply ('largely', 7) allayed his thirst for knowledge and made this very friendly gesture of coming down to his own level ('condescention', 9) to explain things he would otherwise not be able to enquire into. One problem still perplexes him, which only Raphael could sort out for him. When he considers the well-constructed framework ('goodly Frame', 15) of the universe as a whole, consisting of the sky ('Heav'n', 16) and the earth, and calculates their respective magnitudes, then the earth is a mere grain or atom in comparison with the size of the firmament and its numerous stars. The stars seem to roll unimaginable distances day by day merely to supply light around the unshining ('opacous', 23) earth, itself nothing more than a minute point. The vast journeying survey that each star makes daily seems to serve no other purpose ('Useless besides', 25). Pondering such things, Adam is frequently astonished ('admire', 25) that Nature, wise and economical, should allow for such disproportion, making so many 'nobler' and much greater bodies unnecessarily – all apparently for the sole purpose already mentioned – to repeat their restless revolutions every day while the earth (which in fact could itself move through a much smaller revolution – with 'far less compass', 33) sits still, being waited upon by bodies 'more noble' than herself, and gets what she needs without having to stir, receiving warmth and light like tribute brought from those incalculable astral journeys at a speed beyond the maximum scope of physical movement.

As Adam speaks, Eve sees from his face that he is bent on pursuing abstruse thoughts and gets up from where she has been sitting withdrawn from view. Her movements are none the less majestic and graceful for being unassuming and unobtrusive. She goes out to see how the fruits and flowers that she is tending are faring. It is not that she can take no pleasure in the lofty intellectual discourse of Adam and Raphael, still less that she is incapable of understanding it. But she would rather have it recounted to her in a more personal context by Adam alone. He would add pleasing ('Grateful', 55) digressions to the account and smooth the way through complex argument with husbandly caresses and kisses. Though Eve goes out alone, she is like a queen always attended by a retinue ('pomp', 61) of alluring graces.

Raphael now replies to the well-meaning ('Benevolent', 65) but naïve ('facil', 65) question posed ('propos'd', 64) by Adam. He assures Adam that there is nothing blameworthy in his enquiry. The sky is like the 'Book of God'. It is laid open so that man can there read the works of God, and be instructed in the orderly measurement of time with its recurring seasons and cycles. In order to understand this system of sequence and measurement it is not necessary to know whether the sky or the earth is moving, provided you make your calculations correctly. God in his wisdom has concealed the rest from 'Man or Angel' (so Raphael himself does not know either). He will not divulge his secrets to be scrutinized ('scann'd', 74) by people who ought rather to marvel at them ('admire', 75). Or if men wish to test their hypotheses ('Conjecture', 76), he has left the structure of the universe open to rival theorizing, perhaps so as to find amusement in the quaint, erroneous ('wide', 78) theories to be postulated in the future, when they come to make a model of the solar universe and read the stars, and God sees how they hold the mighty frame of the universe at their disposal, how they make correspondences and differentiations in the effort to manufacture theories that fit all the data, how they surround the earth with a massively complex system of cycles on common or different centres, on common or different planes, in order to frame hypotheses that fully accommodate the observed motions of the planetary system.

Raphael observes that he can foresee ('guess', 85) this kind of science in the future from the way Adam is already reasoning: for Adam is to be the instructor of his children. He first corrects Adam's initial blunder in assuming that it is unfitting for the brighter or greater body to serve the duller or lesser one, or for the heavenly body to run a journey while the earth sits still and receives the benefits of it. *Great* and *Bright* are not in themselves criteria of excellence (remember the picture of Satan enthroned at the beginning of Book II). The small thing may contain more good than the big thing, the unshining thing than the glistering thing. Thus the value and importance of the earth, over against the sun, needs to be reconsidered by Adam. The sun, for all its shining, is in itself barren: the potency radiated by its life produces fruitfulness when it touches the earth, but has no such effect on the body of the sun itself. The beams of the sun, otherwise ineffective, become operative when they strike the earth. (Is the Miltonic Eve, correspondingly pregnable by Adam, more important than we thought?) In any case, the sun, moon and stars are not – as Adam's arguments implied – dutiful attendants upon the earth's needs; but upon the needs of man, the earth's inhabitants (so the contrast between small earth and large universe is irrelevant). As for the incalculable ('numberless', 108) speed at which the heavenly bodies move, Adam must account for this by reference to the omnipotence of God who could make material objects ('corporeal substances', 109) capable of swift movement through space almost matching that of bodiless beings (107–10). Raphael adds that he himself has this very morning travelled the mathematically incalculable ('inexpressible/By numbers', 113–14) distance from Heaven to Earth.

There is now an important development in the argument. All that has been said so far has been on the basis of assuming that it *is* the heavenly bodies that move (i.e. 'Admitting Motion in the Heav'ns', 115) – and not the earth. Raphael has been at pains to press this argument ('urge', 114) in order to prove Adam's own doubt invalid (i.e. Adam's case about the apparent disproportions and wastefulness of the system, voiced in VIII. 25–38). Hitherto Raphael has accepted the Ptolemaic system for purposes of argument. He will not 'affirm' (117) that it is correct, though it may well seem so to the earthly observer. It is part of the divine plan that man should not fully understand these things. God has placed the earth at such a distance from Heaven that if men become too presumptuous in intellectual curiosity over things outside the grasp of their faculties, they will reach wrong conclusions and thus not reap any advantage from their presumption (119–22).

Raphael now posits the Copernican theory as an alternative hypothesis to the Ptolemaic in order to illustrate his point. Suppose the sun, and not the earth, is the centre of the universe, and the other stars, under the influence both of its power of attraction and of their own power of attraction, orbit around it in various courses ('rounds', 125). You can see how the six planets (Moon, Mercury, Venus, Mars, Jupiter and Saturn) move in their 'wandering course': suppose the seventh is not the sun, moving similarly (as the Ptolemaic system presupposes), but the earth, which seems to be fixed. And suppose this planet, the earth, moves imperceptibly in three different ways. The 'three different Motions' (130) attributed to the earth by the Copernican theory are the daily revolution of the earth around its own axis, the annual circuit around the sun, and the earth's corrective swivelling during her orbital course, which keeps its axis parallel to the axis of the universe (the last named is the 'Trepidation talkt', III. 483). Either you have got to attribute some such intricate combination of different modes of movement to several separate spheres moving in opposite directions and crossing one another's courses obliquely (131–2) (as required by the Ptolemaic system, and as referred to previously, VIII. 80–4); or else you must save the sun the trouble of going round the earth and get rid of the hypothesis of a rapid daily circuit of the earth made by some vast heavenly wheel not otherwise visible than in the apparent movement of the stars. The strains imposed on Adam's credulity (as evidenced in VIII. 24–38) by his reasoning on a Ptolemaic basis can be removed (–'which needs not thy beleefe', 136) if Earth (far from being the 'sedentarie' recipient of 'Tribute' – see 32 and 36) is herself busily active ('industrious', 137), one hemisphere bringing back the day in the east and the other ('her part averse', 138) meeting the night.

Raphael has supposed the earth a planet. As such it will shine in the darkness of their night upon moon and stars as moon and stars shine on the earth. And possible inhabitants of the moon for whom the moon is their 'terrestrial' (142) equivalent will have a 'reciprocal' (144) relationship with ourselves. The moon is then pictured by Raphael as a possible other earth: the spots discernible on her surface could be clouds, and if clouds there could be rain, fruitful soil and eating inhabitants. Thus, having pictured the sun as centre of the planetary system that the earth belongs to, Raphael allows for the discovery of other possible suns at the centre of comparable systems, each with their attendant moons, and each system a cosmic family in which sun and moon communicate 'Male and Female light'. That *male* and *female* light means original and reflected light corroborates important correspondences. For there are other families, too: the family of the Trinity with the original and reflected glory of Father and Son; the family of man with the original and reflected goodness of Adam and Eve; the family of Hell with the original and reflected evil of Satan and Sin.

Ultimately Raphael's argument comes full circle. He grants the reasonableness of Adam's first objection. It is an 'obvious' (158) thing to do to question the notion of a vast ininhabited system of heavenly bodies serving no other purpose than that of conveying light over an immense distance to this single habitable place, the earth, and each one individually able to contribute scarcely a glimpse of light at that.

In conclusion Raphael seems to treat the rival Ptolemaic and Copernican theories equivalently. Whether the sun rises and moves, or the earth moves – on a 'silent course' with forward 'pace' and 'spinning' movement so gentle and smooth (like sleep, 164-5) that they are undetectable, Adam should not harass his thoughts with matters hidden from him, but rather concentrate on serving and fearing God. Likewise he has no cause to give thought to other possible living creatures like himself. Wherever they may be, God will govern them as he pleases. It is Adam's business to rejoice in the blessed gifts of Paradise and beautiful Eve. Heaven is too exalted a place for Adam to understand what happens there. He should be humbly ('lowlie', 173) wise, not brooding about the situation or status of possible creatures in other worlds, but content with what now has been revealed to him not only of the earth (in the full account of Creation) but also of highest Heaven (the story of the war and the Fall of the Angels).

179-356 *Adam accepts Raphael's exhortation to be content within the limits of human knowledge (–197). He would like to tell his own story to Raphael (–216). Raphael gladly agrees to hear (–228), for he was absent from Heaven when man was made on the sixth day (–248). Adam describes his awakening, his first experience of the world and his first questions about it (–282). He tells how he fell asleep, was led by a seemingly divine being to Paradise (–309), then woke to find his dream true and himself in God's presence (–314).*

God forbids him the Tree of Knowledge (–337) *but grants him lordship over all else* (–356).

Adam addresses Raphael as a pure 'Intelligence' (181, *spirit*) of Heaven who has freed him from perplexing problems ('intricacies', 182) and taught him to live unharassed by anxieties that God will keep us clear of, provided we do not provoke them by indisciplined and fruitless brooding and pondering (180–7). The imagination readily roams without restraint or conclusion unless we are warned, or learn by experience, that the basis of wisdom is not to have an unparticularized knowledge ('know at large', 191) of things removed from our experience ('use', 192), difficult to picture and grasp ('obscure and suttle', 192), but to understand what is in front of us in daily life. Other speculation is nebulous, vain or foolishly irrelevant (194–5) and leaves us such that we are ill equipped and always caught unawares ('still to seek', 197) in the things important to us. So, says Adam, let us come down to earth and talk of immediate matters. Perhaps then something may crop up which it will be fitting for me to enquire about – with your permission ('By sufferance', 202) and your usual good will. Thus Adam tactfully proposes to tell his own story. The note of polite deference is sounded: You see how subtly I am plotting to detain you (207) by asking you to listen while I talk, a foolish thing to do ('Fond', 209), were it not done in the hope that you will have something to say in reply, for while I sit in your presence I feel as though I am in Heaven, and your conversation is sweeter to the taste than the pleasantest fruits of Paradise: moreover, whereas these fruits quickly satisfy, your words, imbued 'with Grace Divine' (215), 'bring to thir sweetness no satietie' (216).

We must not over-sophisticate our reading here. Unfallen man has no need to employ deceptive etiquettes in order to serve his egocentric ambitions as a raconteur by fettering a captive audience. Unfallen man can afford to enjoy the tentative gestures that ease relationships. He can play the host as innocently as unfallen woman can enjoy her own beauty.

There is immense delight for Adam in the sheer presence of Raphael, the angel; richer delight in what he has to tell and the way he tells it. The delight is the philosopher's delight in being let into secrets that constitute the mystery of things; the scholar's delight in finding the full facts of a complex network of events, causes, and purposes sorted out, clarified and synthesized; every man's delight in experiences of discovery, illumination, and new understanding. The food supplied to Adam as rational man has been rich and nourishing. We have just had hundreds of lines of it. In a variety of forms it has presented us with the Good of the Intellect as surely as Hell's speeches and thought-sequences illustrated the Bad of the Intellect perverted and eroded. It would make the point more aptly, perhaps, to say that, whereas we have now seen the intellect in action, before we saw the intellect broken down by the sheer weight of self-centredness, passion, and lust – of uncontrollable envy, ambition, and possessiveness. The contrast is again between the creational and the discreational. Moreover, innocent Adam concedes that the sweetest fruits of Paradise quickly satisfy – 'they satiate, and soon fill' (214): that seems to be the most that can be expected of any purely terrestrial and bodily delight, however choice and rich; but the angelic words and presence bring nourishment *of a different order*. They take one even out of Paradise (210). They convey a 'Grace Divine', which answers a human taste unanswerable otherwise even in Eden; for even at the conclusion of the connubial delights in Book IV, when we left the lovers embracing under a shower of roses, we left them asleep (IV. 771–5); but here there is a sweetness without satiety.

In reply the angel's heavenly meekness matches Adam's human meekness (217). The angel takes reciprocal delight in man's graceful and eloquent speech. Man is God's image upon whom divine gifts have been poured in respect of both inner and outer faculties. We think of you, says Raphael, as of our 'fellow servant' (225) and the words ring with a telling parallel. It is right at the end of Revelation, when the great mysteries and the beatific vision have been laid open before St John, that he falls down 'to worship before the feet of the angel which showed me these things'. But the angel will have none of it. 'Then saith he unto me, See thou do it not: for I am thy fellow servant, and of thy brethren the prophets, and of them which keep the sayings of this book: worship God.' (Revelation xxii. 8–9.) Milton adds a touching additional parallel. If our minds revert (at 225) to 'the sayings of this book' (in Revelation), as Milton's clearly did, they will also note that line 226, referring to Raphael's delight in knowing of 'the wayes of God with Man', firmly recalls the summary of Milton's purpose in his poem – to 'justifie the wayes of God to men' (1. 25–6). It is to them which keep the sayings of *this* book too that the angelic voice speaks.

Raphael's interest in Adam's narrative is made more humanly convincing by the fact that on the sixth day of creation he happened to be absent from Heaven on a weekend 'excursion' with a difference. He was despatched with a legion on a strange ('uncouth', 230) and dark journey to make sure that no one came out of Hell to spy or make an attack while God's work was afoot. A logical explanation is provided for this special precaution. God would not have wished to mix his creational work with the destructive work to which due anger at the eruption of discreational forces at such a time might have led him. Not, adds Raphael, that the fallen angels dare try anything at all without God's permission (the man who has just heard about the war in Heaven and will soon have to face depraved angelic power turned against him no doubt *needs* this reassurance about the rock-bottom incorruptibility of things), but God sends us on expeditions of this kind in order to habituate ('enure', 239) us to prompt obedience. It is a free world. It is a world in which free creatures will be tested: this is indeed the voice of a 'fellow servant'. But the gates of Hell were found firmly shut on the sixth day. There was no sound of dance or song heard from within, only the noise of torment, lamentation and rage. Raphael and his legions returned to Heaven, their duty done. And now he is ready for Adam's story.

Waking as from sleep, Adam registers first the 'flourie herb' (254), his bed, then the 'ample Skie' (258). With a 'quick instinctive motion' he stands 'upright' (260). He discovers the country and the animals, then with great delight examines his own body, limb by limb, and tests it in vigorous movement. He does not yet know who he is, or where, or what has brought his existence about, but he rapidly discovers his power of speech (270–3). Thus he addresses the sun and the earth and the creatures around him, hoping that they can tell him how he has come to be. He recognizes that since he is not self-made he must have a maker, and that maker must be in 'goodness and in power praeeminent' (279), and it is his natural desire to know him and to learn how to adore him, to whom is due the very fact that now he himself moves and lives. The recall here of St Paul ('For in him we live, and move', Acts XVII. 28) is significant because Paul is addressing the Athenians who in their ignorance have set up an altar 'TO THE UNKNOWN GOD' (Acts XVII. 23). 'Whom therefore ye ignorantly worship, him declare I unto you,' St Paul says, and straightway reveals the 'God that made the world and all things therein' (Acts XVII. 24).

Adam receives no answer to his call from the world around him. He sits down and has his first experience of sleep. It is an 'untroubl'd' (289) drowsiness and oppression that overtakes him, so that he imagines he must be returning to the very same unconscious ('insensible', 291) condition from which he so recently awoke to life. In sleep there comes to him a dream in which a being of 'shape Divine' summons him to his 'Mansion' (296), to the 'Garden of Bliss, thy seat prepar'd' (299). He is led up the 'woodie Mountain' (303) to the level Garden, as described in Book IV (132 ff.) and in the manner recorded in Genesis I (v. 15). The Garden surpasses all that he encountered before he slept. Every tree and fruit stirs the appetite to pluck and eat. Suddenly he awakes to find the dream true. Everything about him has in reality what the dream vividly 'shadowd' (311). The 'Guide' of his dream appears, a 'Presence Divine', and he falls at his feet. The guide reveals himself as God, Creator ('Author', 317) of everything around him, and gives him the freedom of Paradise, excepting only the Tree whose effect ('operation', 323) is to bring knowledge of good and evil. If Adam transgresses God's only command, then on the day on which he eats he shall become inescapably subject to death. He will be 'mortal' (331), will lose his present happy state of being, will be expelled from the Garden, and go into a 'World/Of woe and sorrow' (332–3).

Adam now recalls the stern words with a sense of dread, but recognizes that it lies in his own free 'choice' (335) not to incur the threatened penalty. As he takes up his story again, we hear how God then granted him and his descendants lordship over all the Earth and everything that lives in it. In token of this lordship God calls all birds and beasts to come in pairs and do homage to Adam, who in turn gives them their names. The fish are exempt from this duty, being unable to leave the water, but God makes it clear that their subjection is to be understood as no less guaranteed. The beasts crouch down in 'blandishment' (351) while the birds dip their wings in salute. Adam names them as they pass: God endues him with an immediate power of perception whereby he can understand the nature of each one of them. But he misses among all these creatures something which he believes he lacks, and in this matter presumes to speak his thoughts to his Maker.

357–451 *Adam adores his Maker for his goodness, but laments his solitude (–368). God indicates that he is not alone (–377), but Adam voices his need for an equal partner (–397). God observes that he himself has no such consort (–411). Adam replies that God is perfect in self-sufficiency (–421) whereas man's one-ness must be complemented if he is to multiply his kind (–436). God admits that such has been his purpose all along and grants his request (–451).*

But how shall he address him? The naming of beasts in subjection to him is one thing, the naming of the Maker high above mankind, and indeed high above whatever is above mankind, is another thing. How can man name or adore him who is Author of the Universe and of all the good

things here given to man in such ample and generous provision for his well-being? The address is difficult; the need
is simple: he cannot see anyone here to share his lot with
him (animals and birds have all just made their bows to him
in pairs). What happiness can there be in solitude? What
contentment in enjoying oneself alone? If the question
sounds presumptuous, the bright divine smile declares it
innocent.

God enjoys himself with innocent man's request. Father
may not be giving anything away yet to the child, but ob-
servers know that there *is* a bar of chocolate in his pocket
and that Father himself is itching to give it him. So we
follow God's gentle irony. Where is the solitude that Adam
speaks of? We have just seen a multitudinous procession of
bird-life and animal-kind moving before him; and God has
taught him their language and their ways. Moreover these
creatures may be said to 'know' (373) and to 'reason not
contemptibly' (374). God's posture turns playfully magis-
terial. Hell, after all, is not the only place for acting. Find
your pastime with these creatures, God's firmness declares.
Rule them. Your realm is 'large' (375). The Universal Lord
can give brusque orders. But we have heard something in
the New Testament about persistence in just supplication to
the point at which God is, as it were, *bullied* into response
(Luke XI. 8). Adam senses that it is not unfit to implore
leave of speech further; and we may well feel, remembering
what is at issue, that he is right not to be fobbed off.

So in 'humble deprecation' (378) Adam asks God to be
well disposed ('propitious', 380) to him, and makes his very
natural request for a partner equal with himself. What
fellowship ('societie', 383) can accord ('sort', 384) with relationships that are unequal? Delight must be mutually
interchangeable between giver and receiver in 'proportion
due' (385): if the disparity is such that one party in a relationship is intensely and the other always negligently attached,
neither party will be satisfied. The 'fellowship' (389) of
which Adam speaks here is of a kind that, since it must admit of the sharing of all 'rational' delight, cannot exist

between man and beast. He asks for a human consort after the pattern God has followed in the creation of the animal world.

God's irony is maintained (398–411). He pokes fun and enjoys himself. I see you are planning for yourself a charming and ingenious kind of happiness, God says (399–400), and however much enjoyment there is about you, you are resolved not to relish it on your own (401–2). What about me, then? Do I seem happy enough? I am alone, with no one second to me, still less equal with me. I am in the same superior position *vis-à-vis* all the creatures I have made as you claim to be when you say you cannot have true fellowship with the creatures around you (God repeats Adam's key word 'converse', 396 and 408) and, indeed, the gap of superiority is much bigger in my case.

Adam's reply has that blend of humility and dignity that Milton so strenuously maintains in his study of unfallen man. Man's mind cannot grapple with the dimensions in which God lives (412–14). God is perfect and complete in himself. Man is only relatively ('in degree', 417) a perfect being – that is, only within the limits of his hierarchical placing and his derivative existence: and *this* is what makes him desirous of a companion like himself who can compensate, or comfort him, for those limitations ('defects', 419). Because God is infinite he has no need to multiply his kind: indeed to speak of multiplying what is already infinite is nonsensical (that is what lines 419–20 amount to). Though there is only one God, this is not a numerical restriction, but a transcendence of all number, all multiplicity (421). God's singleness is an infinite extension of being, man's singleness is a restriction. (Using the language of formal logic, one would be tempted to say: God's singleness is connotative of all, man's singleness is denotative of one.) In that sense man is limited by his one-ness ('In unitie defective', 425). He must multiply instances of his humanity. His singleness must be offset by love and fellowship on his own hierarchical level ('Collateral', 426). God's privacy and solitariness do not constitute deficiencies: God's own company is the best company he can keep: he has no cause to look for 'Social communication' (429) with any being; yet if it pleases him to do so he can raise any one of his own creatures to any level he chooses in order to participate in fellowship or union with him. But, Adam concludes, reverting to the key word of controversy, I cannot by fellowship ('conversing', 432) with any of these creatures around me exalt them from their 'prone' (belly-downwards, 433) animality to my 'erect' (432) humanity. Nor can I find shared pleasure ('complacence', 433) with them by coming down to their level. Adam is now aware that he has taken great liberty in speaking so boldly; but God has heard him without demur.

Indeed God is gratified. He admits that he has been testing Adam (437), and is glad to see Adam not only 'knowing' the animals but also 'knowing' (438) himself, and freely manifesting the divine likeness in which he has been fashioned, a likeness ('Image', 441) not given to the animal world. God confirms that the fellowship of animals *is* 'unmeet' (442) for Adam, and that he is right to 'dislike' (443) the thought of it. Finally God grants that all along he 'knew it not good for man to be alone' (445 and Genesis II. 18), and has only been testing his judgement.

The reiteration, 'free' (440) and 'freely' (443), indicates how significant this trial is in illustrating the character of human freedom. The trial of man's judgement is a necessary complement of the trial of his obedience that is to come. This is important because if man's machinery of independent judgement is not adequate to sustain him – even in argument against God – then the freedom to disobey may be said to be an unjust burden to impose on it. Thus this passage reveals that man has all the equipment needed to make his moral freedom of will a privilege and not a disadvantage. If he can stand up against God, then he should be able to cope with Eve or Satan. There is another significant point, too. Man's freedom does not just consist in knowing his hierarchical status as inferior to Godhead and accepting the subjection of obedience in that direction: it also consists in knowing his status as superior to the animal world and accepting the superiority of his lordship over the natural order.

452–559 Adam falls asleep (–459) and in his sleep sees God fashioning Eve from one of his ribs (–477). He awakes and finds her coming towards him, guided by God (–490). Adam praises God for her beauty (–499). He leads Eve to the nuptial bower (–520). Adam concludes his story, stressing his delight in Eve (–559).

The dialogue ('Colloquie', 455) with God has strained Adam to the uttermost, and now, his faculties blinded and exhausted by the unequal contact with what so much outpowers them, his being needs to be recharged ('repair', 457) by sleep. God closes his eyes to keep the inner sight of 'Fancie' (461, imagination) operative, so that drawn away from himself ('Abstract', 462) as in a trance, he can witness what happens as God extracts a rib from his side. There is 'Life-blood streaming' (467) from the wide wound, as it is to stream later from the wounded side of the second Adam nailed to the second Tree; but this wound is quickly healed, and the new creature is so 'lovly faire' that what has previously seemed to Adam to be beautiful is now seen either as inferior ('Mean', 473) by comparison with her beauty or as epitomized and compassed in her beauty (473–4). Her looks pour a new sweetness into his heart. Her presence breathes the 'spirit of love and amorous delight' (477) into all things around. When Adam wakes he once more finds his dream true (482; cf. 309–11). Eve comes towards him. God is no longer visible (485), but his voice is her guide and she has had the benefit of pre-marital instruction covering spiritual and physical matters (486–7) in a blend that fallen man has reason to envy. There is grace in her walk and Heaven in her eye.

Adam breaks out into praise of God's goodness for this fairest of his gifts, and declares the pattern of marriage whereby man and wife shall be again 'one Flesh, one Heart, one Soule' (499).

Though Eve has been 'divinely brought' (500) into Adam's presence, her innocence and modesty and the consciousness ('conscience', 502) of her own worth, which requires her to be wooed, prevent her from directly putting herself at Adam's disposal ('obvious', 504) forwardly. It is a fact of her feminine nature that – without there being any question of shame or guilt – she should appropriately know herself to be 'more desirable' (505) if she withdraws. Hence, as she sees Adam, she turns. Adam has to follow her and plead with her as with another creature of 'reason', and when she accepts him it is with 'obsequious Majestie' (509) – a phrase which finely conveys that blend of compliance and regality in the mutual interchange of love, which marks the marriage of Adam and Eve as an earthly image of the divine co-inherence. (Note 'retir'd' above, 504, as well as 'obsequious', 509, then cf. how, at the approach of the Son, the uprooted hills of Heaven 'retired' 'Obsequious', VI. 781, 783.) It is fitting that all Heaven and all stars should pour out their choicest blessing on this new instance and symbol of joy and accord; that the living things of the earth should likewise rejoice in the consummation in which, to look back to Adam's earlier words, all their lovely and fruitful abundances are summed up and contained (cf. 473).

In concluding his story, Adam attempts to define what it is that makes his delight in Eve's beauty and love distinctive. Other things that delight the senses, whether enjoyed or merely observed ('us'd or not', 525), do not bring about any 'change' (525) in his mind or produce any vehemence of desire. But Eve's beauty takes him out of himself with rapture. Adam finds his sense of his own natural superiority imperturbable by anything around him, except Eve's beauty. It is as if Nature had not made him in all respects sufficiently woman-proof (534-5); or as if Nature had subtracted 'more than enough' (537) from his own resources in making woman. Woman seems to be too finished in outward beauty, though inwardly less finely wrought ('exact', 539). Adam knows her inferiority in mind and inner faculties; also that her form less exactly reflects the divine image, less surely expresses the human lordship over other creatures. This knowledge falls away from him when he approaches her.

She seems so complete in herself and so assured in her insight that what she wants to do or say seems best. Higher knowledge is down-graded ('Degraded', 552) in her company, and in dialogue with her wisdom loses face and begins to look foolish. Authority and Reason dance attendance on her as though she were the human being initially purposed by God, and not opportunely ('Occasionally', 556) added as an afterthought. To crown all, magnanimity and loftiness of mind (557) find in her their most beautiful point of repose and surround her with an awesome mystique, like an angelic guard.

We must keep our heads over this outburst on Adam's part. These are not the words of a man unbalanced by an excess of uxoriousness or already half-way seduced by passion (such a man would be speaking very differently). Adam is carefully analysing the effects of feminine beauty and allure upon himself. The fact that he can so clearly distinguish between what *is*, what he *knows*, and what *seems*, what he *begins to think* when in Eve's presence, is crucial. Adam himself stresses his own awareness of the distinction later (607–11).

560–653 *Raphael warns Adam against loss of judgement in love (–578). Earthly love should be a step to heavenly love (–594). Adam accepts this (–611), then asks whether and how angels love (–617). Raphael assures him that they love but does not explain how (–629). With a final word of advice he takes his leave (–643). Adam blesses him and they part (–653).*

Raphael, replying with knitted ('contracted', 560) brow, need not be assumed to be displeased – thoughtful, rather. Adam must not blame Nature (see 534 ff.). She has done her part: it is up to him to do his. He must have no lack of confidence in his own wisdom. Wisdom will not desert him unless he himself dismisses her by overvaluing things less worthy than she is – as you yourself observe, Raphael adds (566), in appreciation of Adam's self-knowledge. The external beauty of Eve, at which Adam marvels and which transports him, is worthy to be cherished and honoured and

loved – but not to be served in 'subjection' (570). Adam
should weigh his own qualities against Eve's. Raphael
recommends a well-balanced self-esteem. The surer Adam
shows himself in this respect, the more readily Eve will
accept him as 'her Head' and put her own external qualities
in subjection to his real inner strengths (573-5). Her beauty
is made rich to give him pleasure: it is made inspiring to
enable him to honour her as well as love her; and she notices
when his own judgement falters in her presence.

If Adam is tempted to set too high a store on sexual
pleasure based on the sense of touch, he should remember
that this pleasure is common to animals and men; and this
would certainly not be the case if there was anything in this
enjoyment fit to overpower reason. Whatever attraction
Adam finds in Eve's companionship that is higher than the
physical, being human and rational, he should continue to
love. Love purifies the mind, extends one's sympathies; it is
based on reason and is well considered ('judicious', 591).
Such love, at the earthly level, is an experience whereby one
can climb nearer to the experience of heavenly love. It is
precisely because man should not sink into mere carnal
pleasure that no fit mate could be found for man among the
beasts.

Adam assures Raphael that neither Eve's physical beauty
in itself nor the procreational system common to man and
beasts is what most delights him – though he adds that the
intercourse of the nuptial ('genial', 598) bed is a far more
exalted and awesome experience than that of animals: rather
it is the numberless words and actions of Eve, which are
marked by graciousness and fitness, by loving agreement
('compliance', 603), and which express the genuine unity of
mind and spirit that binds them together. And Adam repeats
that he is revealing to Raphael (see 528-59) what he inwardly
feels in Eve's presence, not as a person overpowered ('foild',
608) by such feelings. He meets with a variety of objects
and sense-impressions (609-10) but remains free to approve
only of the best of them and to follow where his approval
leads. Raphael has spoken of earthly love as a way to

heavenly love: may Adam enquire whether heavenly spirits love, and if so how they express their love? Is it a matter of interchanging looks only; or is there some mingling of transmitted radiance, some blending of contiguous immediacies (616–17)?

Raphael smiles and blushes: and it is the kind of blush that is peculiar ('proper', 619) to love. It is sufficient for you to know that we are happy, and there is no happiness without love. Whatever pure physical delights you enjoy, we enjoy outstandingly, unimpeded by the inconveniences of the body's framework. This, of course, is the talk of an angel to whom the machinery of human sexuality looks awkward, if not crude. The talk is not likely to find a sympathetic echo in Eden – though fallen, civilized man has perhaps enough experience to sense what Raphael is getting at. For him the total easy mixing of spiritual beings, as of air with air, makes the angelic lot compare very favourably with the human need to have recourse to the cluttering mechanisms of coition. This is obviously not a matter on which the human critic can pass unprejudiced judgement: he must move on.

Raphael, too, feels the need to change the subject abruptly. The sun is setting. He gives Adam a final warning against allowing passion to sway his judgement till he does something which his unbiased will, free of swaying influences, would never permit him to do. On this hangs the future well-being or the misery of Adam and his whole race. To stand or to fall is an issue lying wholly within Adam's own free decision ('Arbitrament', 641). Angel and man part, Raphael having assured Adam that in Heaven there will be rejoicing over him as long as he perseveres (639–40), Adam thanking Raphael for the kindly and courteous openness with which he has condescended to converse with him (648–9).

Book IX

1–47 *Address by the poet to the reader, to mark the approaching tragic climax of the poem (–47).*

There is to be no more now of easy and friendly intercourse between God or angel and man. The poet must sound the tragic note, tell of the disobedience of man, the consequent alienation of Heaven, and the judgement that brings death and sin into the world (the emphatic words 'disobedience . . . World . . . world . . . woe . . . Death', 8, 11, 12, firmly echo the opening of Book I: 'Disobedience . . . Death . . . World . . . woe', I. 1–3, and help to tie the total fabric together). It is a lamentable task; yet the subject is even more heroic than that of the ten-year siege of Troy in Homer's *Iliad*, with its climactic account of the fierce contest between Greek Achilles and Trojan Hector (15–16); more heroic than that of Aeneas's wanderings from fallen Troy to found the Roman state in Italy, in Virgil's *Aeneid*, with Aeneas's eventual marriage to Lavinia, princess of Latium, whose betrothal to Turnus was thereby broken (17); more heroic, too, than that of Homer's *Odyssey*, which relates the wanderings of Odysseus after the fall of Troy, wanderings protracted by the hostility of the sea god, Neptune, which beset him with difficulties ('Perplex'd the Greek', 19) as the goddess Juno's hostility beset Aeneas ('*Cytherea*'s Son' – Venus's son, 19) in the *Aeneid*.

Milton has once more firmly placed his work alongside the major Classical epics. The grand universality of his theme thus asserted, he now puts his trust in his muse to grant him the outflow of a style of corresponding ('answerable', 20) dignity to his subject. The muse has been endowing him night by night with an inspired fluency through visitations

in his sleep, so that composition has been easy and spon-
taneous ('unpremeditated', 24). Milton lets the reader into
a few more secrets about the choice of subject for his epic.
It was after long deliberation that he made his choice. He
postponed the enterprise because he was not keen to describe
wars, previously considered to be the only possible subject
for epic poetry; it was not his talent to analyse the long and
tedious devastations of legendary knights in imaginary
battles, while leaving the superior heroic courage of suffering
and martyrdom uncelebrated in verse; nor was it for him to
describe 'Races and Games' (33) as Homer and Virgil did,
nor to go into details about the trappings and paraphernalia
of medieval chivalry with its heraldic finery, its jousts and
tournaments and formal banquets ('impreses', 35 – heraldic
devices on shields; 'Bases', 36 – skirts worn by knights; the
function of the *marshal*, 37, was to arrange a feast; the *sewer*,
38, led in the food; the *seneschal*, 38, was the domestic
steward). Such subjects demand only the skill of inferior
craftsmanship ('Artifice', 39) and application, not the gifts
that win epic status for a poet and his poem. Having neither
ability nor zeal in these directions, for Milton the higher subject remains: and it is sufficient to win for him the name he
seeks, provided that his age is not an age too late in history
for great poetic achievements (44) and that his purposed
imaginative flight is not prevented by the cold climate and
the damp – as it well might be if composition depended
on himself and not on the muse who nightly inspires
him.

48–191 *Satan returns to the earth by night (–57), having compassed it for seven nights in succession (–69). He comes to Eden
(–86) and chooses the serpent as the creature he will enter in order
to disguise himself (–96). He is moved to appreciation of earth and
man (–113) and laments the misery of his exclusion; but envy makes
him hate all good, so that he is determined to destroy man (–134) and
frustrate God's purpose in creation (–143) – i.e. to replace the fallen
angels (–157). Further lamenting his changed lot (–171), yet bent on
revenge (–178), he finds the serpent and enters into him (–191).*

The last direct contact with Satan was at the end of Book IV when Satan narrowly escaped a trial of strength with Gabriel. The intervention of the divine scales saved him: he took Gabriel's warning and fled (IV. 996–1015). From that point the narrative thread is taken up here. (What has been heard of Satan since that point has come to us indirectly through the long narration of Raphael – v. 469 to the end of Book VII, and has related to events preceding the direct narrative opening of the poem.)

The veil of darkness has been drawn round the hemispherical sky. Satan returns, now augmented ('improvd', 54) in calculated ('meditated', 55) deception and malice, intent ('bent', 55) on the destruction of mankind, in spite of ('maugre', 56) whatever might result from it in the way of heavier penalties upon himself. As he fled at night, so he returns. He has been circling the earth, avoiding ('cautious of', 59) the daylight, since Uriel observed ('descri'd', 60) his previous entry (see IV. 124–30) and forewarned Gabriel and his guard who were keeping watch on the Garden (IV. 555–76) – as a result of which he was driven away 'full of anguish' (62; see IV. 1113–15). For seven successive ('continu'd', 63) nights he has ridden round the earth in darkness. For three days he has circled the earth latitudinally; for four days he has ridden longitudinally through the poles, following the course of ('traversing', 66) the colures (66 – two circles which intersect each other at right angles at the poles: one goes through the equinoctial, the other through the solstitial, points). Now, on the eighth night, he returns and effects a secret entry ('unsuspected way', 69) from the side of Paradise away ('averse', 67) from that of the guarded gateway.

Milton briefly recapitulates what he told us in Book IV about the river that flows southward through Eden, taking a subterranean course under the Garden, from which a fountain rises near the Tree of Life (73) to irrigate the Garden (see IV. 223 ff., and see p. 97). He calls it *'Tigris'* (71) here, though he did not name it before. Satan goes down with the river, comes up, wrapped around ('involv'd', 75) in mist, in the Garden, and looks for a place to hide. He has roamed the earth, making a close ('narrow', 83) search, and considered every creature with penetrating scrutiny ('inspection deep', 83) to see which might most conveniently assist his cunning plot. The course of his search has taken him northwards beyond the 'River *Ob*' (78) in Siberia, which flows into the Arctic Sea, southwards to the Antarctic (79), westwards to where the Caribbean Sea is 'barr'd' (80) by the Isthmus of '*Darien*' (81) (in Panama, between Central and South America) and round to India in the east.

Satan's selection of the serpent is made only 'after long debate' (87) with himself, in which he cannot make up his mind ('irresolute', 87) between the thoughts turned over and over ('revolv'd', 88). His final opinion ('sentence', 88) is that the serpent is the fit vessel to contain him, the fittest to be the offspring ('Imp', 89) of fraud in whom the dark insinuations ('suggestions', 90) can be concealed from detection by the sharpest sight. The choice is made because the 'wilie Snake' is so naturally cunning and subtle that whatever sly tricks ('sleights', 92) he might employ no one would regard them as suspicious, whereas if observed in other animals they might arouse the suspicion that diabolical power was operative there beyond the range of animal behaviour (91-6). Before he enters into the serpent, however, Satan indulges in an outburst of lamentation, envy and malice.

In order to understand the placing of this outburst, one should note that so far in this book Milton has been consciously preparing the ground for the climax of the story. The early lines constitute a miniature second introduction, invocation and dedication, harking back to the beginning of the poem (IX. 1-47). The presentation of Satan is made in order to link back to Book IV and recall the 'story so far' (53-86). The poet's eye has ranged in godlike sweeps over universal perspectives, theological, literary, historical, cosmic, and topographical, touching the immense overall themes of the pre-fallen and fallen worlds (1-13), the vast literary background of epic and history (13-41), the diabolical orbiting of earth's sphere (53–69), the sweeping survey of the earth's surface (76–83). All the time we have been spiralling down, from dimension to dimension, towards the spot in space, the spot in time, the spot in the poem, where the drama is to be played out. We have arrived. But before the action moves, Milton chooses to insert a recapitulary presentation of the satanic persona, with which mankind will soon have to contend. Since we have kept close company with Adam for many hundreds of lines, the reminder of exactly what he is up against is a fit one. We do not learn anything new from it; but it puts the record straight on the brink of the crucial collision between humanity and devilry.

Satan sees immediately that the new earth is 'like to Heav'n' (99), as indeed it was divinely made to be (VII. 329); but the satanic mind, capable of seeing the truth, twists it immediately out of shape, into falsehood – the earth is perhaps preferable to Heaven, a residence ('Seat', 100) worthier of gods, as built with 'second thoughts', making the most of past experience and thus 'reforming what was old'. One cannot but notice that the devilry is familiar. The argument presupposes that what is new will be better than what is old, that there is inevitable progress whereby second thoughts are always better than first thoughts. Along with the now familiar implicit Satanic doctrine of progress is the insinuation that Heaven is defective – that it can be improved upon and is therefore not completely perfect. The conclusive argument – 'For what God after better worse would build?' (102)– is based on the concealed key fallacy whereby different *kinds* of good are assumed to lie within the identical scale of measurement, so that a placing of one justifies a lineally comparable placing of the other, and a system of relative evaluation that is like an examination mark list can be brought into play. God is implicitly denigrated, and the 'old' devalued (101): the satanic mind seems to adopt a humanistic slant that would overstate Earth's heavenlike status (103) and man's godlike stature.

The earth is seen by Satan as a heaven-like centre around

which the dancing stars carry their lamps in dutiful ('offi-
cious', 104) attendance, shedding beams of centripetal
influence. The phrase, 'Light above Light' (105), the words
'precious' (106) and 'sacred' (107), strengthen the comparison
with God in Heaven at the centre of the worshipping angels,
receiving their worship. It is in the earth that the known
potency of the stars produces its visible manifestations in the
whole graded ('gradual', 112) scale of vegetable, animal, and
rational life, whose peak and epitome is man. Satan's wish
that he could himself enjoy earth's scenery suddenly calls
back by firm echo ('Rocks, Dens, and Caves', 118) the universe of death for which he has exchanged his own home
('Rocks, Caves, Lakes, Fens, Bogs, Dens – II. 621: the
metrical chaos is of course replaced by an ordered, rhythmic
line). But in him the sight of pleasure produces only torment.
And once more the dreary sequence of self-analysis, so
prevalent in egocentricity, is set on its familiar course. Good
to him is a curse ('Bane', 123). He would be worse off in
Heaven. He would not want to dwell either in earth or in
Heaven – unless it were by mastering God. He no longer
hopes by what he does to reduce his own misery, but to
make others as miserable as he is, even at the cost of making
things worse for himself. The pressure of his own relentless
thoughts can be eased only by acts of destruction. Hence he
can make it his aim to destroy, or win to action that will
effect his ruin (131), the creature for whom 'all this (i.e.
earth) was made' (132). Then, having linked mankind to
himself in woe (134) and provoked wide-ranging divine
destruction, he will himself have the sole glory among the
devils to have ruined ('marr'd', 136) in one day what the
so-called ('styl'd', 137) Almighty took six successive days to
create – and who knows how long to plan? – though perhaps, Satan reflects, the planning dates back no further than
to the time when in a single night he himself freed almost
half the angels from slavery and left the crowd of heavenly
worshippers looking rather thin. Whether it was that God
had lost the knack of creating angels – if indeed they *are* of
God's making (Satan's most crucial argument in raising

rebellion was that they were *not*, v. 853–63; see p. 145) – or was determined to snub the rebels by replacing them with creatures made of earth and endowing these uplifted low-bred beings with their (the devils') spoils, he decided, as an act of vengeance, and as a way of making up his losses in personnel ('numbers thus impair'd', 144), to make man. What he decided he did; made man, made the magnificent world for him, the earth for his residence, proclaimed him lord of it all and, biggest blow of all, made it the duty of angels to watch over him.

He dreads the watchfulness of these angels, and in order to elude them wraps himself in mist and glides dimly by on his search for a serpent. There is one more outburst about the degradation from competing for God's throne (163–4) to compressing yourself into a slimy serpent. Milton rings a resounding note in his vocabulary here by using the word 'incarnate' and its intensified parodic parallel 'imbrute' (166) of the descent of heavenly essence into the flesh. *This* incarnation is in the cause of 'Ambition and Revenge' (168). It will be paid for by another incarnation, by another descent otherwise motivated. The aspirer must be prepared to go down as deeply as he soared upwards, expos-ing himself ('obnoxious', 170) to contact with the basest things.

Round and round the thoughts still go in the mazy tergiversations of labyrinthine egocentricity. Revenge, though sweet at first, quickly produces a bitter backlash. Let it, Satan ends, so long as it hits its target. Since he has failed in his higher aim, he will attack the next best object of envy, the new favourite of Heaven, the product of scorn, made from dust purposely to spite the fallen. He finds his serpent – labyrinthinally in many a round self-rolled (183) after the fashion of his own evil thinking, as just evidenced, and therefore indeed 'fit vessel' (see 89) to contain him. The creature is not yet harmful ('nocent', 186). In its sleep Satan takes possession of it, permeating its animal ('brutal', 188) faculties with the power of intellect, and waits in hiding ('close', 191) the approach of morning.

192–289 Next morning Adam and Eve rise, worship, and discuss the day's work (–203). Eve proposes that they work apart (–225). Adam says it is pleasanter to work together (–250) and that they are safer together against any possible assault by Satan (–269). Eve does not like the implied doubt about her individual firmness in faith and love (–289).

The 'sacred light' of dawn provokes the living world of nature to worship at 'Earth's great Altar', incense rising from scented flowers, silent praise from all things that breathe. Adam and Eve rise and join in with words, giving voice to the praise of dumb animals. They share in savouring ('partake', 199) the morning fragrance and perfume; then consider together ('commune', 201) how they can most effectively tackle ('ply', 201) their increasing work – which is outgrowing the capacity of two people.

Eve says that, until they have more hands to help them in the pleasant work laid upon them ('enjoyn'd', 207), they cannot keep up with it. The gardening is the more luxuriant ('Luxurious', 209) after all their cutting back ('restraint', 209). What they achieve by a day's lopping and pruning is rendered laughably inadequate by one night or two of the 'wanton' growth moving back ('Tending', 212) to wildness (see IV. 628–9 and p. 113). The words here – 'Luxurious', 'wanton', 'Tending to wilde', 209–12 – indicate the potential uncontrollability of nature's richness and beauty (the garden's reluctance to be disciplined), which has a symbolic association with Eve's own beauty. Nature and she have just worshipped together. Eve's proposal is that Adam and she should work separately. Adam's symbolic task is to direct and discipline climbing honeysuckle ('woodbine', 216) and the parasitical ivy, which need to cling to something else for support (as Eve does), while Eve's is to spend her time amid the thicket where the roses are intermixed with myrtle ('held sacred to Venus . . . and used as an emblem of love', *O.E.D.*). Eve argues that while they garden closely together, glances and smiles and casual talk about things freshly noticed interrupt and slow up their work.

Adam praises Eve for what she has proposed ('motion'd', 229) in that she has been thinking out the best way of working. There is nothing finer in a woman than to set her mind on what is good for her home and will strengthen her husband in worth-while work (232–4). But God has not imposed work as a duty so strict that it precludes the intermittent refreshment of food – food for the body, talk, which is food for the mind, glances and smiles, which are the food of love for creatures of reason. God did not make man to work but to take delight in things, 'delight to Reason joyn'd' (243). Their 'joynt hands' (244) will keep the 'paths and Bowers' from becoming wild. Delight joined to reason: Eve's hand joined to Adam's: this is the way to keep at bay the dangers inherent in that abundance in garden or woman, which might become 'luxurious' or 'wanton', which could so easily 'tend to wilde' (see 209–12). Of course, if Eve has had her fill of 'converse' (cf. the reiteration of the word, VIII. 396, 408, 432), he could readily on those grounds grant her the refreshment of temporary solitude, which quickly makes the return to companionship all the sweeter. But there is fear that harm might befall her if separated from him. Adam recalls Raphael's warning of Satan's envy and determination to undo them (VI. 900–8). It may be that he is even now secretly at hand waiting and hoping for the opportunity of catching them apart, knowing, as he must, that he can have no hope of practising his deceit upon them as long as they are together ('joynd', 259). Adam's native insight enables him to conjecture that their conjugal love must excite Satan's special envy. Eve should not leave the 'faithful side' that gave her being (265–6: cf. VIII. 467 and see p. 202).

Eve has been addressed by Adam as the 'Wife' (267) by the 'Husband' (232–4, 268). In reply she seems to assume the remoter queenliness of a 'Virgin' (270). She is like one who has encountered some unkindness where she was looking only for love. Her calmness is sweet but sober. She knows of their enemy both from Adam's own words and from what she overheard Raphael say when he took his leave. But she is surprised to have her constancy brought into question on this account. You cannot fear violence from the enemy, she says, since we are not susceptible to pain or death. It follows that you fear his deceptiveness: from which it must be deduced that you likewise distrust the firmness of my faith and love in the face of deception designed to shake and seduce them. How could you harbour thoughts so wrongly entertained ('misthought', 289) of her who loves you so dearly?

290–411 Adam replies. He does not distrust her but would not wish her to be affronted by an attempt against her (–305). She should not underestimate either the foe or the quality of their joint strength (–317). Eve insists on their separate incorruptibility (–341), Adam that the emphasis on their need to be together springs from love, not from distrust (–358), but he would not wish her to stay with him unwillingly (–375). Eve accepts the permission (–384) and leaves him (–403). The poet laments what is to follow from their parting (–411).

Adam addresses Eve once more as 'Daughter of God and Man', as he did on the memorable night of their rapturous love recorded in Book IV (660). On that occasion, when Satan and the reader first sighted them, 'hand in hand they passd' (IV. 321). And soon after they were to move 'hand in hand' (IV. 689) to their inmost bower of union, which they entered 'Handed' (IV. 739). On *this* occasion they are going *from* their bower, and though Adam has pressed strongly for 'joynt hands' (IX. 244), when the time for this very different climax approaches, hand is drawn from hand ('from her Husbands hand her hand soft she withdrew', 385–6). As the phrase takes us far backward, it takes us far forward, too. The hands of a different Adam and a different Eve are to be rejoined at a third momentous point in the penultimate line of the poem. We should note also that this is the last time Adam can call Eve 'immortal' (291) and describe her as untouched ('entire', 292) by sin and blame.

It is not in distrust ('diffident', 293) of her that he discourages separation. He would avoid any hostile attempt against her. Anyone who tries to tempt another, however vainly, does sling mud ('asperses . . . with dishonour foul',

296-7) in supposing that the person he assaults may be corruptible. No doubt Eve would respond with scorn, anger and resentment against any such temptation presented to her – and the temptation would thus prove ineffectual. Adam would save her from meeting alone with a distasteful affront, which the foe would scarcely dare to make on them both together: and if he did so dare, it would be right that Adam should be the one to meet it.

Adam advises Eve not to write off too contemptuously the malicious cunning and subtlety of a foe who proved capable of seducing angels to revolt. Nor should she look on the help of another as unnecessary. From the influence of her presence and her looks he himself receives increase ('Access', 310) in every quality – wisdom, watchfulness, and strength. If she were looking on, the shame of being over-come or overreached in front of her would raise up his utmost vigour. Why should not Eve feel within herself a similar sense of increased resources when he is present with her – and therefore choose to be tried with him, the best person to be present at such a test? The phrases, 'domestick Adam' (318) and 'Matrimonial Love' (319), weight the emphasis on joint strength and married harmony.

Eve still thinks Adam is not giving her her due in respect of her faith and sincerity. If our lot is to be confined within a narrow compass by the threat of a foe, ourselves not being fully equipped to match him in subtlety or strength, wherever he turns up, then how can we be said to be happy, always ('still', 326) apprehensive of injury? Injury does not necessarily lead to sin. By tempting us the foe insults us – casting an aspersion on our integrity: such an aspersion does not stick disgrace on our forehead ('Front', 330) but recoils on his own head. So why should we either shun or fear him, since we gain a double honour by proving his innuendo false – attaining inner peace and winning approval of God, witness of the result. And what is the value of a person's faith, love or virtue if it has not been tested alone, unsup-ported by help from outside? We must not suspect that our happy condition has been left so incomplete by the wise

Maker that it is not secure whether we are single or together. It would be a fragile happiness were that the case. An Eden so vulnerable would not be Eden.

Adam firmly insists that there is no defect in anything made by God, least of all in man. The only danger lies in man himself, but it is within his own control. He cannot be harmed against his will. Man's will is free – freely obedient to his reason; and his reason is sound, but needs to be cautious and always alert ('still erect', 353) lest she should be taken off guard ('surpris'd', 354) by something that falsely has the appearance of being good (354) and therefore issues the wrong orders ('dictate false', 355), leading the misinformed will to do what God has explicitly forbidden. It is not mistrust but love which prescribes that he should be often mindful of her and she of him. They stand firm, yet it is possible for them to stray, since reason may conceivably meet some plausible instrument ('specious object', 361) corrupted by the foe, and 'fall into deception unaware' (362) – that is, if reason does not heed the warning and keep strict watch. Adam's advice, then, is still that she should not go out of her way to find temptation, rather avoid it, and the likeliest way to do so is to stay with him. The test will come without being looked for. If you want to prove your firmness, he says, give proof of your obedience first. If no one sees you tested, how can they know anything of your firmness? Who could give evidence of it? But if you think that an unexpected test might find the two of us less on our guard than you yourself seem to be now that you have been warned, then go (370–2: he has now, fatally, allowed to her reasoning a possible priority over his own); for to stay, other than of your own free will, would be a bigger separation than your physical absence.

Eve is submissive but persistent; and she has the last word. She accepts, as the basis for her decision, the hint given her in her husband's last concession; that an unexpected test might find the two of them less prepared. She does not expect a proud foe to tackle the weaker of them: if he *were* so inclined ('bent', 384) then his repulse would be all the more shameful. With that, hand from hand is withdrawn.

In her going, she is likened to *'Oread* or *Dryad'* (387), mountain nymph or wood nymph of Greek mythology, to one of the train of Diana (*'Delia'*, 387) virgin-goddess of the hunt; not, however, armed like Diana with bow and quiver, but equipped with such gardening tools as might have been brought by angels or manufactured by the art of man still innocent of fire (cf. IV. 714–19; and see p. 115). She is also likened to *'Pales'* and *'Pomona'* (393), Roman goddesses of flocks and fruit, and to *'Ceres'* (395), goddess of agriculture and mother of *'Proserpina'* (396).

The comparisons are not fortuitous. Eve, now severed from her 'Author and Disposer' (IV. 635) who is 'Offspring of Heav'n and Earth' (IX. 273), whose 'Best Image' she is and 'dearer half' (V. 95), in going from the faithful side of him whose 'faithful side' (IX. 265) gave her being, in leaving the care of 'domestick Adam' (IX. 318) with his 'Matrimonial Love' (IX. 319), is symbolically returning to the ideal but unhallowed natural world of Oread and Dryad, and not even armed like the chaste Diana. She has the purity of Diana, but is unfenced; she has the gardening tools of Pales and Pomona, and she will be cunningly wooed by Satan in disguise as Pomona was by *'Vertumnus'* (395). As mother of the human race, she has the associations of generative fruitfulness that belong to Ceres. But perhaps the dominant note in all these correspondences is that which suddenly rings us right out of the world of 'Patriarch' (376) and angels, Eden and Heaven, to leave us drenched for a few lines in the imagery of a dangerously wanton world. However that may be, Eve's wilful severance from her husband will have to be paid for in a willing severance already made known to us in the Father's words: 'I spare/Thee from my bosom and right hand, to save . . . the whole Race lost' (III. 278–80).

The momentousness of the parting comes over us in Adam's lingering pursuit of her with his eyes, and in the reiterated promises of a quick return for lunch. The poet's intrusive lamentation on what is to follow underlines the pathos (404–11).

412–531 The serpent is seeking his prey (–424). He sees Eve gardening and winds his way nearer (–444). The close sight of her at first delights (–466), then torments him (–472). He pulls himself together (–493), approaches her, neck upright (–522), and stops, as in admiration, before her (–531).

Wholly disguised as a serpent ('Meer Serpent', 413), Satan is seeking Adam and Eve – or rather the whole human race involved ('included', 416) with them as his intended prey. He is seeking some patch of ground that they specially cultivate ('Thir tendance', 419) or delight in. He is looking for them both, would like to think his luck ('hap', 421) might be to find Eve separate, but is not really expecting that so rare an eventuality will turn up, when his hopes are exceeded and there she is, behind a veil of perfume, a flower among the flowers, a 'stooping' (427) flower among the 'drooping' (430) flowers, an 'unsupported Flour' (432) bending 'to support' (427) their lovely hanging heads, gently upstaying them, unthinking ('mindless', 431) how the loveliest of them all, herself, is far from 'her best prop' (433), while the storm is ready to break. (Satan will pay eventually when, 'spoild' of his 'spoile' by the Son, it is his turn to 'stoop/Inglorious', III. 252–3.) Some idea of the care with which *Paradise Lost* is constructed may be gained from noting that the description here of Eve, the 'fairest unsupported Flour' (432) is related to that of Proserpina by the comparison we have just had (IX. 396) and by some lines in Book IV – 'Her self a fairer Floure by gloomie *Dis*/Was gatherd, which cost Ceres all that pain/To seek her through the world . . .' (IV. 269–72). Pluto ('Dis') carried off Proserpina to the dark underworld. Eve is another flower in danger of being gathered by the prince from the black realm of Tartarus. This other ruler of the infernal regions would also like to take a captive back to Hell (see p. 99, and for more on 'stooping' p. 275).

Before he finds her among the drooping flowers, Satan rolls across past many walks where stately, upstanding cedars, pines and palms stand as reminders of the erect husband whose side Eve has foolishly forsaken. The re-

minder is intentional: we know it not only by virtue of the
now established imagery of upstanding trees and support-
needing plants and flowers, but also because the word
'Covert' was used especially in law 'of a married woman:
Under the cover, authority, or protection of her husband'
(*O.E.D.*). It is possible that 'voluble', 'hid', 'seen' (436),
apply to 'walk' and not to Satan, as others seem to have
assumed. In which case the meaning here would be that
Satan followed the course of ('travers'd', 434; cf. IX. 66)
many a walk under the stately cover of tall trees, a path
winding and clear to see ('bold') and then a path at one
moment hidden, at the next moment visible, among the
bushes (434–7). The syntax is not obvious here. 'Spot' (439)
is the delayed object of the verb 'drew' (434). Thus the
'Flourie Plat' (456 – plot) is the 'Spot' (439) that Satan is
approaching (434). It is more delicious than the imaginary
Gardens of *Adonis*, who was 'revivd' (440) by Proserpina
after being killed by a wild boar (cf. I. 446–52, and see
p. 17). Proserpina (Persephone) shared him with Aphrodite
(Venus) who kept him in the garden that Spenser turns into
a place of blissful love in *Faerie Queene* III. vi. It is more
delicious, too, than the Garden of Alcinous, king of
Phaeacia, who royally entertained Odysseus ('*Laertes* Son',
441) when his daughter Nausicaa found him cast upon the
shore (cf. V. 340–1; see p. 132). The third garden mentioned
is that in which Solomon ('the Sapient King', 442: cf. 797
and 1018, and see p. 236) entertained Pharaoh's daughter
(I Kings III. i).

If Satan marvels at the beauty of the place, he marvels even
more at the beauty of the person. Line 444 corroborates the
already implicit correspondence between garden and woman
(strengthened by the indirect allusion to the Song of
Solomon). When a man who has been for a long time
imprisoned ('pent', 445) in the overcrowded city, with its
tightly packed houses and its stinking open drains, takes a
summer morning walk, he is delighted with the country
smells, sounds and sights, and most of all with the sight of
a pretty country girl. The emphasis is upon sudden freshness

after long enclosure in what is foul and noisome, because Eve's beauty, grace and innocence momentarily knock the dirt out of Satan. They submerge his malice under awe; they commit a sweet ravishing of his ferocity, which leaves him temporarily bereft of his fierce purpose ('intent', 462). For a brief time ('space', 463) Satan is torn away ('abstracted', 463) from his own evil and stands there in a stupor of unintentional goodness ('Stupidly good', 465), involuntarily stripped of his vices. This is what innocence and beauty will do to evil if evil loses its grip in the confrontation. But 'hot Hell' (467) ('The Hell within him, for within him Hell/He brings', IV. 20–1) comes quickly rushing back to burn up his delight. The torture is the greater for the sight of pleasure not prescribed ('ordain'd', 470) for him. He regathers ('recollects', 471) and stimulates his ferocity and hatred.

He dismisses the sweet thoughts that have compulsorily carried him out of himself to forgetfulness of his purpose, which is hate, not love. There is no hope of Paradise (and its pleasure) for Hell (and its inhabitants). Hell's aim is to destroy all pleasure except the pleasure of destroying. He must not let go the opportunity ('Occasion', 480). The woman is alone, well placed ('opportune', 481) for any assault. He cannot see the husband near, with his superior intellect and strength a more formidable foe – and invulnerable as he, Satan, since his debasement by Hell, no longer is. Eve, though divinely beautiful, is not frightening – though there is a power to be feared in love and beauty if they are not accosted ('approacht', 491) by a greater strength of hate, hate that is stronger (against love and beauty) if it is well disguised under a show of love. That is the way he is pursuing to bring about her downfall.

The devil-inhabited serpent does not approach with undulating ('indented', 496) wave, belly-downwards ('Prone', 497) on the ground. His crested head and burnished green-gold neck rise above a towering spiral of folds. He is beautiful, more beautiful than Cadmus and his wife Harmonia (here '*Hermione*', 506) who came to Illyria and were changed into serpents, fitly remembered here because it was Cadmus who sowed the dragon's teeth from which armed warriors sprang up and destroyed one another; more beautiful than Aesculapius, god of medicine, worshipped in '*Epidaurus*' (507), who appeared in the form of a serpent to check a plague at Rome; and more beautiful than the serpent-forms in which Jupiter allegedly made appearances to the mother ('*Olympias*', 509) of Alexander the Great and to the mother of Scipio Africanus.

At first Satan acts the part of one who seeks to approach but is loath to interrupt. He zig-zags on an indirect track ('tract', 510) like a ship tacking off an estuary or a foreland in a veering wind. He is vain enough to curl his twisting ('tortuous', 516) body in 'many a wanton wreath' (517) in the hope of catching and luring Eve's eye. She hears him rustling the leaves; but she is busy. She is accustomed to having animals at play around her: they are all more dutiful at her call than the herd of men-turned-monsters by the enchantress *Circe* (Milton's Comus is made the son of Circe and endowed with her bewitching powers; Circe changed Odysseus' followers into swine, and he narrowly escaped the same fate: see Joyce's *Ulysses*, episode 15). Eventually he stands before her, gazing, as it were, in wonderment. He bows his towering crest and his sleek, richly coloured ('enamel'd', 525) neck: he fawns and licks the ground she treads on. But it is none of these tricks that catches Eve's eye: it is his 'gentle dumb expression' (527). Whether it is that he turns the serpent's tongue itself into an organ of speech, or that he sends out appropriate impulses into the air, Satan speaks through the serpent.

532–646 *Satan addresses Eve flatteringly (–548). Eve replies. She is surprised to hear the serpent speak (–566). The serpent explains. He ate the fruit of a wonderful tree and gained the power of reason and utterance (–612). Eve asks where the tree is (–624). Satan offers to show her (–630). Eve accepts, and he leads her to the forbidden tree (–646).*

'Do not wonder – if wondering is a possible experience for you who are in yourself the epitome of all wonder; do not cover the heavenly mildness of your looks with an expression of scorn or displeasure that I approach you on my own, like this, and stare at you with insatiable admiration, overcoming even the awesome reverence you inspire, especially when you are withdrawn and alone.' Such is the satanic idiom with its roots in the specious gallantries of a permissive society. Eve is the most beautiful image of her beautiful maker. Her heavenly beauty is most fittingly seen where it is marvelled at by a whole universe of living spectators. Is it enough for her to be seen only by the insensitive and undiscriminating (544) animals here around her – and otherwise by one man only?

The question raised by Satan here – about the implied wastefulness of Eve's beauty that ought to be enjoyed by a whole universe of admirers – has been at issue twice before. Eve asked the question of Adam about the beauty of the stars – for whom did they shine all night when everyone was asleep? (IV. 657–8: see p. 113) – and Adam told her in reply of the unseen spiritual creatures walking the earth and praising God in his works (IV. 674–80). That Milton intends us to make the connection is clear from his emphatic words, 'beheld, there best behold' (IX. 541), which recall the earlier passage: 'These then, though unbeheld . . . All these his works behold . . .' (IV. 674, 679: see p. 114). The question was also at issue, in a converse form, when Adam first asked Raphael about the heavenly bodies whose apparently disproportionate function was to pay tribute to the earth 'in all thir vast survey/Useless besides' (VIII. 24–5: see pp. 188–9); a question to which Raphael gave a substantial reply (VIII. 85 ff.: see p. 190).

Thus the tempter flatters ('gloz'd', 549, glossed, glossary: the usage arises from the notion of interpreting a text to suit your fancy or convenience; see III. 93 for Satan's 'glozing lies'). Thus he tunes his introduction ('Proem', 549). Eve is amazed to hear human language spoken by an animal, and 'human sense' (554) expressed in it. On the former point she understood God to have made animals dumb ('mute', 557) in respect of speech. On the latter point she hesitates to express an opinion ('demurre', 558) since animals often seem by their looks and actions to have 'reason'. She knew the serpent was the subtlest beast – but not to have speech. She wants him to 'redouble' the miracle by speaking about his power of speech. How comes it?

The serpent explains that he was as subrational as the other animals until the day when he came upon a tree whose fruit gave off a smell sweeter than that of fennel (supposed to be a favourite food of serpents: hence Ophelia gives it to Claudius in *Hamlet*) or of the milk-laden teats of ewes and goats. (Milton seems to be alluding to the habits of the incubus in sucking the teats of animals and the breasts of women. The woman who was assailed by the blandishments of the incubus and submitted to them would be removed from the side of her husband during the night.) The appeal to his appetite was irresistible. He wound himself round the tree's trunk, to the envy of other watching animals who could not reach. He plucked, ate his fill, for the pleasure was greater than any he had known. Afterwards there came over him a strange transformation to the extent ('degree', 599) that the power of reason was added to his inner faculties, and thereafter power of speech was not lacking ('Wanted not', 601) for long – though his outer shape did not change. After this transformation he was able to ponder and comprehend all things beautiful and good in Heaven, or Earth, or the air between. Now he has found all things beautiful and good united in herself, the matchless image ('semblance', 607) of divinity. Hence his perhaps troublesome ('importune', 610) but compulsive visit here to worship her.

Thus speaks the sly snake possessed by the Devil ('spirited', 613). Eve observes that his excessive praise of the fruit puts in doubt its efficacy ('vertue', 616), presumed to be evidenced in his acquisition of reason. But Eve's curiosity is aroused. She wants to know where the tree grows amid all the abundance of untouched fruit that hangs waiting for the human family-to-be: and the reference to the future beings who will grow up to enjoy what is here in the fruit provided ('thir provision', 623) and what in itself 'hangs incorruptible' (622) adds a grave note of irony.

Satan offers to lead her to the tree, which grows just past a thicket of blossoming ('blowing', 629) myrrh and 'Balme'. Myrrh is the thorny shrub producing the gum resin from which incense is made; from the balsam tree, or balme, is derived a healing ointment. The incarnational and cruci-fixional associations of these two hint at the price to be paid for Eve's decisive 'Lead then – ' (631), an ironic phrase, since she has rejected her husband's guidance so recently. The serpent's winding guidance makes the intricate path to the forbidden tree easy to follow. He is like the will-o'-the-wisp or *ignis fatuus*, the wandering light sometimes produced by ignited marsh gas. Milton's technical explanation of it as an oily ('unctuous', 635) vapour that condenses in the night air and is kindled to a flame through 'agitation' is perhaps less interesting than the popular belief that the 'delusive Light', which misleads night-wanderers to their deaths in bogs and pools, marks the presence of hovering evil spirits. We have already noted the hint of devilry in terms of current demonology in lines 581–3 above. Moreover, the devil who deceives one class and sex at the midnight masquerade with such polished flattery as Eve has just listened to may mislead on a different social level with cruder flashes of delusive light. There is more than one mode of being 'amaz'd' (cf. 614 and 640) and of wandering from the way – misled by 'fancy lights' and 'menaced by monsters' (*East Coker* 92). The snake glisters and our credulous Mother is led to the forbidden Tree, 'root of all our woe'.

647–779 *Eve explains that this is the one forbidden tree (–654). Satan feigns a curious interest (–658) and Eve repeats the divine prohibition (–663). The serpent puts on an act of astonished in-dignation (–678), praises the benefits the tree confers (–699), and disputes that a just God would deny them to man (–709). The fruit would raise man to godhead (–732). Eve is touched in mind by his persuasiveness, in appetite by the fruit (–744). She argues round the prohibition under the double influence and decides to eat (–779).*

Eve's observation that though there is plenty of fruit here, this has been a fruitless visit for her (648), confirms that the corresponding pun (fruit/result) is present in the first line of *Paradise Lost*. The reliability ('credit', 649) of the fruit's efficacy ('vertue', 649) must depend ('rest', 649) on his evidence alone, since she and Adam have been forbidden to taste or touch it. The tempter affects an aroused curiosity and Eve repeats God's prohibition. At this Satan assumes a posture of mingled zeal and love on mankind's behalf, and outraged indignation at the wrong apparently done to man. The flexibility with which the serpentine frame undulates ('Fluctuats', 668) makes him highly effective at this kind of emotional performance. He is like an orator completely master of himself in mind ('in himself collected', 673) whose every gesture and movement speaks eloquently to the audience before he even opens his mouth. The high-pitched outburst of his opening words expresses passionate zeal, which can brook no delay in utterance.

He speaks as one in whom the tree itself is at last bearing its full fruit – in a new reach of insight given to him. It is the mother of knowledge ('Science', 680). He has gained from it the double power of distinguishing things according to the fundamental purposes they serve and of tracking down the true motives and intentions of those who set things in motion, however exalted they are, however wise they may be assumed to be (680–3). He turns on Eve as 'Queen of this Universe' with a new uncontainable frankness. She must not believe the threats of death. He himself has tasted only to reach a higher level of life than fate destined for him; this by venturing higher than his lot prescribed. Will God shut off from man what is open to the beast? Will he stoke up his anger for so petty a trespass and not rather praise Eve's courage in not being deterred by a threat of death from attaining what might lead to greater happiness – knowledge of good and evil. It cannot but be just to know good. As for evil – if it is real – why should it not be clearly known, since it will then be more easily avoided? In short, God cannot punish you for this if he is just: and if he is not just, he is not God: and if he is not God, he should be neither feared nor obeyed.

Satan declares the only possible divine motive for forbidding the tree to be the resolve to keep man 'low and ignorant,/His worshippers' (704–5). God knows that when Adam and Eve eat of the tree they 'shall be as Gods,/Knowing both Good and Evil as they know' (708–9). He, a serpent, has been made internally a man by the fruit: they – by a corresponding development – will become as gods. In *that* sense they may *die* – putting off humanity and assuming divinity – a highly desirable kind of death. And indeed what do gods have that men may not attain to if they partake of 'God-like food' (717)? 'The Gods are first' means 'The Gods ante-date us'; and they use that advantage to impose on our credulity, Satan argues, the belief that everything derives from them. Satan questions the assumption: he sees the earth productive of much, the gods of nothing. If the gods really *are* the source of all things, then who was it that enclosed the knowledge of good and evil within this tree in such a way that whoever eats it will attain some wisdom that the gods would deny them? And in what respect can a man's desire to attain knowledge in this way be considered damaging? In what way can your knowledge hurt him, or this tree supply something he does not want you to have, if he is lord of everything? Is it just envy?

After piling up the tangled perversities of guileful reasoning and the furtive appeals to self-aggrandizement, Satan's conclusive device is to proclaim Eve in advance the new being that the fruit will make of her – 'Goddess humane', the first of the new species that devilry forecasts in all ages: Godwoman, Godman, Superman, Man-come-of-age and released at last from the fetters of obedience and the blindness of finitude.

The sight of the fruit is of itself enough temptation to Eve's eyes. In her ears the serpent's ringing words seem to be impregnated ('impregn'd', 737) with reason. To the temptations of sight and sound are added those of smell and taste, as noon draws on and whets her appetite. A desire to touch completes the fivefold appeal to the senses. Yet she pauses on the brink, musing.

There is another echo of the poem's seminal lines. The 'Fruit . . . whose mortal taste/Brought Death into the World, and all our woe' (I. 1-3) has become, in Eve's mind, the 'best of Fruits/Whose taste . . . Gave elocution to the mute' (745-8). Man has 'too long forborn' to try what at first tasting has taught the tongue of the dumb animal to praise it. God too, in forbidding enjoyment ('use', 750) of the tree, has in his way praised it by naming it the 'Tree of Knowledge'. The divine prohibition is really a commendation of the tree in that it implies that the tree has something good (because desirable) to offer which human beings lack (753-5). An unknown good is simply an unpossessed good: if it is possessed and still unknown, the possession is meaningless. Therefore to forbid knowledge of good is to forbid possession of it. Such perverse prohibitions of wisdom cannot be binding.

There remains one point to be argued away; the threat of the death penalty. The serpent has eaten and not only lives but enjoys a higher level of being. Is death then an invention devised for human beings only – and devised to keep from them an intellectual food reserved for animals? For Eve now the serpent is self-evidently a reliable source of information ('Author unsuspect', 771), emphatically 'Friendly to man, farr from deceit or guile' (772). In this conviction, the divine prohibition is swept away, the 'Fruit Divine' (776) taken and eaten.

Within the compass of her final musings, Eve has revealed her conquest by Satan to be so blinding that she has mentally reduced God to one who would himself speak the praise of a tree (as in reality Satan does), as one who would deny benefits to men and envy them (as in reality Satan does), as one who would plan death for them (as in reality Satan does). Correspondingly and logically Satan has been designated 'Author unsuspect' (771). The irony is heavy. He is indeed the unsuspected author of her doom: he is the new author she has substituted (unsuspectingly) for Adam, her true

'Author and Disposer' (IV. 635) and for the God the two of them should adore as 'Author of this Universe' (VIII. 360), the God who indeed at Adam's first introduction to Paradise personally proclaimed himself 'Author of all this thou seeest' (VIII. 317). (We may add that Milton has already stretched the meaning of the word so far as to make Adam 'Our Authour', that is, Author of the human race, v. 397.) Eve has accepted instead the one whom the angels know as 'Author of evil' (VI. 262). So doing, she has put herself unwittingly (unsuspectingly) at the side of Sin, the only other person to apply the term approvingly to Satan – 'Thou art my Father, thou my Author' (II. 864). Sin went on to ask, 'Whom should I obey but thee?' (II. 865–6). Eve has (unsuspectingly) given Satan the same authority over her. (That future literary critics might virtually turn Satan also into the 'Author unsuspect' of *Paradise Lost* is conceivably an irony that Milton himself anticipated. We for our part may be pardoned for suspecting that he is indeed the Author unsuspect of much that they have written.)

780–885 Eve eats the fruit and Satan moves away (–794). She breaks into praise of the tree and its effects (–817). She ponders whether to tell Adam about it, and decides to (–833). She returns to Adam, who comes to meet her (–855). She tells what she has done and asks him to do the same (–885).

Eve's act of plucking and eating is felt as a 'wound' by the earth and a threat of ruin to the entire natural order (782–4) because she has undermined the law of obedience whereby the whole hierarchical system is governed. She eats greedily, stuffing her mind with expectant notions of higher knowledge, even of godhead, as she gorges her body. She is physically soon satisfied to the point of inebriated cheerfulness and self-satisfaction.

Her first words are in praise of the tree, which now draws from her the language of a devout worshipper. Its hitherto hidden ('obscur'd', 797) power of producing wisdom ('Sapience', 797) makes it the most 'precious of all Trees' (there would seem to be some parody of hymnology in praise of the cross, the sacred tree, here as elsewhere). It is to be henceforward the object of daily worship and tendance (800–1) till, nourished by what hangs on its branches 'offer'd free to all' (Crucifixional echoes again obtrude), she grows 'mature in knowledge, as the Gods'. Eve's second tribute is to 'Experience' as her 'Best guide'. Through following it (instead of Obedience), she has found access to Wisdom, even though Wisdom may as yet be withdrawn into hiddenness (the unreality of her new thinking is becoming painfully evident). Perhaps she herself is 'secret', too, hidden from high Heaven, which is too remote for a close watch on earth to be maintained. Perhaps 'Our great Forbidder' (815 – the foe's name for the Christian God in all ages) may have had his attention diverted from us.

Shall she make known her changed status to Adam so that he can share her full happiness; or shall she keep her additional knowledge to herself? This would right the balance between the two sexes, compensating for what is lacking in the female sex, giving her a surer power over him, and perhaps even making her superior. For 'inferior who is free?' she asks, illustrating the total collapse of hierarchical thinking according to which there is no freedom except in obedience (cf. v. 520 ff.). The recollection of the threatened death penalty halts this train of thought. It is intolerable to imagine herself 'extinct' and Adam married to a second wife. She resolves that he must share with her 'in bliss or woe'.

She does reverent genuflection to the tree in leaving it, an act of homage directed to the indwelling power whose presence in it has infused it with knowledge-conferring sap, derivative from the drink of pagan divinities. Eve is at this moment something like a practising pantheist. The implicit philosophy of naturalism that she is embracing makes more ironically touching the reception Adam is meantime preparing for her as he weaves a garland of flowers to crown her hair. It is not surprising that intermittently an undercurrent of foreboding disturbs him so that there is an unsteadiness in his heart-beat ('faultring measure', 846) as he sets out to meet her. By the Tree of Knowledge she comes towards him, carrying the bough of fruit. Milton adds a flavour of theatrical stagey-ness to Eve's prepared features and gestures – for she is now under the authority of the 'Author unsuspect' who is past master of disguise. Excuse comes Prologue, and Apology is at hand to prompt him. The 'bland words' come 'at will' (855). She seems to have an immediate fluency in falsehood. She speaks as though every moment of absence from him has been an agony – an agony never more to be repeated. The strange and wonderful cause of her delay is laid before him. The Tree is not after all dangerous to taste but divinely efficacious in endowing those who taste it with insight and godhead. 'The wise serpent, either not being under our prohibition ('not restraind as wee', 868), or being disobedient, has eaten of it, and acquired human speech and understanding, so that he can reason astonishingly well, and has persuaded me also to taste.' The fruit has had corresponding effects on her, opening her eyes, expanding her spirits and enlarging her heart, so that she is 'growing up to Godhead' (877). The ghastly parody of what was foreseen by Raphael when angel and men shared the same human food at the meal in the bower is now fully apparent. The angel forecast that perhaps the time would come when men might duly participate with angels in feeding on heavenly food, and thereby ascend to a higher level of being – 'If ye be found obedient' (v. 501). Eve crowns her pretence with a lie. It was chiefly for Adam's sake, she says, that she sought this new state of being (877–8). Her only bliss is what he shares with her (but see how she thought twice about sharing her new experience with him, 817–26). The hollow declaration is full of ironic pathos when set beside the lyrical outburst of IV. 641–56, which it caricatures. Her final persuasive argument verges on self-burlesque. 'You must also taste, to ensure that we both enjoy an equality of fortune and joy as we do of love: otherwise, through your failing to taste, we might find ourselves living on different levels of being, myself too late attempting to renounce my divinity in order to come back down to your side.'

886–1033 *Adam is shocked* (–895). *He sees clearly what has happened* (–904), *yet declares that he must share Eve's fall* (–916). *He broods aloud on her sin and its consequences* (–951), *then repeats his decision to be at one with her* (–959). *Eve breaks out in praise of their love and unity* (–976) *and the new life opened to them* (–989). *They embrace and Adam eats* (–999). *Intoxicated, they lust after each other* (–1016). *Adam expresses gratitude for Eve's initiative and the pleasure it has won them* (–1033).

In a sequence of vivid brush-strokes Milton shows us Eve's blithe expression and flushed cheek, Adam's blank astonishment, the running chill through his veins, the relaxing of his joints, and the down-dropping from his slackened hand of all the faded roses, tragic reminder of that down-dropping of showered roses that covered their innocent nakedness in the bower of love (IV. 772–3).

Adam, for whom no words can be too rich to describe innocent Eve's excellence (896–9), sees her now lost, defaced and deflowered. He detects the hand of the fraudulent enemy at the back of what he immediately accepts as their joint ruin. For, in Adam's case, the resolution to die with her is a single-minded one. There is no selfish pondering of the pros and cons of sharing everything with her, as there was in Eve's case (817–31). The 'Link of Nature' is too strong.

He achieves the calmness of one who has gathered his strength after a shock and submitted to resignation after an inner turmoil. To Eve he stresses the audacity of her presumptuous act and the great peril it will have provoked. But what is past is done. Unfallen Adam does not fall into recrimination. He tries to find some hope to cling to: that perhaps the death penalty may not apply; that perhaps the deed is not so grave in that the fruit had been already tasted by the serpent, its sacrosanctity profaned before Eve tasted it. And indeed the serpent, the first taster, is still alive, Eve has said, climbing to manhood – a strong inducement to the two of them who, similarly tasting, may climb correspondingly to godhead or angelhood. For that matter Adam cannot

think that the wise Creator will in earnest destroy the two
creatures set over the new Creation, thereby defeating the
entire project of which they are key figures. In any such act
God would turn discreational, be thwarted and undo what
he has done. Adam cannot think of God abolishing his
creatures and thus enabling the adversary to mock the pre-
carious condition of those he favours. He cannot see Satan
being given the opportunity to say – God destroyed me;
now he has destroyed man; whom will he destroy next? The
reasoning is defectively oversimplified, but Adam, still
unfallen, has not yet embroiled himself in a sequence of
irrationalities. All the more striking is the impact of his
resolution to undergo whatever doom is in store for Eve.
The 'Bond of Nature' (956) proves stronger than the law of
obedience.

It is left to Eve to translate this concession to their unity
in the flesh into an illustration of romantic love. It is a
shining manifestation ('Illustrious evidence', 962) of love
that lays on her the obligation to emulate it, though she
must fall short of his perfection. Glad to hear Adam speak
of their unity in the flesh, she amplifies the bond: they are
'One Heart, one Soul in both' (967), as evidenced by Adam's
noble resolve to share with her 'one Guilt, one Crime' (971).
That is, she adds, if there be any crime in tasting of the fruit
whose effect has been, directly or indirectly, to present this
fortunate trial and proof of Adam's love, which otherwise
would never have been so eminently revealed. The whole
sequence thus shows how good proceeds from good. The
argument here (973–6) is a brief profane parody of the doctrine of how God brings good out of evil by using man's fall
as a starting-point for the new manifestation and trial of
divine love in the Son's incarnation and redeeming self-
sacrifice. Eve is bringing her earthly Author, Adam, to a
perverted test of fleshly love in crude imitation of the test
to which divine love ultimately submits. The showing forth
of divine Love in Atonement is parodied in this showing
forth of fleshly love in a different at-one-ment.

Eve continues. 'If I thought the threatened death would

result from my testing of the tree (977–8), I would wish to go through the worst alone and not persuade you to join me (see 826–31 for proof that Eve is lying). I would rather die deserted than make you guilty of a deed ('oblige thee with a fact', 980) dangerous to your peace, especially now that I have been so strongly convinced of your true and matchless love. I feel that the result ('event', 984) will be, not death, but life enriched with new insights, hopes and joys, whose divine flavour already makes the sweet experiences I had before seem flat and crude by comparison.

Eve is touched by Adam's readiness to incur God's displeasure and even death for her sake. It is a bad acquiescence ('compliance', 994), Milton tells us, and deserves a bad return. That is what it gets. She gives him the fruit with 'liberal hand' (997). Adam eats 'Against his better knowledge, not deceav'd,/But fondly (i.e. foolishly) overcome with Femal charm' (998–9).

The 'bad compliance' (994) is bad because Eve is leading Adam into sin, because it is compliance of husband with wife, of man with woman. The faint note of subjection in the connotation of the word *compliance* is important. Adam spoke to Raphael of Eve's 'sweet compliance', which declared genuine ('unfeign'd') 'Union of Mind, or in us both one Soule' (VIII. 604). The *unfeigned* Union was based on female, wifely compliance. Here has been established a 'Union ... One Heart, one Soul' (967) on the basis of a masculine, husbandly compliance, which is not genuine (note, too, that 'Heart and Soul' has replaced 'Mind and Soul'). The key contrast resides in the fact that in Book VIII Adam made a clear distinction between what he felt ('I feel', 608) inwardly and what he knew to be right and did (VIII. 610–11). Now, compliant with the female, 'overcome' (999) in feelings, when before he was not 'foild' (VIII. 608) by them, he knows what is the best but refuses to follow it. The fact that some critics defend Adam's preference (as some indeed have an admiration for Satan) perhaps only serves to illustrate how powerfully Milton has made his point and reproduced human emotional and psychological sequences.

We are fallen men, and naturally side with Adam in so far as we cannot disentangle ourselves from the pleas of Eve, from our own weaknesses, and from the subtle snares laid by the 'Author unsuspect'.

The living world of Nature weeps and groans at the completing of the 'mortal Sin/Original' – and the evident double meaning carried by the word *mortal* (*fatal* and *human*) will corroborate the reading of the same double connotation in Book I, line 2. Adam takes no heed of the thunder and Eve does not fear to repeat ('iterate', 1005) her trespass. The two of them are intoxicated; they reel in mirth and imagine that they feel divinity developing within them, giving them wings to lift them above the earth. In fact the deceptive fruit works far otherwise, enflaming them with lust.

Adam now declares Eve 'exact of taste', praising her fine palate and her precise judgement in neat ambiguities. The 'Sapience' (1018) he attributes to her is not only *wisdom* but *tastefulness*; and as it is Adam's first praise of Eve after eating, so it was Eve's first praise of the Tree after eating ('of operation blest/To Sapience', IX. 797). 'Sapient' was Milton's adjective for Solomon when referring to the garden where he 'held dalliance' with Pharaoh's daughter, IX. 442–3 (see p. 221). Moreover, in his first references to Solomon (I. 400–3, I. 444–6) – linked verbally to later events by the Miltonic key words, *fraud* and *guile* – the emphasis is correspondingly on how his 'wisest heart' was 'led by fraud' (I. 400–1) to build a temple of idolatry. He is the 'uxorious King, whose heart though large,/Beguil'd by fair Idolatresses, fell/To Idols foul' (I. 444–6). One should note the double emphasis on the betrayed 'heart' and relate it to what is said on p. 249. If Eve rapidly became a tree-worshipper, Adam as rapidly becomes a woman-worshipper (1020–1). His lascivious invitation to sexual activity is notably different in idiom from the innocent nuptial joys of their unfallen condition. There is a new note of self-consciousness and contrivance, a new awareness of their bodies as instruments to be exploited. The key phrase is, 'now let us play' (1027). Adam is not lost in wonder at her beauty, but conscious that they have a machinery of pleasure at their disposal and aware of his own enflamed sense calling for gratification.

1034-1189 They satisfy their lust, then sleep (–1045). Awaking, they feel guilt and shame (–1066). Adam upbraids Eve over their loss of innocence (–1080) and cries out in shame for coverage (–1098). They go into a wood, cut fig leaves and make loin cloths (–1118), then give vent to angry passions (–1133). Adam blames Eve for her wilfulness (–1142); Eve blames the serpent's deception (–1154) and Adam's lack of firmness with her (–1161). Adam defends himself, and they fall to mutual recrimination (–1189).

There is no reverent approach or sweet reluctance, still less any amorous delay about the sexual experience that follows. It is a case of purposive eyeings and toyings, well understood, of darting infectious glances and a suddenly seized hand. They take their fill of love and its 'disport' (1042) until they are tired of the game. The sleep that oppresses them is a heavy ('grosser', 1049), drugged, dream-cluttered sleep, bred of the unnatural ('unkindly', 1050) fumes of inebriation. From it they wake, not refreshed, but 'As from unrest' (1052). They find their *eyes* indeed *opened* (1053), but not in the way anticipated (cf. 706–8, 985). They are opened to the recognition of their own darkened minds, to the disappearance of that 'veile' (1054) of innocence that has 'shadow'd' them from knowledge of evil (our loveliest views of Eve have been through a veil, IV. 304, IX. 425, as of Raphael in full splendour, V. 250). Adam's waking to guilt is like Samson's waking from the lap of Delilah, who, in his sleep, had cut off his hair and thereby deprived him of his strength. The correspondence underlines the concept of innocence as positive power, which it is important for the modern reader to sense. The loss of innocence is a virtual emasculation. 'Shorn of strength . . . destitute and bare/Of all their vertue' (1062–3); this is their new condition.

Adam sees the irony of Eve's having given ear to the voice of the 'false Worm' – a counterfeit of the human voice. The 'true' (1069) thing about the serpent was that in it human reason and articulation had descended to the bestial level: *there* was a fall to foreshadow their own 'Fall' (1069). The false thing about the serpent was that it 'promis'd' their 'Rising' (1070). Indeed now they find their 'Eyes/Op'nd' (1070–1). The reiteration corroborates the emphasis above (1053), taking us back to the temptation (706–8, 985). They know good lost, evil got. This is the bad fruit of knowing – to know yourself stripped of innocence, faith and purity, to see in each other's faces the expressions of lecherous desire, which forebodes evil, even shame, the worst of evils.

In shame and remorse Adam recalls the faces and shapes of God and angels, which he will never dare to look upon again. He cries out for a solitary and savage life concealed within woods impenetrable by light. Such is their sorry plight, they must devise a means of hiding their unseemly sexual parts, which newly acquired shame causes them to find unclean. They seek out the fig tree (the Indian Banyan tree) whose branches grow so long that the bended twigs take root in the ground and further trees ('Daughters', 1105) spring up around the 'Mother Tree' (1106) and create a network of over-arched spaces through which 'echoing Walks' (1107) and 'Loopholes' (1110) can easily be cut. The symbolic appropriateness of the ever-increasing network of mother tree and daughter trees, in connection with the covering up of those parts from which the human family is to derive, is obvious, but unfortunately Milton is repeating an error made in Gerard's *Herball*. It is the *Banana* tree, not the *Banyan* Indian fig tree, that has the large leaves. The *Banyan* leaves are small. They gather leaves, broad as an Amazonian shield ('targe', 1111) and sew them into loin cloths, such as more recently Columbus found the American natives wearing, along with girdles of feathers. Thus protected ('fenc't', 1119), they sit down and give vent to the violent passions which tear their inner 'State of Mind', once a peaceful region, with discord and turbulence. For 'Understanding', which is the sovereign of the ordered kingdom that constitutes man's being, no longer rules. Sensual appetite has usurped the sovereignty of Reason (Understanding). The passions and desires that should be subject to Reason and Will are themselves exercising 'Superior sway' (1131).

Adam reproaches Eve for not staying with him as he begged when the strange desire of wandering, for some unknown reason ('I know not whence', 1137), possessed her. In future let no one look for an unnecessary situation to demonstrate the faith to which they are in duty bound; when they begin to look earnestly for opportunity to demonstrate, you can conclude they have already begun to lapse from duty (1140–2).

Eve complains that Adam is being too severe in imputing to her wilful wandering something which might just as easily have happened had he been there, or might indeed have happened to him. Had he been where she was, or had the attempt been made on him, he would not have been able to detect the fraudulence of the serpent, speaking as he spoke, and there being no known grounds for hostility between serpent and man. Could she be expected to be always at his side? If so she might just as well have remained a lifeless rib. And anyway why had he not commanded her firmly, being the head? He was too easy ('facil', 1158) with her, did not oppose her enough, virtually approved her departure by his kind words of dismissal.

Adam is incensed. Is this his reward for self-sacrificingly joining her in her disobedience? Is this the unchanging love she promised in return when she was fallen and he was not, but still free to live in bliss, yet chose death in order to be with her? Is he now reproached as the cause of her transgression, and blamed for not being strict enough in restraining her? He recalls the care he took in warning her. There was nothing more he could have done, unless he had used force – and there is no place for force where the will is free. Her own self-confidence misled her. She thought herself secure in that either she would meet no danger or find an attempt upon her an opportunity to achieve a glorious victory. Perhaps he erred in being so overcome by her qualities that he thought her unassailable by evil. He rues the excessive admiration (which has now become his crime) of a woman (who has now become his accuser). Such is the lot of the man who puts too much trust in the worth of a woman and lets her will govern his. She will kick against his attempts to restrain her: then, when left to herself, if the results are evil, she will first of all put the blame on his weakness in indulging her.

The mutual recrimination fills the now 'fruitless' hours. Neither blames himself.

Book X

The hate-packed, spite-packed ('despightfull', 1) deed done
by Satan in Paradise is known in Heaven. We recall the
comment on the first unfolding of the diabolical plan in
Heaven; that it was 'done all to *spite*/The great Creator. But
their *spite* still serves/His glory to augment' (II. 384–5). And
Raphael summed up the satanic plot as 'all his solace and
revenge,/As a *despite* don against the most High . . .' (VI.
905–6). And lest there should still be any doubt about
Milton's feeling for this key word, hear Satan summing up
the position before taking possession of the serpent. He will
destroy this new man, 'Son of *despite*,/Whom us the more to
spite his Maker rais'd/From dust: *spite* then with *spite* is best
repaid' (IX. 176–8).

The two falls, of angels and men, are seen together in
Heaven. Two points are underlined. God did not hinder
Satan in his resolve to assault ('attempt', 8) the mind of man;
but man was armed with fully adequate resistance in terms
of strength and will-power. He could have uncovered
('discover'd', 10) Satan's fraud and repelled his 'wiles', however hypocritically practised (cf. III. 95 ff., and especially – 'I
made him just and right/Sufficient to have stood, though
free to fall', III. 98–9). Adam and Eve knew the 'high
Injunction'. They always ('still', 12) *knew* it, even when Eve

was being tempted and Adam was being tempted. They ought to have *always* ('still', 12) borne it in mind. They did not obey it. Not obeying, they incurred the penalty. Given up to a multitudinous ('manifold', 16) sinfulness, they deserve to fall.

The angelic guards return to Heaven 'mute and sad' (18) for man. The angels, whose glory is utterance of praise, are silenced because the serpent, who in reality is 'mute' (IX. 563, 748), assumed articulate speech. The angels, whose glory is joy, are saddened because the devil who is in reality author of all woe, came to Eve with words and expressions 'blithe' and glad (IX. 625: infected Eve's countenance became 'blithe' too, IX. 886). It is a characteristic of Heaven not fully comprehensible to the human mind that the displeasure and sadness evident in the angelic faces, being mingled with compassion ('pitie', 25), does not violate their bliss. The point is important. If it did real damage to heavenly happiness, then evil would have in its hand a power of blackmail that a loving God could never allow to created beings. Angel and man are free to destroy – themselves and their happiness. All evil is self-destructive. It cannot damage good. It can only subtract itself from good.

The celestial to-do is apparent as the 'ethereal People' (27) run in multitudes to find out what exactly has happened. The guards from the garden, who must account for the satanic invasion of it, easily prove that they exercised the maximum vigilance. God assures them that the failure of their mission ('charge', 35) is not their fault. Not the most exact oversight ('sincerest care', 37) on their part could have prevented what has happened. He himself foretold that Satan would prevail and succeed ('speed', 40) on his bad mission ('errand', 41) (see III. 92 ff.). This does not mean that any divine decision contributed ('Concurring', 44) to make man's fall inevitable, or even to touch his free will with a featherweight of influence ('impulse', 45). The free will was left with two perfectly balanced scale pans. The tilting ('inclining', 46) of the scales was wholly in its charge. What remains ('rests', 48) but to pass the human-death ('mortal', 48) sentence, which he is already beginning to think null and void just because it was not inflicted in an immediate stroke. Before the end of the day he will learn that postponement is not discharge ('Forbearance no acquittance', 53: both terms are loaded with joint legal and moral significations). Man may have thrown God's bounty back at God in scorn: he cannot do the same thing with God's justice (54). Whom shall God send? The Son. Then it will be clear ('Easie . . . seen', 58) that 'I intend/Mercie collegue (*in league with*) with Justice, sending thee . . .' (58–9). *I* intend. The Father will be, as ever, present in the Son, justice and mercy inseparably bound within the mystery of the co-inherence. He will be present in man's 'design'd' (*intended* – and intended by the Father) 'Both Ransom and Redeemer voluntarie' (60–1). The Son is 'collegue' with the Father as mercy is 'collegue' with justice, as Eve ought to have remained 'collegue' with Adam, unsevered from his side, in voluntary obedience.

Unclouded deity blazes forth from Father on to Son as the glory unfolds towards that 'right hand' (64) from which the image and reflection can never sever itself. The Son, full resplendent, plainly shows forth '*all his Father*' (66) as he speaks of mercy and mitigation. For, as the Son says, it is for the Father 'to decree' (68), for the Son 'to do' his will (69). Going to judge man, the Son recalls that he himself must bear the worst penalty (73) (cf. III. 236–8, 245–6), and claims the agreed right to mitigate their punishment ('doom', 76) which in its full severity has been diverted ('deriv'd', 77) on to his own shoulders. He will so blend justice and mercy as to show them forth ('illustrate', 79) both fully satisfied without there being any violation of the divine peace ('thee appease', 79). The Son will go unaccompanied to Adam and Eve. As for Satan, he is self-convicted, self-condemned. It is no one's duty or business to establish his guilt. Thus saying, the Son rises from the seat of the side-by-side ('collateral', 86) glory, which he never leaves but by permission of him whose only-begotten he is. His descent is swift. The sun is low in its westward fall ('cadence', 92) from the noontide heat, and the gentle cooling airs of evening (see Genesis III.

8) are at work on the earth as this other Son comes down with the heat of divine wrath likewise cooled ('from wrauth more coole', 95), to voice to man the sentence of the 'mild Judge and Intercessor both' (96). The elaborate parallel is pressed home. The voice of God is brought to the ears of Adam and Eve 'by soft windes' (98) as they are 'walking in the Garden' (98: Genesis III. 8 again). They hide away till God calls them aloud.

103–228 Adam and Eve come forward and God questions them (–123). Adam tells how Eve gave him the fruit and he ate (–143). God rebukes Adam, then questions Eve (–158). She briefly confesses (–162) and God passes judgement on the serpent in a prophetic curse (–181). The poet explains the prophecy (–192). God then passes judgement on Eve (–196) and on Adam (–208). He has pity on them, clothes their nakedness (–223), and returns to the Father (–228).

God summons Adam with the gentle remonstrances of a guest who finds no one to entertain him at his arrival (105) where formerly there was a dutiful, unsought eagerness to meet him ('obvious' – *coming to meet*, 106). Is my coming less evident? What change keeps you away? What chance makes you late? Both come forward, out of countenance and ill at ease ('discount'nanc̣t', 'discompos'd', 110). In their looks there is no love; but evident guilt and shame. Adam answers, 'faultring long' (115), the poet says, reminding us of the 'faultring' (IX. 846) heart-beat with which he went to an earlier momentous meeting, tragic forerunner of this one. (And connect the 'faultring' and the 'discompos'd' condition with the 'faultring speech and visage incompos'd' of that master of confusion worse confounded, old Anarch, II. 989.) He heard God and hid himself, being naked and afraid. God asks the cause of the shame and the fear.

Adam laments that he must either take the whole crime upon himself or accuse his wife whose failing he should conceal so long as she is faithful to him. The inevitabilities and limitations imposed by the calamity (the need to be truthful is one of them) are such that he cannot allow the whole insupportable load of sin and punishment to descend on his own head: and in any case concealment is to no purpose when you are speaking to God. The woman, God's perfect gift, from whose hand he could 'suspect no ill' (140) and whose every act seemed to be its own self-justification, gave him fruit and he ate it.

God's reply plays firmly with Miltonic key words. Was she 'God', 'guide', 'Superior', that he should 'obey' her, resigning his 'manhood', his 'Place', his 'dignitie', giving 'Subjection', where he should have given 'Love'? The 'Gifts' she had were such as 'seem'd' well 'under Government', but were 'Unseemly' to beare 'rule'. Then God turns to Eve, and she answers with 'brevity', 'sad', and 'with shame'. The serpent 'beguild' her and she ate.

God lays his curse on the serpent. The serpent cannot have its guilt transferred to Satan. In making it 'instrument of mischief', Satan exploited it in such a way as to pervert it from its purpose ('end', 167) in the created order. This perversion is a pollution (167) of its being; and its entire nature is 'vitiated' (169). The serpent is not a being misled but an instrument marred. The curse is voiced (175–81) in close paraphrase of Genesis III. 14–15. The serpent is to continue to bear in itself the marks of its possession by Satan. Satan sinned first: God nevertheless applies the doom of Satan to the serpent. It will grovel on its belly and eat dust all its life. The poet takes up the second part of the prophecy: 'I will put enmity between thee and the woman, and between thy seed and her seed; it shall bruise thy head, and thou shalt bruise his heel.' (Genesis III. 15). The prophecy came true (was 'verifi'd', 182) when *Jesus*, son of *Mary*, second *Eve*, finally overcame the powers of Hell through his act of Redemption. In the act of Ascension the powers of darkness are finally dragged captive through the air whose region they have usurpingly made their thoroughfare (cf. III. 250–6). They are at last trodden down under the feet of God made man.

Eve's sentence is to bring forth children in sorrow and to be in subjection to her husband. Adam's sentence is com-

parable. If the labour and fruitfulness of woman's productivity in childbirth is to be marked with sorrow, so the
labour of man's productive work on the earth is to be a
compulsory burden. The earth will bring forth thorns and
thistles spontaneously, and bread-winning will be accompanied by toil and sweat. Man, born of dust and due to
return to dust, will labour in servitude to the earth.

The death penalty is deferred, but the Son, foreseeing the
change of environment in store for Adam and Eve (see
651 ff.), takes pity on their nakedness. He anticipates the
accepted humiliations of the Incarnation, when he is to take
on himself 'the form of a servant' (Philippians II. 7) and even
wash his disciples' feet (John XIII. 4–5): he clothes them
with the skins of animals. The compound allusiveness of
line 219 makes it difficult. The reference would appear to be
to the Sermon on the Mount: 'And if any man will sue thee
at the law, and take away thy coat, let him have thy cloak
also' (Matthew v. 40). Christ's recommendation of not just
clothing your enemy, but double-clothing him ('Enemies',
here, 219, in the sense of those who have alienated themselves by sin and implicitly sued him for the self-sacrifice he
has already guaranteed, III. 236 ff.) is partly realized in the
Father's clothing of his disobedient family (216: and see
Luke XII. 28, 'how much more will he clothe you': the
word 'Arraying', 223, helps to make this link – 'Consider the
lilies . . . Solomon in all his glory was not arrayed like one
of these', Luke XII. 27). It is fully realized in the Son's
clothing of their 'inward nakedness' (221; for they are now
stripped of innocence, IX. 1074) with his own robe of
righteousness; a metaphorical expression for his taking their
sinfulness upon himself and decking their guilty humanity
in his own sinlessness for re-presentation of that humanity
before the throne of God (cf. 'He hath clothed me with the
garments of salvation, he hath covered me with the robe of
righteousness . . .', Isaiah LXI. 10). Our eyes having been
thus cast forward momentarily to that momentous 'ascension
bright' (187 and cf. III. 313–16), we now see the Son make
a 'swift ascent' (224) back to the bosom of the Father,

bringing pacification with his self-alienated children ('to him appeas'd/All', 226–7).

229–353 *We return to Sin and Death at the gates of Hell (–234). Sin senses Satan's success (–249) and proposes the construction of a bridge to the world (–263). Death agrees, sniffing the scent of prey (–281). They build a great highway through Chaos (–311), which follows Satan's route (–320) and forms a junction with the way to Heaven from the world (–324). They meet Satan, in disguise, making his return journey to Hell (–353).*

Sin and Death sit facing each other at the gates of Hell, where we left them after Sin had opened the gates and Satan passed through into Chaos on his journey to the world (II. 871 ff.). Sin judges that Satan must have succeeded in his enterprise since, had he met with failure, he would have come fleeing back from his avenger to this, his only fit place of punishment. She feels within her a new access of strength. Some strange sympathetic force, some powerful natural attraction of like for like, that links similars in a hidden telepathic connectedness, lures her. She addresses Death as her 'Shade/Inseparable' (249–50). Death is her shadow – her dark negative image and reflection.

Sin considers it possible that Satan's return may have been delayed by difficulty in crossing the impenetrable ('impervious', 254) gulf of Chaos. She proposes that they undertake the congenial task of constructing a highway to the world, a highly useful and worthy commemorative edifice ('Monument/Of merit' is thus ambiguous, 258–9) whereby the movement of devils will be facilitated, whether such movement is a two-way traffic with the world or a one-way emigration from Hell ('for intercourse,/Or transmigration', 260–1). The new instinctive drag pulls so strongly that there can be no mistaking the way.

Death, her lean ('meager', 264) shadow, agrees. He will stick to Sin. He is lured, too, by the scent of carnage, and tastes the 'savour of Death' (269), as Eve was lured 'by the smell/So savorie' (IX. 740–1) to touch and taste. And thus the change to mortality ('mortal change', 273) on Earth has

brought its pervasive smell. The anticipatory flocking of
vultures and kites to a battlefield makes an apt, if unscientific
comparison.

The two launch out 'Hovering upon the Waters' (285) in
mockery of the Holy Spirit at the Creation (I. 19–22; VII.
233–5; Genesis I. 2). They scoop up a mixture of dry and
moist aggregate from either side of the roadway-to-be and
pack it together, then cram it down towards the mouth of
Hell, just as contrary polar winds drive masses of ice together
and block up Arctic sea routes. Death smites the accumulated
soil with his petrifying mace till it is dry and firm. (For *Delos*,
296, see v. 264–5 and p. 129.) He cements the rest with slimy
asphalt. His own look (with its '*Gorgonian*', 297, power – for
the gorgon's head turned all who looked on it to stone) is
enough to bind the concrete immovably. They fasten this
basic structure of concretized shingle ('beach', 299) to the
roots of Hell, and then work on the immense pier-like
structure ('Mole', 300) arching the deep and connecting with
the wall of the now undefended ('fenceless', 303) world, so
as to make a broad, easy and unobstructed ('inoffensive')
pathway to Hell. So Xerxes came from Susa in Persia (whose
citadel was built by Memnon; hence 'Memnonian', 308) to
invade and enslave Greece and had to build a bridge of boats
to cross the Hellespont. Because a storm destroyed it, he
commanded the scourging of the waters (311).

The skill of Sin and Death in bridge-building (their 'Art/
Pontifical', 312–13) produces a vast arched viaduct, which
follows Satan's route to where he landed on the bare outside
(see III. 418–30) of the universe. Thus three different ways,
to Heaven, to the Earth, and to Hell, lead off from a common point (see III. 523–8). As Sin and Death get their first
view of their way to Earth, Satan comes rising straight upwards ('stearing/His *Zenith*', 328–9) between the constellations *Centaure* and *Scorpion*. (The Sun was supposed to be in
the sign of *Aries*, 329, at the Creation.) He wears the disguise
of a bright angel, but his own family are quick to see
through it. After the seduction of Eve he slunk away
unnoticed ('unminded', 332) and changed shape in order to

keep watch on what happened. He saw Eve unknowingly ('unweeting', 335) repeat the same trickery on Adam that he had practised on her, and saw their shame and their vain attempts at self-concealment ('covertures', 337). When he saw the Son of God come down to judge them he fled, not imagining that he could escape all punishment, but anxious to get away from what God's immediate wrath might inflict upon him. He returned later by night to eavesdrop on the conversation of Adam and Eve, now sadly talking over their plight. Thus he had indirectly gathered what his own sentence was to be (i.e. the curse explained in lines 182–90), which seemed to postpone his punishment. The meeting with his family has the character of a happy reunion: the sight of the bridge makes it all the happier for Satan.

354–459 *Sin praises Satan for his conquest of the new world (–382). Satan praises Sin and Death for the new bridge (–393), and sends them to be his representatives on Earth (–409). They go their way (–414) while he goes down to Hell to find the chiefs in council in Pandaemonium (–441). He enters unnoticed, ascends his throne (–448) and is recognized with acclamation (–459).*

Sin attributes all that she has done in bridge-building to Satan. Her deeds are his deeds, as the Son's deeds are the Father's deeds. Satan is their 'Author and prime Architect' (356). It is interesting that Satan and Sin are 'joynd in connexion sweet' (359), which has its basis in the union of heart with heart (357–8), and that this is how Sin 'divin'd' (357) that Satan must have succeeded; because whereas after her fall Eve stresses the union between herself and Adam as of 'One Heart, one Soul' in both (IX. 967), Adam, before the fall, speaks of their union as of 'Mind' and 'Soule' (VIII. 604), and it is with a faultering of his 'heart, divine of something ill' (IX. 845) that unfallen Adam first detects something amiss. The emphasis on the betrayed and betraying heart of Solomon has already been noted (see p. 236; and cf. I. 400 and 444). Satan's looks now prove ('evidence', 361) that Sin was right in that instinctive divination of his success which impelled her to pursue him. Satan, Death, and herself are so united over what results from Satan's venture (364) that nothing could prevent her from following him, however distant. Satan has freed them from Hell and given them power to build this marvellous and menacing ('portentous', 371, is double-edged) bridge. The whole world is now his. His courage and initiative ('vertue', 372) have gained for him what his hands did not make; his wisdom has gained as much and more than was lost in Heaven by war. Thus the only-begotten Daughter praises and magnifies her Father and his works. Their defeat ('foile', 375) in Heaven has been fully avenged. Let God keep his rule in Heaven, which victory in battle assigned to him (376–7), and withdraw from this new world, which his own judgement has alienated from him. God and Satan shall be twin monarchs over Heaven and this new world respectively. God shall rule his four-square kingdom ('Quadrature', 381) and Satan his spherical ('Orbicular', 381) world. Allusion to the four-square heavenly city of Revelation XXI. 16 takes us back to the view of Heaven first given us through Satan's eyes, 'In circuit, undetermind square or round' (II. 1048; see p. 63).

Satan takes up the thread of mutual congratulation. Sin and Death deserve the thanks of the entire 'Infernal Empire' (389) that they have matched his own effort in moral and spiritual bridge-building (for that is what it amounts to) with the appropriate material structure, making one realm of Hell and the world, with easy access either way. (R. E. Houghton, in his annotated edition of *Paradise Lost*, Books IX and X (O.U.P.), notes the 'ironic contrast' between this union and that looked forward to in Raphael's narrative to Adam: 'And Earth be chang'd to Heav'n, and Heav'n to Earth,/One Kingdom, Joy and Union without end', VII. 160–1.) Therefore Satan will take the now easy road back to Hell, while the two of them make their way down between the 'numerous Orbs' (397), which are now all within their domain, to Paradise, where they can exercise their new lordship over the earth and over man especially. The commission is assigned to them in the grand official idiom in which high responsibilities are conferred. They shall be his substitutes, invested with full authority ('Plenipotent', 404). His own exploit has opened up the new kingdom to Death through Sin. His hold on it depends on them. If their joint power maintains its grip there, Hell's interests ('affaires', 408) should suffer no harm ('detriment', 409: Verity notes that the word echoes a Roman formula for conferring special emergency powers on consuls: 'Videant consules ne quid res publica detrimenti capiat' – Let the consuls see to it that the state suffers no damage).

Sin and Death speed through the constellations, shedding their evil influence ('bane', 412). The stars, whose very nature it is to shed influence, good or evil, to infuse with virtue or to *blast* and *strike* with bane, become in the proximity of Sin and Death the recipients, not the dispensers of influence. They are themselves 'blasted' (412), stricken (413) and made pale ('wan', 412). Such is the pervasive evil now threading its way between them. Meantime Satan proceeds down the highway ('causey', 415 – causeway) to the gate of Hell. On either side of the bridge the clamour of divided ('Disparted', 416 – cut through by the structure) Chaos surges and resurges against the unyielding fabric (415-18). Within the wide-open and unguarded gate Satan finds desolation. Sin and Death have gone to the world, the rest of the inhabitants far inland to the city of Pandaemonium (cf. 1. 756: see pp. 23-4), the seat of Lucifer, so called through Satan's being compared ('paragond', 426) to the morning star (see p. 141). Here the chiefs sit in council, as Satan commanded before leaving, concerned to know ('sollicitous', 428) what might have overtaken him. The retirement of the devils to their inner fortress leaves the outermost ('utmost', 437) regions of Hell dark and deserted. They have been withdrawn ('reduc't', 438) to keep a vigilant guard over the metropolis. The action is compared to the withdrawal of Tartars from their Russian enemies: Ivan the Terrible defeated them and annexed Astrakhan (432) in 1556. It is likewise compared to the withdrawal of the Persian Shah ('*Bactrian* Sophi', 433) from his Turkish enemies to his own cities, Tabriz ('*Tauris*', 436), ancient capital of the province of Azerbaijan (it often changed hands during the Turkish–Persian wars of the sixteenth and seventeenth centuries), and Kazvin ('*Casbeen*', 436) ('*Aladule*' was part of Armenia). It seems unlikely that much more could be conveyed by this use of names (made familiar to Milton by the work he did on his *History of Muscovia*) than a general impression of desolation over a vast and remote terrain, though no doubt the watchful suspense of withdrawn armies, who have reason to anticipate a possible pursuit by forces as dreaded as the Russians and the Turks, adds an additional emotive relevance to the comparison.

Into this tense gathering Satan slips unnoticed in the guise of an angelic soldier of the lowest rank. He is playing the epic hero, the Great Wanderer Returned, in a big way. One thinks of Odysseus returning to Ithaca. The Hall is called '*Plutonian*' (444) because Pluto was king of the Classical Underworld (cf. IV. 270 and see p. 220). Unseen he ascends his high throne, royally splendid under a richly woven canopy ('state', 445), surveys the scene around him, then suddenly emerges, as from a cloud, with shining head and shape of star-like brightness – wearing indeed all the 'false glitter' (452) of 'permissive glory' (451) left him since the Fall. The sudden blaze of his brightness astonishes all. They turn their eyes on him ('bent thir aspect', 454), see the very person they wished to see, and acclaim him. They rush forward, putting an end to their secret consultation ('dark *Divan*', 457). With a wave of the hand he calls them to silence.

460–609 *Satan announces the successful conquest of the world (–469), sums up the difficulties he encountered and how he overcame them (–503). There is a great hiss instead of a shout (–509), for all are suddenly changed into serpents (–528) and Satan into a dragon (–532). They go out, and the waiting legions are then transformed likewise (–547). They are tormented by baited trees, unassuageable appetite (–560), and bitter delusive fruit (–572), before being restored to their normal shape (–584). Meanwhile Sin and Death arrive in Paradise (–601) where Death is to feed on all living things (–609).*

Satan addresses the demons by their former heavenly titles of rule and authority, insisting that these titles are theirs now not only by right but by actual possession of dominion. They are rulers *de facto* as well as *de iure*. For he has returned successful beyond all expectations to lead them out of Hell to the rule of the new world. It would take a long time to tell, he says ('Long were to tell', 469), the difficulties of his journey, which they can now make with ease over the new highway. He had to toil through an uncharted ('uncouth' – unknown, 475) route, traverse the unmanageable Abyss, plunged in the pre-creative realm of Night and Chaos. Satan's false account of the opposition he met with from Night and Chaos (cf. II. 1007–9) is as misleading as the initial pretence that the demons are now restored to something like their former dignities (460–2). His summing up of the Fall of Man is distorted by scornful simplifications – that nothing more than an apple was needed to seduce Adam and Eve, and that God, angered by their fall ('thereat/Offended', 487–8), has been so laughably foolish as to hand over his beloved new creature and creation, lock, stock and barrel, to Sin, Death and themselves; all this without their having to make any great effort or take any great risk. They can now range as they please over the new world and rule over man as God should have ruled. It is true, Satan adds, that God has passed judgement on me, too – or rather, not on me but on the serpent in whose shape I deceived man: the part of the penalty that applies to me is that I am to bruise the heel of Adam's progeny, and they – the time is not yet fixed ('set', 499) – shall bruise my head. And who would not gladly purchase a world at the cost of a mere bruise? That is the end of Satan's account. He invites them to rise and enter immediately 'into full bliss' (503).

Instead of full bliss there follows a 'universal hiss' (508). The sound of public scorn, instead of applause, bewilders Satan: bewilderment at his own condition quickly follows.

His face is pulled into a new shape, pointed and thin (511), his arms become tied to his sides, his legs are entwined to-gether, he loses his footing ('supplanted', 513) and falls flat on his belly as a serpent. So he is punished in the shape in which he sinned, while a few moments ago he was boasting that the serpent he possessed bore the main brunt of punish-ment and that only the latter part of God's sentence applied to himself (495–501). A further irony is that he gave voice to the serpent and now a serpent's voice has usurped his own, a forked tongue his articulate tongue (517–18). Moreover, the clinging of his 'Armes' to his 'Ribs' (512) in the transforma-tion is a sharp reminder of how Eve was torn from Adam's side, her hand from his, herself from the shelter of the ribs from which she was shaped.

The others, as Satan's accessories, are likewise trans-formed. The 'thick swarming' (522) of the twisted ('com-plicated', 523) monsters takes us back mentally to the first gathering at Pandaemonium when the very different 'hiss' (1. 768) of wings was noted as the demons 'swarm'd' (1. 767 and 776) together like 'Bees/In spring-time' (1. 769). Milton seems to press the connection (N.B. 'Thick swarm'd' . . . 'Swarm'd', 1. 767, 776; 'thick swarm'd', x. 526; 'thick swarming', x. 522). On the first occasion demons voluntarily transformed themselves into creatures of pigmy size in order to get into a smaller space while the evil plotting was afoot (1. 789–90). Likewise Satan voluntarily took over a serpent at the execution of the plot. Now all are involuntarily trans-formed. The deterioration of *being-hood* marks the increase of devilry. You cannot enter into possession of a beast without a corresponding bestialization of yourself.

The associations of the various reptiles and monsters (actual and mythical) named make for a concentration of horror. 'Scorpion' is the familiar biblical name for a whip of knotted cords, lead weights or steel spikes (cf. 1 Kings XII. 11: and Death threatens to use just such a 'whip of scorpions', II. 701, at Satan's first meeting with him), as well as the name of the creature whose sting is proverbially of maximum painfulness. The venomous asp is closely akin to the English adder. The *'Amphisboena'* (524) is a mythical two-headed (one at each end) serpent. The *'Cerastes'* (525) is a horned African viper, the *'Hydrus'* (525) a fabulous sea-serpent. There would appear to be no connection between the serpentine *'Ellops'* (525) of ancient writers and the elops of the herring family. The *'Dipsas'* (526) was a serpent whose bite, fitly, was fabled to cause a tormenting thirst: the corresponding South American dipsas is a non-venomous snake – though its appearance is formidable. There have been previous references to Medusa, the gorgon (II. 611, p. 49), whose face could not be looked upon or the spectator turned to stone, and who had serpents in her hair. There is a story that after Perseus slew her, blood dripped from her severed head and bred serpents where it fell. The island of *'Ophiusa'* (528) was reputed to abound in serpents. The story of the monstrous serpent *'Python'* (531), bred by the sun from the mud after the flood of Deucalion, is told in Ovid, *Metamorphoses* I.

The grim flock of monsters follows the gigantic satanic dragon out of the hall. ('And there was war in heaven: Michael and his angels fought against the dragon; and the dragon fought and his angels ... And the great dragon was cast out, that old serpent called the Devil, and Satan, which deceiveth the whole world ...', Revelation XII. 7–9.) Outside, the other demons stand on guard ('in station', 535) or drawn up in formation ('just array', 535), their spirits raised ('Sublime', 536) in expectation of a triumphal processional egress led by the 'glorious Chief' (537). The sight of the ugly serpents strikes them with horror – a fellow-horror ('horrid sympathie', 540) as the same transformation overtakes themselves. Serpentinism spreads like an infection. The intended burst of applause becomes, uncontrollably, a burst of hissing. The demons no longer have the power of voluntary approval (with its basis in worship and hierarchy) but only of compulsive disapproval. They who could not appreciate others now cannot express appreciation of themselves.

To coincide with this change God has arranged the sudden growth of a nearby grove laden with fruit like that with which Satan tempted Eve. Instead of one forbidden tree they see a large number of trees sent to tantalize them, yet they are so parched with burning thirst and ravenous hunger that they cannot resist the bait. They roll to the trees and climb them. The comparison with '*Megaera*' (560), one of the Furies (Eumenides), who were often represented with snakes in their hair, is perhaps made because of the association between the Furies and the avenging of crime, especially of crime against the ties of kinship. The tempting apples are like those on the trees that grew in the ashes near Sodom, which were supposed to turn to ashes in the hand when plucked. Those deceived the touch: these deceive the taste (563–4). The reference to the Dead Sea ('bituminous Lake', 562) is interesting, because Death used its '*Asphaltic* slime' (298) to cement the bridge to the world. The demons foolishly ('fondly', 564) think they can satisfy their appetite by tasting ('gust', 565) but the fruit turns to 'bitter Ashes' (566) in their mouths, and they spit them out. Their hunger and thirst compel them to repeat the experience time after time until their jaws are writhing with detestation of the soot and cinders packed between them. So they fall repeatedly into the 'illusion' into which man fell once. Eventually they are allowed to resume their 'lost shape' (574), though it is said that annual repetitions of periodic transformation into serpents is imposed as part of their continuing penalty. Preparing to take leave of the demons, the poet mentions that some people hand on the belief that the demons scattered themselves among the heathen, whom they won over, and that Satan can be identified with Ophion, ruler of Olympus, while Eurynome, his wife, might perhaps be equated with Eve, in the mythological hierarchy that preceded that of Saturn and Ops (his wife), and its successor, that of Jupiter (or Zeus). The name 'Eurynome' means 'wide-ruling'. In hypothetically equating Eve with Eurynome Milton notes Eve's presumptous over-reaching of herself in the phrase 'wide-Encroaching *Eve* (581–2).

We move briefly to Paradise. Sin has already been present there in act ('Once actual', 586), now she is there in body and is to be an established resident ('Habitual habitant', 588). Death follows her, step by step, not yet mounted on the 'pale Horse' (590) on which he is pictured in Revelation (VI. 8). Sin asks Death what he thinks of their new empire and the more lavish food supply it promises him. Death can only reply that Hell, Paradise, and Heaven are all alike to him. His hunger is unsatisfiable. All plenteousness is inadequate to stuff the loose-hanging sack of his belly. Whereupon Sin helpfully draws up a menu, vegetables first, meat course next, with 'Fish and Fowle' to follow. These are not exactly everyday snacks ('homely morsels', 605). Time's scythe will keep up a steady supply for his devouring. She herself, dwelling within man, will infect the human race and season him to be Death's last and most tasteful dish.

610–719 *God sees Sin and Death at work (–628) but also foresees the Son's conquest of them (–640). The angels praise God (–648). God adjusts the course of Nature to produce climatic variations and extremes (–667) and the familiar seasonal cycles (–691). Hail and snow and whirlwind become known on Earth (–706), while comparable discord affects living creatures with internecine hostilities (–714), which Adam observes with remorse (–719).*

As Sin and Death set about their destructive work, God observes them, the 'Dogs of Hell' (616), Furies who spread desolation (are 'wastful', 620) and who, like Satan and his followers, attribute foolishness to himself for allowing them to take possession of the terrestrial premises ('enter and possess', 623), and by his connivance giving satisfaction to his enemies. They laugh, imagining that God has lost his temper, and handed everything over ('quitted', 627) to them in a fortuitous surrender. They do not realize that he himself called them out like dogs to lick up the mess made by the polluting taint of human sin on what was pure. When they have gorged themselves sick, one sling of the Son's arm will send Sin, Death and the open-mouthed grave spinning through Chaos to block up the open mouth of Hell for ever. New Heaven and Earth shall be pure in stainless sanctity.

The angels sing out in praise that God's ways are just

(which the poet set out to prove, I. 24–6) and that none can disparage ('extenuate', 645) him. Then they praise the Son by whom 'New Heav'n and Earth shall to the Ages rise,/Or down from Heav'n descend.' ('And I saw a new heaven and a new earth . . . And I John saw the holy city, new Jerusalem, coming down from God out of heaven, prepared as a bride *adorned* for her husband.' Revelation xxi. 1–3.) Scarcely any biblical correspondence needs to be pondered as much as this one, which brings into focus much of what we have said or hinted at in reference to the earthly city, earthly garden, and earthly beloved, as potential types and symbols of the New Jerusalem and the mystical bride of the divine spouse. Heaven was 'adorn'd/Of living Saphire' (II. 1049), Eve 'adorn'd' with perfect beauty and 'adorn'd' with naked beauty (IV. 634, 713) under a sky of 'living Saphirs' (IV. 605),

God calls forth his 'mightie Angels' (650) and gives them separate ('several', 650) responsibilities as best befits ('sorted with', 651) the present situation. The sun first gets his instructions ('precept', 652) to move in such a way as to bring about on Earth extremes of cold and heat. The pale ('blanc', 656) moon has her function ('office', 657) prescribed. Likewise the other five planets have their movements and relative positions ('aspects', 658) prescribed. These 'aspects' determine what mixture of planetary influence will reach and affect the earth (see p. 88). '*Sextile*, *Square*, and *Trine*, and *Opposite*' represent the separations of planets at distances of 60, 90, 120, and 180 degrees respectively, as measured from the earth. There is need now for aspects that are harmful in their effect ('Of noxious efficacie', 660), for the kind of combination that will form a malignant conjunction ('Synod unbenigne', 661). The fixed stars, too, have to be taught when to shed ('showre', 662) malignant influence. The angels also arrange ('set', 664) from what quarters ('corners', 665) the winds must blow to produce storm and tempest.

Seasonal changes have to be introduced, too, to replace the ideal paradisal blend in which '*Spring* and *Autumn* . . . Danc'd hand in hand' (v. 394–5). Two rival theories of how this was effected are cited: either by the shifting (turning 'ascance', 668) of the earth's axis into an oblique position in relation to the sun (668-71) or by the diversion of the sun from its former route. The diversion is an adjustment calculated to produce a change identical ('Like distant breadth', 673) to that which the shifting of the earth's axis would produce. The poet traces the new ascending and descending path of the sun required to effect the needful change of seasons, without which there would have been perpetual spring on earth with days and nights of equal length, except for those living so far north or south that they saw the sun going round all day and night level with the horizon. In those conditions the snow would not have spread so far from the north and south poles as in fact it does – into North America, *Estotiland* (686), and into South America, *Magellan* (687). When Atreus killed the two sons of Thyestes, cooked their flesh and served it at table so that Thyestes ate his own children, the sun itself turned aside in horror at the deed (687-9). Likewise the sun must have been diverted by disgust at the tasting of the forbidden fruit in Paradise. Were it not so, the inhabited world, however sinless thereafter, could not have avoided the extremes of frost and heat.

The effect of changes in the heavens is gradually felt on earth – malign influence from the stars ('sideral blast', 693), mists, and disease-ridden exhalations. Arctic winds from America and Siberia (696) bring snow and hail, northern blasts (four are named, 699-70) come tearing into woods and trees; while contrary ('adverse', 701) south winds ('*Notus* and *Afer*', 702), thunder-laden from Sierra Leone, collide with them, and cross-wise from the directions of the rising and setting sun ('*Levant*' and '*Ponent*', 704) east and west winds, south-east and south-west winds ('*Eurus* and *Zephir*', '*Sirocco* and *Libecchio*', respectively, 705-6) cut sideways into them.

Such is the beginning of the derangement ('Outrage', 707) at the inanimate level (fruit, of course, of the initial 'rage' of Satan). Among living things discord is initiated first at the subhuman ('irrational', 708) level in the form of fierce antipathies between animals, which rouse them to devour one another. Likewise animals lose respect for man, fleeing and distrusting him (contrast IV. 340–52). Adam witnesses these developing miseries outside him, and even more laments the passionate derangement within himself.

720–844 *Adam bewails his own state (–729) and that of his seed who will blame him for it (–741). After questioning the justice of what God has done (–755), he recognizes its fairness (–770) and begins to long for death (–782). Then he questions whether death will utterly destroy and whether his miseries will have an end (–816) and thinks again of his posterity, who will all share his guilt and curse him, wishing the punishment and the guilt could be all his own (–837). His thoughts lead him deeper and deeper into misery (–844).*

Adam laments the great change outside him and within him, as he now hides away from the face of God, which it was once his highest joy to look upon. Yet this is not the worst. He feels he could endure his own deserved misery, but all he begets will inherit the curse upon him. To propagate his kind will multiply execrations on his own head for having burdened his progeny with evil. So, in addition to his own miseries, all those that derive from him will flow back ('redound', 739) on him and alight heavily on him as their natural point of attraction ('center', 740). The quickly past joys of Paradise seem now to have been dearly bought at the price of lasting misery. He did not ask God to make him, and since his own will did not acquiesce ('Concurd not', 747) in his creation, it would seem appropriate to reduce him to dust again, as one ready to give back everything he was involuntarily given, conceding that the terms and conditions of a good but unrequested existence have proved too hard. Why should God have added to the loss of what was worth having (a sufficient punishment in itself) this additional punishment of continuing existence in which the loss must be mourned? God's justice seems inexplicable.

But he is too late to dispute ('contest', 756) this point. The time to reject the terms of paradisal life was when they were first put before him. He accepted them. He enjoyed the life.

He cannot now cavil at those terms. God made him without his permission. His own sons will be begotten without their permission. Suppose they too prove disobedient and, when reproved, turn round and ask him why he begot them. Would he accept that excuse for disobedience from his own offspring? Yet, he argues, it is not by his own choice ('election', 764) but by the necessity of nature, that he will beget sons, whereas God made him of his own choice: but since the reward opened up to him was of God's free giving ('grace', 767), the converse punishment is also rightly at God's disposal. Thus Adam accepts the judgement upon him as just. It is right that he should die. He would welcome death. Why does God delay it?

The argument is starting all over again, returning to the question that he has already settled once. In short, Adam, we see, is beginning to think like Satan. He is also beginning to talk like a nineteenth-century romantic bred of a naturalistic philosophy. Gladly would he lay himself down in the lap of Mother Earth. Gladly would he become one with her in insensibility, to sleep secure in her keeping. No more thundering of the divine voice in his ears: no fear of worse to come. But suppose he cannot really *die*, suppose the spirit of life within him is imperishable. May there be such a thing as a living death – a corpse in the grave but no annihilation? He consoles himself that it was not his body that sinned but that spirit within him, which must therefore be subject to the death penalty. He will die entirely. Let the doubt be resolved like that, since human knowledge cannot take him further. Quieting such doubts is easier said than done. They persist. Granted that God is infinite, is his wrath unending also? If it is, then man must be doomed to extinction. For how can God go on forever punishing man, when death must finish the matter? Could there be such a thing as deathless death – unending endurance of dying? That would be an absurd contradiction, not conceivable of God, for it would be an expression of weakness rather than of power. Might God stretch out the finite span of human life to an infinity of punishment in order to satisfy a never-satisfiable strictness

(801-4)? That would be to extend the divine judgement beyond the mortal span and thereby to break the law of nature – whereby everything else in the universe can act upon other things only within the limitations of their capacities, *not* beyond those limitations to the extent of its own capacity (804-8); i.e. you can do with a piece of wood only what wood is capable of ('according . . . to the reception of thir matter . . .', 806-7) not what *you* are capable of ('to th'extent of thir own Spheare', 808): you cannot make it breathe. And the interesting thing here is that this natural law has already been broken by Satan; for in making the serpent speak he acted to the 'extent' of his own 'sphere' of rationality and articulacy and was not bound by the 'reception' (the capacity) of the serpent (the 'matter' or object he was dealing with).

But suppose death were not one stroke, which put an end to consciousness ('Bereaving sense', 810), but everlasting misery from this day (once more an argument already closed is being re-opened, after the fashion of the satanic obsessional repetitiveness in self-centred brooding and lamentation: cf. IX. 99-178). That fear thunders back on his defenceless head. (The increasing element of self-dramatization is apparent.) Suppose both he and death are eternal, bound together – and not he as an individual, but bringing all his posterity into the same relationship with death. That is a fine legacy to hand on to his sons. If only he could waste it all himself and disinherit his sons of the legacy of guilt; then his disinherited sons would bless instead of cursing him for their inherited curse ('your Curse', 822, is double-edged: Adam is the supplier and recipient of their curse). Why should all mankind, in themselves guiltless, be condemned for the guilt of one man?* Yet what can proceed from himself, corrupt father, but corrupt sons – a family, depraved, as he is, in both mind and will, not just in individual action ('to do onely', 826), but in sharing in the willing of what he has willed (826-7)? This being the case, how can they be acquitted in

* See my *Word Unheard*, pp. 68-9, for treatment of this theme in Davies's *Nosce Teipsum* and in Eliot's *Four Quartets*.

God's eyes? After all the arguing he is compelled to absolve God of the charge of injustice. All his own fruitless attempts to argue himself out of responsibility ('my evasions vain', 829), however elaborated, lead to the conclusion that he himself is guilty (i.e. to his 'own conviction', 831). From first to last on himself singly, as the source and origin of all the corruption, all the blame quite properly falls (831–3). If only God's anger would also fall only on him! (But we have just been right through an argument that fully disposed of this wish.) It is a foolish wish. (The grounds we now hear are, admittedly, new.) The immense load is incalculably greater than he could bear, even though he shared it with 'that bad Woman', Eve. Thus, Adam tells himself in conclusion, what you desire (to bear all the guilt and punishment) and what you fear (unending punishment) both present a prospect of intolerable and unparalleled misery, comparable only with Satan's in respect of the crime and the punishment. He is thus plunged by introspection into deeper and deeper gloom.

Looking back over this remarkable speech, one should underline, not only the satanic element of obsessionally repetitive introspection and circular reasoning, but also the closeness of the argument over how God's wrath in punishment may work, whether he himself will or will not die, and whether existence is worth having, to the argument worked over several times, in a different context, by the devils in Hell (cf. II. 82–101, 142–59). The 'Mazes' (830) through which Adam's mind wanders are as vain and endless as those 'wandring mazes' (II. 561) in which the cerebrally active devils occupied themselves in Hell. The crucial difference, of course, is that all the arguing in Hell led up to a new, though indirect, assault upon God, whereas Adam's arguing leads here to acceptance of his 'own conviction' (guilt, 831), and eventually to a new approach to God in repentance.

845–1009 *Plunged in despair, Adam cries out for death* (–862). *Eve approaches him with soft words, but he repels her as the cause of his woe* (–888). *He laments the making of woman* (–895) *and the miseries she will bring on mankind* (–908). *Eve begs his forgiveness*

(–929), *admits in tears her greater share of guilt* (–940). *Adam relents* (–957). *They must comfort each other* (–965). *Eve proposes that they forestall the growth of a guilty race by forbearing to beget children* (–991), *or else commit suicide* (–1009).

Adam lies on the cold ground, in the now damp and frightening blackness of night, curses his own creation, and laments the long delay in the carrying out ('execution', 853) of the death penalty passed ('denounc't', 853) on the day of his crime. 'On the ground/Outstretcht he lay, on the cold ground' (850–1): the repeated emphasis on his reduction to the serpent's proper posture, reminds us that the tempting serpent assumed the human posture in its approach to Eve, 'not with indented wave,/Prone on the ground' (IX. 496–7). The single stroke of death would be 'thrice acceptable' (855) in that it would satisfy him by ending his misery, meet the demands of truth that one should keep one's word, and quickly fulfil the requirements of divine justice (854–7).

Eve sees his affliction, comes near, and tries to soothe his passion: but he repels her angrily. She is a serpent in falsehood and hatefulness, lacks only the outer shape of a serpent, which would express her inner deceptiveness and warn off other creatures, so that her 'too heav'nly form' (872), hiddenly devoted ('pretended', 872) to falsehood, shall not trap them. The packed summary of her crime that follows (873–88) is touched by some distortions and exaggerations that flow from his bitterness. But for her he would have continued in happiness. When it was least safe to do so, she rejected his advice out of pride and vanity. She thought herself too grand to be untrusted (876–7). She wanted to be looked at, even by the Devil, preening herself on her ability to outwit him. But when she actually met the serpent, she was completely taken in; just as he had been taken in by her, in trusting her on her own, in believing her wise and firm, in not realizing that it was all a sham – not solid quality, but a show put on by a crooked rib, bent from birth, a left-hand product of his anatomy, which should have been scrapped as superfluous.

He laments the divine lapse whereby God finally created this novelty, this beautiful blunder, instead of devising some other mode of human procreation. Not only would this present mischief have been thus prevented, but also innumerable earthly troubles to come. The troubles listed, in addition to those produced by feminine wiles, are those that spring from not being able to find the right partner and having to put up with the one that fortuitously comes your way, from making a mistaken choice, from falling in love with someone who does not want you or is not allowed to have you, or from marrying the wrong one and then meeting the right one only to discover that she has married your worst enemy. The list is a brief catalogue of matrimonial calamities familiar to all ages.

If Adam's plaint has a masculine ring heard often since the days of Eden, Eve's response is equally close to later experience. It is a touching outburst of distress. She protests her sincere love and 'reverence' for Adam. She committed her offence ignorantly ('unweeting', 916): she was taken in. She begs him not to deprive ('bereave', 918) her of what her life depends on – his sympathy, help and wise guidance in the depths of their distress. He is her only 'strength and stay' (921). (It is notable that Eve is now reversing the attitudes that led her away from Adam's side into temptation.) Bereft ('forlorn', 921) of him, where could she go, where live? So long as they live – and that may be but briefly – let the two of them live in harmony; and as they were joined together in the injury they suffered, let them join together in hostility to the serpent explicitly proclaimed their enemy (in God's judgement, x. 179–81). She begs Adam not to turn his hatred on her for their misery. She is more wretched than he. His sin was against God alone: hers was against both God and Adam (this is the counterbalance to the difference in their respective allegiances noted in the much-discussed line IV. 299). Her last cry is that she will beg Heaven to put the entire weight of punishment on herself alone, as the sole cause of Adam's woe and the just object of God's anger. (The implication would seem to be extravagant – that God's anger against Adam is less than 'just'. It does not make her humanly less lovable, of course.)

Adam is touched by her insistence on remaining at his feet ('her lowlie plight/Immoveable', 937–8: cf. 911–12) until she has wrung from him forgiveness for the fault admitted and lamented. He is disarmed by her distress, her beauty, and her dependence on him, and gently raises her. She is still too incautious, he says, too ready, as she was before, to take on more than she realizes – the burden of punishment for both of them. She must learn to bear her own first. She shows herself ill equipped to put up with God's full wrath, of which she has yet had but a slight taste, if she is so little able to endure Adam's wrath (949–52). If prayers could change God's mind, he would outpray her to have all punishment imposed ('visited', 955) on himself, and to have the weaker sex forgiven, for she was entrusted to his keeping yet he allowed her to be unguarded (952–7). Let her rise; let them put an end to rivalling or blaming each other, but do their best, in dutiful acts ('offices', 960) of love to lighten each other's sad burden, since it appears that the death penalty is not going to be carried out suddenly but in a slow process, dragged out to increase their pain and that of their descendants.

Eve replies. She knows by sad experience ('experiment', 967) how little weight her words must carry with him, since they have proved untrue and led to unfortunate consequences ('event', 969) in the past. Nevertheless, however despicable, she has been accepted again by Adam, hopes to regain his love, and will not conceal her thoughts about how to gain relief in their extremity ('of our extremes', 976) or end their misery in a way that would be 'sharp and sad' (977) but endurable in a plight as evil as theirs (978). If concern for their descendants ('care of our descent', 979), subject now to woe and death, is the main worry, it lies in Adam's power to forestall the breeding of an unhappy race before conception. Let him remain childless: then Death will be deprived of his feast ('glut', 990) and will have to be satisfied with the two of them. If on the other hand he thinks it too hard to abstain from coition, and languish with hopeless desire in the presence of the object of his desire (996), who would herself be in the same tormenting predicament, then they could free both themselves and their descendants immediately from what they fear by committing suicide. Why should they tremble any longer in helpless fears that promise nothing but death, when they are in a position to choose the quickest way to death. This would be to destroy destruction with destruction.

Eve's proposal to abstain from breeding is offensive to the feminine principle of fertility as Adam's first reactions were offensive to reason. If Adam's tangled arguments (720–824) showed us the human intellect corrupted, Eve's proposal threatens us with the corruption of natural human fruitfulness. The Good of the human Intellect and the Good of the human Body are both being eroded. Adam's cerebral masturbation led to the same cul-de-sac, frustration and death, at the intellectual level, as Eve's proposal for physical sterility would lead to by the route of desire and emotion taunted and denied. The endless self-centred, intellectual self-abuse, which left Adam stretched out on the cold ground, cursing his creation (850–4), is balanced by Eve's notion of natural physical faculties endlessly teased and denied fulfilment. Eve's plan amounts to a second disobedience, since they live under the divine command to increase and multiply (x. 730). Of God's two injunctions, the positive and the negative, they have already broken the latter. Eve's proposal is that they should get out of their predicament by breaking the former, too. The alternative proposal, to commit suicide, is the logical conclusion of the sequence. Endless frustration and sterility is the negation of life. The fruit of feeding on the forbidden fruit is ultimately total fruitlessness.

Two crucial correspondences must be noted. Eve's proposal, like Adam's reasoning, is closely in line with the state of mind revealed by the devils in the debate in Hell in Book II. It reflects the identical tendency towards discreation. Its way and its end are destruction (see pp. 49–50).

Again, Eve's proposal to defeat death by dying, to destroy destruction by self-destruction, is a parodic perversion of the Son's readiness to defeat death by dying (see p. 272). If the Son takes up the Father's plan to destroy destruction by a voluntary acceptance of self-destruction, Eve lays before Adam a blasphemous burlesque of the redemptive pattern. The divine purpose is to save free human beings from subjection to sin and death. Though Eve's purpose has its altruistic aspect, the end is the abolition of free existence. *I* will voluntarily accept death, says the Son. *They* shall involuntarily have no life, says Eve.

1010–1104 *Adam points out the flaws in Eve's arguments (–1028) and rejects her proposals (–1046). God has not been harsh in judging them (–1059). He may help them to make their lot tolerable if they pray to him in penitence (–1096). Whereupon they fall down in penitent prayer (–1104).*

Adam corrects Eve's reasoning. The readiness to surrender life and pleasure *seems* to suggest that there is in her a superiority to what she is devaluing; but in fact her motives for self-destruction disprove her superiority: they reveal, not a real disregard for life and pleasure, but an excessive attachment to them and painful remorse at their loss. If she seeks death as an end to misery, hoping to evade full punishment by that means, no doubt God is far too wise to be forestalled like that. They cannot snatch death so as to get out of the penalty they are due to pay. Any such act of obstinate resistance would provoke God to make death, not a conclusion, but a continuing thing in their lives. (Belial went over this argumentative ground, II. 155–9, in reply to Moloch's suggestion that self-provoked extinction might be better than continuation of present misery, II. 85–98. As the hellish and the diabolical are the decisive perversions of the heavenly and the divine, the earthly and the human have it in their power to image the one or to be eroded by the other.)

Adam is now asserting himself in the firm rational leadership which it is proper for him to exercise. Of course it was Eve's genuine display of affection that restored him from despair (x. 909 ff.). There is no all-round superiority in Adam. The warmth and sympathy she brought him plays no lesser part in the movement towards repentance than does his own rational thought. Indeed his intellect is restored to healthy reasoning by her love. That said, the dominance of his thinking is her only sure support. Thus he recalls the prophecy that Eve's progeny shall bruise the serpent's head (x. 179–81). A poor consolation this, unless, as he assumes, it applies to Satan, who deceived them. If they either die, or refuse to breed, there would be no due revenge on Satan, their deceiver. Their enemy would escape his punishment, and they would double their own instead. There must be no more talk of violence against themselves, or of wilful barrenness, which smacks of rancour and pride, unreadiness to suffer, and stubbornness against God.

Adam recalls God's mildness in judging them, when they were expecting immediate extinction. Instead, Eve's burden of pain in labour will be immediately compensated for by joy in the new-born child. The phrase 'Fruit of thy Womb' (1053) is used so often of Christ and the Virgin Mary that its special relevance to the prophesied bruising of the Serpent's head must be noted. The new Adam, in whom all shall be saved, will be born of the new Eve (cf. XI. 158). And the new Eve, the Virgin Mary, will be of that progeny of the old Adam and Eve, which would never exist were the fruitfulness of the old Eve to be frustrated. The word 'Fruit', which has had its own epic career, rich in changes, contrasts, and manifold correspondences, since it was launched in the first line of *Paradise Lost*, here perhaps reaches its fullest fruitfulness in the foretaste of the Incarnation.

As for the curse on himself, that glanced off him on to the ground, as the penalty of Eve glanced off her on to the serpent. He must earn his bread with labour, and there is no harm in that. Moreover God has already shown his 'timely care' and pity by clothing them, unasked. ('Cloath'd ... How much more ...', 1059–60: see Luke XII. 28 – 'How much more will he clothe you.' This takes us forward again to the Incarnate Christ and his representation of the continuing 'timely care', 1057. The lines hereabouts are rich in biblical echoes.) If they pray, he will further teach them how to cope with the climate, now deteriorating about them. The keen winds are scattering ('shattering', 1066) the 'graceful locks' of the trees in the garden, as Eve's tresses were first 'discompos'd' (v. 10) during the dream induced by Satan, and more recently 'all disorderd' (x. 911) in her lowly plight at Adam's feet. They need some better shelter ('shroud', 1068) before the sun ('diurnal Starr', 1069) sets. They must learn how to gather its reflected beams and keep alive their warmth in dry material (1070-1), or else how to rub two substances together to produce such friction of the air that the grinding sets it alight (1072-3) in the same way as the clouds are jostled together by colliding winds till they kindle ('Tine', 1075 – *tind*) zig-zag lightning, whose cross-flame sets fire to the gummy bark of trees, and they send out a comforting heat, which could make up for the lack of ('supply', 1078) sun. Adam trusts now that God will aid them with remedies for evils which they have brought upon themselves, if they pray and beseech him to do so 'of Grace' (1081), that is, of his own good favour, and not because they deserve to have their prayers heard. In this way they may hope to pass their lives bearably ('commodiously', 1083). Going back ('Repairing', 1087) to the place where God judged them, they must 'confess/Humbly' their faults, water the ground with their tears, filling ('frequenting', 1091) the air with their sighs in token of their genuine sorrow and humiliation (the involvement of the offended earth and air in this their contrition is significant). Undoubtedly God will then relent and turn from his displeasure: for grace and mercy shone in his tranquil look when he seemed most angry and severe. Adam has caught more than a glimpse of the divine love behind the judgement and is rebuilding his faith upon it. So the two of them, repairing to the place where he judged them, fall, not now into disobedience, but flat on their faces to confess humbly their fault, and to beg forgiveness with contrite hearts. (Their repairing fall is voluntary. Satan fell flat on his belly involuntarily: cf. x. 1099 with x. 513.)

Book XI

1–133 The prayers of Adam and Eve, inspired by Heaven, are heard in Heaven (–20), where the Son intercedes with the Father for them (–44). The Father accepts that, though man must leave Paradise, death shall be his way to new life, not his end (–71). The angels are summoned (–83) and God tells them of man's penitence (–98). He commands Michael to go and dismiss them from the Garden, but to comfort them with a prophecy of the future (–125). Michael and the cherubim set out (–133).

Adam and Eve remain in penitent prayer. The use of the phrase 'lowliest plight' (cf. 'lowlie plight' – grovelling position, x. 937) in the first line makes it certain that 'stood' (1) must mean *remained* where they 'prostrate fell' (x. 1099) at the end of the last book. It is the 'Prevenient Grace' (3) of God, guiding and strengthening them in advance of their own decisions, that has removed the hardness of their hearts (cf. Ezekiel xi. 19) and made 'new flesh/Regenerate' (4–5) grow there instead. Thus the flesh corrupted deathwardly to discreation is reborn to new creation in a miniature microcosmic anticipation of what the human race will experience through the Son's future incarnation. Divine grace can be *prevenient* (anticipatory) in more ways than one. The divine spirit makes their sighs articulate (though they are 'mute', see 31 – serpentine word; cf. ix. 748 and x. 18) as it turned the devils' articulation into involuntary hisses (x. 517–18). Their status ('port', 8) is not insignificant, for they are the representatives of the whole human race, whose future existence depends on them, as it depended on *Deucalion* and *Pyrrha* (12), only survivors of the Deluge with which Jupiter flooded the earth in his wrath at human impiety. They consulted the oracle of *Themis* (14) about how to repair the loss of mankind. The prayers of Adam and Eve (uncluttered by the religious paraphernalia which gets blown into Limbo by cross-winds, iii. 489–93), are not blown erratically and vainly off course: being pure of form or verbiage in spiritual nakedness ('Dimentionless', 17), they pass into Heaven and *there* are clothed in incense, to be offered up by the one interceding divine Priest at the smoking altar before the Father's throne. These prayers are the 'first fruits' of the grace that God has 'implanted' (23) in Man (he 'supplanted' the Devil, x. 513), sweeter smelling fruits (the word is repeated, 26) than any that man's own tending ('manuring', 28) could have brought forth in Paradise. The Son will give voice and articulation to man's wordless ('mute', 31; cf. 'Unutterable', 6, and 'Dimentionless', 17) prayer. He will express man's meaning ('Interpret', 33); he will be man's word as he is the Father's Word. He will be man's spokesman and means of conciliation, the 'Advocate/And propitiation' (33-4) of 1 John II. 1 and 2. For this purpose all man's deeds, good or bad, must be grafted into the Son's own self (the metaphorical sequence from gardening is maintained from line 22). The Son's own merit shall bring man's good deeds to completeness and fulfilment before the Father; the Son's death shall pay for his evil deeds, curing the inevitable death-wardness of corruption by realizing it, living it (which means dying it), so that *that*, too, has reached its perverse completeness and fulfilment and, death having died (in the way that Eve's parody vainly tried to mimic, x. 989–1006), death-free life can be restored to man. The full implicit argument is here briefly summed up (34–6). The Son begs that his priestly self-sacrificial offering (cf. 18 and 25) be accepted (37) to the reconciliation of man. The Son is not seeking the removal of the death penalty, a judgement (40) he wishes to see mitigated (cf. x. 76), not reversed. He wants man to die the death along with himself, whose dying will be the death of death. Thus man's days on earth will be 'sad' but numbered (40), and their end a new life of joy in union with the Son, who lives in union with the Father.

It would be misleading to say that the Father relents. There is no divine change of mind. We are above the sphere of change or decay. The Father, tranquil, 'serene' (45) now as the Son was in passing judgement on man (x. 1094), speaks for once with no cloud to veil him. Everything the Son has asked is his own 'Decree' (47). But man cannot stay in Paradise. His corrupted nature is a fact now: what is immortally pure and untaintable cannot assimilate what is soiled by any admixture of pollution. Man was endowed with happiness and immortality at his creation. He has foolishly ('fondly', 59) lost happiness. And, happiness once lost, immortality would be a burden, for it would serve but to make woe everlasting. Death is therefore man's 'final remedie': after the trials and tribulations of life, which will sharpen man's faith and discipline him in good works, death will hand him over at the re-awakening of just men and their restoration in the new Heaven and new Earth (prophesied in III. 333–5). The Son is bidden to call the angels to council, so that they can learn of God's dealings with man as they did of his dealings with the sinful ('peccant', 70) angels. The Son gives the signal. The trumpet sounds, the trumpet heard once since, perhaps, at the giving of the law to Moses (cf. I. 7), and to be heard again perhaps at the day of judgement. The Sons of Light come from bowers of '*Amarantin* Shade' (78; cf. III. 352; and see pp. 81–2) and from round about the 'waters of life' (79; cf. III.357, the 'Fount of Life') and take their seats before the throne.

God tells his 'Sons', the angels, how man has come to know good and evil since tasting of the forbidden ('defended', 86) fruit. He is now repenting and praying in contrition: this is the effect of impulses I have stirred in him, God says. When such impulses are no longer stirred by me and he is left to his own resources, I know how changeable and shallow his nature is. To make sure therefore that he does not eat now of the Tree of Life and thereby obtain an immortality of corruptedness, even if only subjective ('dream at least', 95), I decree his removal from the Garden. (Since death, we now know, though a penalty in man's eyes, has been turned into his 'final remedie' in God's eyes, 61 ff., eating of the Tree of Life in this condition would be to frustrate the cure and perpetuate the disease.)

Therefore God commands Michael to take chosen

cherubim, for fear Satan raises new trouble either on man's behalf or in the hope of occupying vacated territory (102–3), to drive out sinful Adam and Eve without compunction ('remorse', 105), and to pronounce perpetual banishment on them and their descendants. Adam and Eve might be overcome if the sentence were pronounced with vehemence, so Michael is to make no show of terror, but rather, if they obey the command with resignation, to comfort them. He shall reveal the future to them as God himself will make it known, including how a new Covenant between God and man will be established in Eve's own lineage. Thus the pair shall be sent out in sorrow but in peace. An angelic guard shall be placed on the Garden to keep foul spirits out.

Michael sets out with a bright cohort of watchful cherubim; the *verbatim* echo 'four faces each' (128) takes us back to VI. 753, and the more extended account of the Son's setting out to battle (see p. 166). As two-faced *Janus* (129) was the god and guardian of doors and gates, and the hundred-eyed *Argus* (some eyes slept while the others kept awake) was set by Hera to keep watch over Io, the combined associations of watch and ward are very appropriate. The cherubic eyes are 'more wakeful' (131) than those of *Argus* who was sent drowsily to sleep, charmed by the lyre of *Hermes* (133) or by his notorious wand ('opiate Rod', 133), which was fitly entwined with serpents.

133–292 *It is next morning* (–140). *Adam tells how he has been comforted through prayer* (–161). *Humbled and chastened, Eve proposes that they go to work* (–180). *There are signs of hostility among birds and animals* (–192). *Adam reads the signs as warnings* (–207). *Michael and the angels alight* (–225). *Adam sees Michael coming and tells Eve to withdraw* (–250). *Michael announces the postponement of death and their banishment from the Garden* (–262). *Adam is struck with horror. Eve has overheard* (–267) *and laments that she must leave* (–285). *Michael recommends patience* (–292).

Next morning, after a night spent in prayer (cf. 173), Adam and Eve find themselves strengthened and consoled. Adam thinks it not easy to believe that anything they say should be important ('prevalent', 144) enough to be worth attention or response from God; yet in fact human prayer does have this effect. Praying humbly, he was aware of God's gentle and friendly ('placable', 151) interest. This brought him inner peace and a reminder of the promise that Eve's descendants will 'bruise' (155) their enemy, Satan (x. 179–81). When the promise was made, he had not given it much attention ('not minded', 156), such was their dismay at the time: but now it reassures him with the knowledge that they are to live. Thus he hails the Old Eve, 'Mother of all Mankind', from whose seed will spring the New Eve, the Virgin Mary, who will be hailed at the Annunciation as the Mother of him by whom correspondingly 'Man is to live' (161: see x. 1053, 'Fruit of thy Womb', and the comment on p. 269).

Eve is self-reproachful. She feels unworthy of the high title, and of God's mercy in gracing her with the gift of being the source of human life, when she is really the bringer of death. She is grateful for Adam's pardon, too. Meantime the dawn promises a good day: Eve promises always hereafter to be at Adam's side; and proposes that they go back to their work in contentment.

It is not quite so simple as that. The new humble Eve has spoken, but fate does not sign on the dotted line ('Subscrib'd not', 182). The sky is suddenly darkened. Nearby an eagle ('Bird of *Jove*', 185) swoops down ('stoopt', 185 – the word is so used in falconry) in pursuit of two colourful birds, and a lion pursues a hart and hind (cf. the *drooping* and *stooping* here, of morn and eagle, 178 and 185, with the 'stooping' and 'drooping' of Eve and flower, ix. 427 and 430; and see p. 220). Adam reads these 'mute signs' (194) in Nature as portents ('Forerunners', 195) of God's purpose, or perhaps as warnings to them not to feel too sure ('secure', 196) of their exemption from the death penalty because of their temporary reprieve. Who can say for how long the penalty will be postponed and what kind of life they are to live meanwhile? What do they know except that they are dust and must return to the dust? What else can be the meaning of the double hunt through the air and on the earth, while the dawning eastern sky is darkened and a white morning radiance is shining over the blue sky from behind a descending cloud in the west?

The angelic troop alights now in Paradise and halts ('made alt', 210) on a hill. Doubt and human fear dim Adam's eyes to the full splendour of their glory. It matches the glory of the double angel host that Jacob met encamped before him in the place he called *Mahanaim* (214: see Genesis XXXII. 2), and the glory of that mountain in *Dothan* (217), which was 'full of horses and chariots of fire round about Elisha' (2 Kings, VI. 17), divinely defending him from the encompassing forces of the king of Syria. Michael leaves the bright troop to stand in occupancy of the Garden while he goes to find where Adam has withdrawn ('shelterd', 223). Adam foresees an important communication as he recognizes the authority of the approaching visitor in the aura of majesty wrapped around him. The angel is neither so awesome in appearance as to frighten him, nor so amiably placid (like Raphael) as to make him feel at ease. He is a dignified and lofty ('solemn and sublime', 236) figure: Adam must confront him reverently and bids Eve withdraw.

Michael draws near, not in 'shape Celestial' (239) but as man to meet man, wearing a vividly coloured tunic over his armour (*Meliboea*, in Thessaly, and *Sarra*, the city of Tyre in Phoenicia, were both famous for their purple dyes, 242–3). Important correspondences with Raphael's full celestial splendour in his first approach to Adam should be noted (cf. V. 266 ff.), especially since we recall that the sign portending Michael's visitation was the pursuit of two birds by the eagle stooping from his tower (184), while Raphael on his approach 'within soare/Of Towring Eagles, to all the Fowles' seemed 'A *Phoenix*, gaz'd by all . . .' (V. 270–2). Michael is man and warrior in his prime, the sword at his side with which he wounded Satan in the war in Heaven (VI. 250–3, 320–7). He does not unbend. He comes to the point quickly. Adam's prayers have been heard. Death is to be denied his prey ('Defeated of his seisure', 254) while time is allowed for Adam to repent and cover his one bad deed with many good ones. It may well be, then, that God will fully ransom him from the claim of death upon him. But he may not remain longer in Paradise. Michael has come to send him 'from the Garden forth to till/The ground whence thou wast tak'n, fitter Soile' (261–2: the couplet repeats God's decree *verbatim*, 97–8). A freezing spasm ('gripe', 264) of sorrow paralyses Adam. Eve has overheard: she bursts out audibly, revealing ('Discover'd', 267) where she is withdrawn, lamenting the unexpected banishment as worse than death. She had hoped to spend the time of reprieval ('respit of that day', 272) among the familiar flowers she has daily watched over, tended and named. Who will now cultivate them, place them and water them? And lastly how can she part from her nuptial bower (to which the key word 'adorn'd', 280, once more adds overtones of the heavenly city's earthly image and the heavenly bride's earthly reflection: see p. 258). Michael is firm but gentle in his reply. She must in patience give up what she has justly forfeited: and not, in excessive attachment, set her heart on what is not her own. Her husband is going with her. His home is her home.

293–428 *Adam expresses his sorrowful submission (–314) and his especial regret at leaving the place where he has conversed with God (–333). Michael assures him that God is everywhere present and watchful over his creatures (–354). He will now reveal to Adam a vision of the future while Eve sleeps (–369). Michael and Adam ascend a hill (–384) from which the future kingdoms of the world may be surveyed (–411), and Michael opens his eyes to a vision of the future (–428).*

Adam thanks Michael for announcing gently a punishment that might otherwise have been hurtful to hear and fatal to suffer. He finds banishment painful because of the familiarity of Paradise, but he now humbly submits to God's command. His greatest grief is to be deprived of the sight of God's face (his 'blessed count'nance', 317), to leave the paradisal 'Mount' (320), 'Pines' (321) and 'Fountain' (322), which hold his earthly memories of converse with God. (They image the 'sacred Mount' and 'living Fountain' of Heaven itself.) They would be the fittest place to build altars and offer up the odours of worship. In the world outside the Garden, where can he hope to glimpse the brightness of God's presence or the track of his footprint?

Michael assures Adam that God's presence fills the whole earth: all living things are cherished ('Fomented', 338) and warmed by the divine inner efficacy ('virtual power', 338). God gave Adam lordship over the whole earth: the gift is not to be undervalued, and Adam must not assume that God's presence is limited to the bounds of Paradise. Had there been no Fall, Paradise might have been Adam's sovereign metropolis and home ('Capital Seate', 343) from where all his progeny would have spread over the earth, and to which they would have returned to do homage to their great forefather. But Adam's pre-eminence over the human race has been forfeited. Nevertheless he will find signs of God's presence and loving kindness watching over him everywhere: and to strengthen Adam's faith, before he leaves the Garden, Michael will reveal to him what the future holds for the human family. He must expect to learn how supernatural grace will compete with human sinfulness, and will thereby acquire patience and the capacity to respond with moderated joy and sorrow to the blend of prosperity and adversity that will be the human lot. Such is the surest recipe for living and the best preparation for death. Michael bids Adam ascend the hill of revelation, while Eve sleeps. Adam slept while Eve was brought to life: it is fitting that she shall sleep while he is wakened to understanding of the future (and the coming birth of the new Adam).

Adam gratefully and humbly submits to Michael's guidance, promising to arm his breast with fortitude to confront whatever evils he must suffer. 'In the Visions of God' (377 – a formula to mark the opening of the prophetic passage; cf. Ezekiel XL. 2) the two of them ascend a hill from whose summit the kingdoms of the world can be surveyed. The vast prospect opened to view takes in cities and territories reaching from Mongolian China (388), Samarkand, Pekin

('*Paquin*', 390), India (391) and the East Indies (392) to Russia, Persia and Turkey (393–6); likewise from Abyssinia (397–8), East Africa (400), West Africa (401–2) and Barbary (403–4) to Europe. Such is the sweeping view of the 'Hemisphere of Earth' (379) that the hill of Paradise commands. The poet adds that 'in Spirit' (406) perhaps Adam can also see what lies on the opposite invisible hemisphere on the continent of America (406–11). Michael gives Adam's eyes a threefold treatment in preparation for the coming revelation, first removing the 'Filme' (412) produced by eating the forbidden fruit, then cleansing them with the herbs 'Euphrasie and Rue' (414), and lastly putting in three drops from the 'Well of Life' (416). This infusion penetrates to the innermost centre of intellectual vision (the eyes of the mind referred to in III. 52–3), so that Adam is overpowered by their potency and closes his eyes in a trance. Michael gently raises him and bids him open his eyes to see some of the effects of his original sinfulness that are to be involuntarily inherited by his successors. (A systematic survey of the way the forthcoming sequence of visions is organized is made at the beginning of the commentary on Book XII, when the reader is in a position to look back and see more clearly the shaping of the prophetic episode as a whole, for it extends from XI. 376 to XII. 605: see p. 288.)

429–555 *Adam sees Cain murder Abel (–449) and asks the meaning of it (–452). Michael explains (–460) and Adam laments (–465). Michael tells of death in other forms (–477) and shows disease and death due to intemperance (–495). Adam weeps (–499) and laments man's lot (–514). Michael blames man's intemperance (–525) and Adam asks how such disease can be avoided (–529). Michael advises self-control (–546). Adam acquiesces (–552). Michael introduces another vision (–555).*

Adam sees enacted the murder of Abel (Adam and Eve's second son) by Cain (their first son) as recorded in Genesis IV. 1–15. There is the tilled land ('tilth', 430) of Cain, the 'tiller of the ground' (Genesis IV. 2) and the 'sheep-walks' (431) of Abel, the 'keeper of sheep' (Genesis IV. 2) on either

side of an altar made of grassy sward ('sord', 433). Cain
brings as his offering to God a sheaf of corn picked up
haphazardly ('Uncull'd, as came to hand', 436) whereas Abel,
more 'meek' (437) than his brother, brings the 'choicest and
best' (438) of the firstlings of his flock as an offering, taking
pains over the sacrificial rites. There is a favourable ('propitious', 441) answer from heaven as a quick flash ('nimble
glance', 442) of fire consumes the lamb. Cain rages with envy
at the 'grateful' (442) divine recognition of Abel's sincere
offering and beats out his brother's life with a stone. Adam
wants to know why, and Michael explains that the motive is
envy, and also that the deed ('Fact', 457) will be avenged.

Michael now provides a counterbalance to this illustration
of murderous death due to envy, anger, and injustice, with
a vision of the forms of disease and death brought about by
the fleshly intemperance that Eve's failure to control her
appetite ('inabstinence', 476) has introduced into the human
blood-stream. Hence we see a place like a leper-house
('Lazar-house', 479) in which diseased creatures writhe in
agony and cry out for death. Death, thus 'oft invok't' (492),
delays his stroke. In shape 'deform' (494), as he was seen at
first encounter (II. 706), Death, now 'triumphant' (491),
shakes the dart that shook first in Satan's face (II. 672, 702,
786). Adam, though 'not of Woman born' (496 – echo of
Macbeth, of course) cannot but weep and ask whether it
would not be better not to live. Such is the effect on him of
seeing man, created once in the image of God, 'so goodly
and erect' (509: the adjectives take us back to our first sight
of unfallen Adam and Eve, IV. 288–9, 323), debased by
deformity. Michael points out that the men themselves have
degraded ('villifi'd', 516) their maker's image by becoming
slaves to their appetites. A man takes upon himself the
Image of the divinity or idol he serves. If his vice is a bestial
('brutish', 518) one, the adopted image will be an 'abject'
(520) one – as opposed to an *erect* one. That sensual indulgence is derivative ('Inductive', 519) chiefly from Eve's sin is
obvious. Disfigurement of the human body by self-indulgence
is a self-chosen disfigurement, and Michael stresses that

it is the result of man's failure to reverence God's image 'in themselves' (525), not simply an offence against some objective rule. Adam accepts this but naturally wants to know whether there are less unpleasant ways of dying.

Michael concedes that a temperate life may conclude in a peaceful and easy death, but even so the weaknesses of old age must be faced, when the senses will be blunted ('Obtuse', 541), the spirits dampened and depressed. Adam accepts, and Michael reiterates, that man must be neither over-attached to life nor eager for death.

556–636 *Adam sees groups of Cain's descendants (573), then a tribe descended from his son Seth (–580). Women join them and they revel in music and dance and love (–597). Adam is favourably impressed (–602), but Michael explains that the women are sensual descendants of Cain and the men are corrupted by them (–627). Adam is inclined to blame the women but Michael corrects him (–636).*

The first vision of descendants here bears reference to Genesis IV. 19–22. Lamech, a descendant of Cain, married two wives. The one, Adah, bore Jabal, 'the father of such as dwell in tents' (Genesis IV. 20), and Jubal, 'the father of all such as handle the harp and organ' (Genesis IV. 21). The other wife, Zillah, bore Tubal-cain, 'an instructor of every artificer in brass and iron' (Genesis IV. 22). Hence Milton's threefold picture here of the herdsmen (557–8), the musicians (558–63), and the metal-workers (564–73). The flying ('volant', 561) touch of the organist as he follows through the contrapuntal intercrossing of parts in the rich texture of the fugue is expertly defined. The foundryman's clods of iron and brass come perhaps from the mouth of a cave after a fortuitous fire has burned a wood and penetrated the ground sufficiently to melt the buried ore and bring it to light, or perhaps from some stream which has washed the soil away and thus disinterred it. The ore is melted, drained into moulds, and made into tools and other things able to be cast ('Fusil', 573) or graven.

In the Bible, after the death of Abel, Adam and Eve beget

Seth in his place (Genesis IV. 25). It is the descendants of
Seth who seem to be just, and bent on the due worship of
God (576–8), and who live in freedom and peace. But when
they come down from the hills to dwell in tents on the
plain, they encounter women of rich attire, 'wanton dress'
(583), who sing and dance amorously and catch the eyes of
the grave men from the hills: this seems to be Milton's ex-
pansion of the terse biblical record that 'the sons of God saw
the daughters of men that they were fair; and they took them
wives of all which they chose' (Genesis VI. 2). Marriage,
feasting and music follow, 'all in heat' (589). Adam rejoices
in this vision of peaceful delights, in which Nature 'seems
fulfilled in all her ends' (602); but Michael corrects him.
Judgements must not be made on the basis either of what is
pleasurable or what seems to be in accordance with 'Nature'
(604). Man is created to a nobler purpose than conformity
with Nature – to a 'conformitie divine' (606). The tents of
the vision (that is, of 557 ff.) were tents of wickedness, and
though their inhabitants seemed zealous in pursuit (i.e.
'studious', 609) of the civilized arts (the music and the
metal-work of 559–73), they did not acknowledge their in-
ventive skills as the gifts of God. 'Unmindful' of their
Maker, they established a secular civilization. (We recall that
the devils in Hell indulged in closely comparable foundry-
work and craftsmanship: cf. XI. 558–73 with I. 700–19.) They
were the descendants of Cain: they bred 'beauteous offspring' (613), the troop of seeming 'Goddesses so blithe, so
smooth, so gay' (615: the word 'blithe' smacks of their
questionable spiritual ancestry: cf. IX. 625) described in
582–3. These fair women, empty of all 'domestic' (617) good,
were brought up only to answer lusting appetites with song
and dance, rolling tongue and rolling eye. The sober-minded
descendants of Seth (first described in 576–80), whose religious lives justly entitle them to be named 'Sons of God' (as
in Genesis VI. 2) – for indeed as Adam was made 'in the
likeness of God' (Genesis V. 1) so he begat Seth 'in his own
likeness, after his image' (Genesis V. 3) – are ensnared by the
wiles ('traines', 624) and smiles of the 'fair Atheists' (625).

Now these hedonists 'swim in joy' (625) and laughter: before long they will pay the price, weeping a world of tears.

Adam laments that men who have begun by living so well should be led astray into wrong ('indirect', 631) ways, and notes that the pattern of man's misery tends to be constant in being initiated by woman. Michael quickly disabuses him. Man's misery derives from his 'effeminate slackness' (634) in not firmly sustaining the masculine prerogative of superior wisdom.

637-711 *Adam sees a vision of war (–659) and political conflict (–673), and asks its meaning (–682). Michael explains that there will be ages in which might will be right (–699) and the lonely man of righteousness will be hated of men – but protected by God (–711).*

The close connection with the Old Testament continues (cf. 664–71 and 705–9 with the record of Enoch in Genesis v). Connections with Classical epic hereabouts are equally notable: the sequence of prophetic pictures in this section has often been compared to the descriptions of the figured shields of Achilles and Aeneas in Homer (*Iliad* XVIII) and Virgil (*Aeneid* VIII). Memories of the Civil War (cf. 652–6) and of the political struggles and crises involved in it (cf. 661–73) obviously linger in Milton's mind, as so often in *Paradise Lost*. But the dominating significance lies in the universalized structuring of matter and message, narrative event and moral theme. The rich idiomatic variation is such that the imagination may lightly touch the Old Testament world, the medieval-Spenserian world, the Virgilian–Homeric world, the contemporary world, all within a few lines (642–5, for instance); but underlying this allusive multifariousness is a controlled articulation of thought, deep and comprehensive enough to match the moment and the mood of readers in all ages.

Thus Adam looks on a panoramic sequence of towered cities, mighty men of warlike prowess ('emprise', 642), moving cavalry and infantry, of fruitful countryside given over to slaughter and of towns brutally besieged. Elsewhere he sees warriors and statesmen in factious consultation, unable to agree until a man of wisdom brings the words of morality, religion and truth to bear upon the situation. Then at last there seems to be something like unity among the others for he is hissed ('Exploded', 669) by young and old alike, and saved from their violent hatred only by being snatched up to heaven by a descending cloud. Adam laments the ten thousand-fold multiplication in war of the original murder committed by Cain (675–9) and asks who is the 'Just Man' (681) rescued by Heaven.

Michael explains that the warring people are bred of the ill-matched marriages described in lines 585–92, which he has already condemned (621–7). The good and the bad were partnered in spite of their mutual natural antipathy (685–6). The effect of such heedless mixing is to produce creatures physically and mentally unnatural ('prodigious', 687). Hence these 'Giants' (688: the word derives from Genesis VI. 4: cf. 642), renowned at a time when only brute force is admired and the greatest slaughterers and destroyers are hailed as the greatest of men. Such will be the way to earthly fame while what most deserves fame will remain hidden in obscurity. But the sole righteous man, hated by all for uttering the truth, is Enoch, the 'seventh from Adam' (Jude 14: 700). The more fully developed picture given here of his direct translation to heaven (705–6) decisively recalls Elijah's, however (2 Kings II. 11). Such is the reward of the good. As for the evil, the next vision will reveal what awaits them.

712–901 *Adam sees a vision of Noah; his vain prophecies (–727), the building and peopling of the ark (–737), and the Flood (–753). Adam is stricken with grief (–762), regrets his forevision of what is to come (–776), and asks whether his race will end thus (–786). Michael explains how peace brings its evils as well as war, evils of degeneracy (–807), which the lonely prophet will condemn unheeded (–816). Noah, however, will be saved in the ark (–839). Adam sees the Flood abate, the ark grounded and the land reappearing (–869). He rejoices and asks the meaning of the rainbow (–883). Michael tells of God's promise not to destroy mankind (–901).*

Adam sees a quite different scene. The 'brazen Throat of Warr' has 'ceast to roar' (713): the image is of seventeenth-century cannon. The strife is followed by scenes of sport, lust ('luxurie', 715) and promiscuous casual fornication. A venerable prophet comes where people gather to preach 'Conversion and Repentance' (724) as if to souls under threat of judgement. He is ignored. Whereupon he withdraws; builds the ark, provisions it, and admits one male and female of every beast and bird, all as described in Genesis VI. 14–22. Lastly he takes in his three sons and their wives. Meanwhile clouds gather and to their assistance ('supplie', 740) the hills send up dark ('dusk', 741) and humid mists and vapours. The downpour comes. Only the ark floats. All else is submerged. Howling sea monsters inhabit the palaces where lust so recently reigned. At this moment of crisis for the human race, the voice of the poet himself intervenes to bewail the grief of Adam for his lost children (754–6). Another flood, a flood of tears sinks him, so that Michael has to raise him again to his feet.

Adam now wishes he had remained ignorant of the future, bearing only his own share ('part', 765) of evil. The evils he has seen distributed ('dispenst', 766) are in fact evils spread over many ages, but they here fall all at once on his shoulders, brought to premature ('Abortive', 769) birth by his forevision, to torment him before they have actually occurred with the realization that they must come to be. Henceforward no man should seek to know what the future has in store for him or his children. It will be evil. His fore-knowledge of it will not enable him to forestall it (773) and he will find it just as hard to bear in mental anticipation ('apprehension', 775) as it will later prove in practice ('in substance', 775). But it is too late now to think of warning the human race: that worry ('care', 776) is past, for there is no longer any human race to warn. He had hoped for peace and happiness on earth after war and violence. How is it that peace corrupts, as war destroys?

Michael explains. The great conquerors in war, having achieved fame and wealth, become victims of pleasure, self-indulgence and factious hostilities in peace (787–96). The conquered lose with their freedom both their valour and their fear of God, whom their insincere piety called on vainly during their struggle. Having lost their fervour, they try to make themselves as comfortable as possible under their conquerors on whatever is left over for them; and nature provides more than enough so that human self-control can be tested. So everyone degenerates, except the one just man who shines in the dark age, in his goodness opposed to all precedent around him ('against example good', 809), singly taking his stand ('Offended', 811) against all the world does to entice and habituate men to evil (810). Fearless of hostility, he will denounce wickedness and prophesy divine wrath. He will be derided of men, but observed of God.

This generalized picture of the lonely prophet, known in all ages, once more assumes the specific persona of Noah, as he executes God's command to build the ark and rescue the living nucleus from the world doomed ('devote', 821) to total wreckage ('rack', 821). No sooner, says Michael, will he be lodged in the ark with the men and animals picked out ('select', 823) for survival, than the rain will pour and the floods rise till even the 'Mount/Of Paradise' (829–30) is carried away by the forking ('horned', 831) torrents, to take root later as a bare island in the Persian Gulf, haunted by whales ('Orcs', 835) and gulls ('sea-mews', 835).

Adam sees the ark float ('hull', 840) on the flood, then the flight of the clouds before the dry north wind, the coming of the hot sun, the steadying of currents and the ebbing of waters. The ark is grounded on a mountain, the hilltops appear, a raven is dispatched from the ark, then a dove, which returns with an olive leaf. Noah and his company descend on to dry land, the three-striped ('listed', 866) rainbow appears (red, yellow and blue). Like Noah, Adam rejoices. He now finds less to lament in the loss of the numerous wicked offspring than there is to rejoice over in the one man found so good that another world can be peopled by him. What, he asks, is the meaning of the

coloured streaks stretching out like the unfurrowed brow
of a no-longer-angry God (880)?

Michael commends his skilful conjecture ('Dextrously
thou aim'st', 884). The rainbow is indeed a sign of how
gladly God will put an end to his anger. Once the wicked
are removed, the 'one just Man' (890) shall find such grace
in God's sight that he will make a 'Covenant' (892) never
again to destroy the earth by flood. In future the cloud will
be accompanied by the rainbow, the guarantee of this
covenant, that the cycle of seasons shall hold its course till
the 'coming of the day of God, wherein the heavens being
on fire shall be dissolved', and man shall look for 'new
heavens and a new earth' (2 Peter III. 12–13).

Book XII

In the first edition of *Paradise Lost*, published in 1667, the poem was divided into ten books. In the second edition, of 1674, the original Book VII was divided into the present Books VII and VIII, and the first four lines of Book VIII were added to the text. Likewise the original Book X was divided into the present Books XI and XII, and the first five lines of Book XII were added to the original text. We have now reached a hinge in the unfolding of the future, as in the construction of the poem, and it is a good point at which to clarify the detail of the design. Michael is to continue his prophecy by direct narration, though so far the prophecy has been presented in a series of visions, beginning with the comprehensive view of the 'Hemisphere of Earth' (XI. 379–411) and continuing with the sequence of six particular scenes revealed to Adam, each of which provoked a questioning response from him that led to an explanatory interpretation by Michael. What complicates the structure for the reader is that Michael's attendant commentary is often as much an amplification of the scene as an interpretation of it. The six particular visions are:·

1 The murder of Abel by Cain (XI. 429–47). Michael's explanation (XI. 453–60).
2 The 'Lazar-house' full of people dying of diseases produced by debauchery (XI. 477–95). Michael's explanation (XI. 515–25). Michael's more personal and individual advice to Adam about living temperately and about the strains of old age is really an extension of the explanation (XI. 530–46).
3 The corrupting of the 'Sons of God' (descendants of Seth) by the wanton daughters of the civilized secularists (XI. 556–92). Michael's explanation (XI. 603–27).

4 The land engulfed by warfare and faction, the persecution
and divine rescue of the one just man, Enoch (XI. 638–73).
Michael's explanation (XI. 683–710).
5 The people corrupted by peace and ease, the vain warning
from Noah, his recourse to the ark and the flooding of the
earth (XI. 712–53). Michael's explanation (XI. 787–838).
6 The end of the flood, the saving of Noah, and the appearance of the rainbow (XI. 840–67). Michael's explanation
(XI. 884–901).

1–104 *Michael foretells the history of Jewry after the Flood (–24),
the rise of Nimrod (–37), the building of the tower of Babel (–62).
Adam laments Nimrod's tyranny (–78). Michael explains how
fallen man's loss of true liberty makes tyrannies inevitable (–104).*

The archangel pauses in his prophetic survey as one who on
a journey takes a breather ('bates', 1) at midday. The break
fits neatly into his scheme of revelation, as he is now poised
between his account of a world destroyed in the Flood and
a world to be fully restored in the sequent history of Jewry,
with its culmination in the incarnate Son's redemption of
mankind. The reason Michael gives for now proceeding by
oral narration is that mortal sight and sense grow weak
under the impact of 'objects divine' (9). So he tells how the
descendants of Noah, with recent memories of the Flood to
discipline their thinking, live toilfully, piously and peaceably
under 'paternal rule' (24) till a proud ambitious man arises
who is not content with fraternal equality, arrogates
authority to himself and establishes a tyrannous rule. This
is Nimrod, the 'mighty hunter' of Genesis x. 9, hunter of
men not of beasts in this context (30). Milton has Dante as
precedent for making Nimrod a tyrant (he is pictured alongside Saul and Sennacherib as examples of pride brought low,
Purgatorio XII. 34 ff.). Nimrod claims sovereignty over his
fellow men in defiance of God (34–5).* He leads a 'crew' of
like ambitious men to a plain where a whirlpool ('gurge', 41)

* That Nimrod's name has semantic associations with a word
meaning *rebellion*, 36–7, is an erroneous etymological fancy according
to Verity (*Paradise lost*, ed. A. W. Verity, C.U.P. 1936).

of bituminous liquid boils up from underground. This place, we may assume, is Hit, in Iraq, anciently famous for its bitumen and naphtha pits, and locally known as the 'mouth of Hell' (42). There they try to build their tower 'whose top may reach to Heaven' (44), their motive being sheer arrogant lust for fame. God frustrates their pride by erasing their common language and disseminating among them such a variety of tongues that they cannot understand one another. *Babel* (Assyrian *Bab-ili*) is the native name for Babylon, and memories of the towers of Babylon are assumed to lie behind the story, but scholars deny any connection between *Babel* and the Hebrew word *bālal* ('to confound'), such as is presupposed here ('the work Confusion nam'd', 62) on the basis of Genesis xi. 9.

The tradition associating Nimrod with Babel is extra-biblical. Scriptural references to Nimrod are scanty (he 'began to be mighty upon the earth', 1 Chronicles 1. 10: see also Micah v. 6), but Dante takes up the tradition, and Nimrod is encountered in the *Inferno* on the approach to the Ninth Circle, a gigantic figure half-submerged in a pit –

'questi è Nembrotto, per lo cui mal coto
pure un linguaggio nel mondo non s'usa' (*Inferno* xxxi. 77-8)

Josephus, the Jewish historian of the first century A.D., connects Babel with Nimrod's determination to outwit the God who drowned the world, by making a tower too high to be flooded, and Milton held Josephus to be an author 'not less believed than any under sacred'.* Thus Milton's symbolic use of Nimrod as typifying tyranny and the spread of discord has ample precedent. That Milton associated Nimrod's tyranny with the invention of the institution of monarchy we also know from *Eikonoklastes*, where Milton defends the execution of Charles I, and speaks of 'Babel (which was Nimrod's work, the first king, and the beginning of his kingdom was Babel)'. Here Adam execrates Nimrod for usurping a lordship over his fellowmen, which belongs to God only, man's authority extending only over animal-kind. Michael com-

* *Eikonoklastes.*

mends Adam's abhorrence of the man who caused such trouble in endeavouring ('affecting', 81) to subdue 'Rational Libertie'; but adds that since Adam's fall ('lapse', 83) true liberty, which is inseparably twinned with 'right Reason', is lost. Once the clarity of human reason is 'obscur'd' (86), once its authority is resisted, the human appetites, no longer in their proper subordinate place (but 'inordinate' – out of their hierarchical placing, 87), and usurping ('upstart', 88) human passions, wrest the control from reason's grip, and reduce man to servitude. In correspondence with this inner microcosmic disorder there is an external disorder in the world, which matches it, for God answers man's voluntary inner subjugation of reason to passion by subjecting him externally to an undeserved encroachment on his liberty by men who assume lordship through violence. Thus tyranny is inevitable: though tyrants are not thereby any less culpable. Sometimes nations deteriorate ('decline', 97) so much from the way of reason that no evil men are needed as instruments of tyranny to deprive them of liberty, for justice itself, with some attendant curse brought down on their heads, will deprive them of outward liberty, as they have already forfeited their inner freedom. As instance of this kind of doom, Michael cites the case of Ham (101–4). He is one of the three sons of Noah, Shem, Ham and Japeth, as the relevant story is told in Genesis IX. 18–27. Ham dishonours his father by looking upon his nakedness when he lies drunk in his tent. Shem and Japeth respectfully cover it. Ham, the father of Canaan, in consequence suffers Noah's curse: 'Cursed be Canaan; a servant of servants shall he be unto his brethren' (Genesis IX. 25).

105–269 *Michael continues his prophecy. God selects his chosen people (–113) and calls Abraham, who leaves Ur (–134) and comes to the Promised Land (–146). His descendants, the Israelites, move down to Egypt (–163) and are enslaved to Pharaoh till Moses and Aaron arise (–172). God sends the Plagues (–190), Pharaoh releases the Israelites, then pursues them. They are led safely across the Red Sea, where their pursuers are swallowed up (–214). They*

*journey through the Wilderness, organize themselves (–244), make
the Ark of the Covenant (–256), and eventually reach the Promised
Land (–260). Michael here cuts his story short (–269).*

Michael continues. Like the world before the Flood, the
world after the Flood will go from bad to worse till God
turns his eyes from human iniquity and decides to select 'one
peculiar Nation' (111), which will spring from 'one faithful
man' (113) – Abraham. Difficult as it is to believe that within
the lifetime of 'the Patriark' (117), Noah (350 years after the
Flood, Genesis IX. 28), there could be a forsaking of God,
Abraham has been 'Bred up in Idol-worship' (115), but God
calls him in a vision from his home and kindred to a land
where he will raise a great nation from him, and pour such
blessing upon them that they, his offspring ('seed', 125),
shall be a blessing to all other peoples. Abraham's response
is immediate – 'hee straight obeys,/Not knowing to what
Land, yet firm believes' (126–7) – a response of obedience.
Michael *sees*, though Adam and the reader can only *hear*, how
this man of faith leaves all familiar things – Gods, friends,
native soil ('*Ur* of Chaldaea', 130) – fords the Euphrates
(130), and comes with all his servants and flocks to Canaan,
where he pitches his tents.

Michael defines the geographical limits of the Promised
Land from Hamath (in Upper Syria) in the north to the
Desert of Zin in the south (138–9), from Mount Hermon in
the east to the Mediterranean Sea in the west. Then he relates God's promise in Abraham's vision, 'that all Nations of
the Earth/Shall in his Seed be blessed' (147–8), as previously
quoted (125–6), to the memorable divine promise given to
Adam himself (x. 179–81), from which he has already
derived comfort (x. 1029–32). This seed of Abraham is
the seed of Adam, the great deliverer who shall bruise the
serpent's head. The connection made, Michael postpones the
full explanation of it (150–1) to the appropriate chronological point (see 429–33 and 450). Abraham's son, Isaac,
and his grandson, Jacob (Israel), will match him in faith.
Jacob and his twelve sons will come to sojourn in the land

of Egypt in a time of famine, invited by the 'younger son' (160), Joseph, who has achieved power in the kingdom of Pharaoh (Genesis XXXIX–L).

The enslavement of the Israelites follows. Milton skims over the narrative of the first fourteen chapters of Exodus in just over fifty lines (165–220), as Michael tells how Moses and Aaron arise to lead their people out of enslavement ('enthralment', 171) and back to the Promised Land. He recounts the ten plagues (176–89) by which Pharaoh has to be divinely tormented before he will let the Israelites go: the turning of rivers to blood, the frogs, the lice, the flies, the cattle disease, the boils and blisters ('blaines', 180) that swell up ('imboss', 180) on everyone's skin, the hailstorm, the locusts, the three-day darkness (a dust-storm, presumably), and the slaying of the first born. The plague-wounded 'River-dragon' (191), Pharaoh, who has alternately agreed under stress to release the Israelites and then broken his pledge, at last lets them go, but then pursues them till he and his host are swallowed up in the Red Sea, which has already miraculously opened up a dry way 'between two christal walls' (197) of water to let the Israelites through.

Michael lays stress on the last climactic events. God watches over the Israelites in their journeying by means of the cloud and pillar of fire, their guides by day and night, which perplex their pursuers when Moses commands the waters of the sea to part for their passage through them and to close again over the trapped Egyptians (200–14). Under God's guidance the Israelites choose to avoid the shorter coastal route and probable encounter with the Philistines – from which they might have been driven back into renewed slavery in Egypt (see Exodus XIII. 17–18). An added inducement to take the longer route through the Wilderness is that they have time there to organize themselves in their twelve tribes. God himself will descend on Mount Sinai to give them the Ten Commandments and to lay down laws for them covering both civil justice and religious practice. The latter will symbolically foreshadow the Incarnation and Redemption whereby the pledge about bruising the serpent is to be fulfilled (231–5) (Christ is the 'destind Seed', 233, who will deliver mankind). The Israelites will not hear all this at first hand. The thunder and lightnings, the trumpet, the smoke and the quaking of the mountain, are enough to make them tremble (Exodus XIX. 16–18). Moses is the chosen mediator, in whose office is anticipated and fore-signified the coming mediation of Christ (240–4).

It remains for Michael to tell how God sets up his own symbolic tabernacle among his people. By his instruction ('prescript', 249) they frame a sanctuary and make an Ark within it to contain the 'Records of his Cov'nant' (252). After this brief reference to the elaborate formulations that begin in Exodus XXV, Michael foresees the arrival in the Promised Land, glancing forward (to Joshua X. 12–14, for instance, in 263–6) to the many battles ahead before the seed of Israel is fully established there – a chronicle here, of course, too 'long to tell' (261).

270–371 *Adam rejoices at the forecast of salvation, and asks why so many laws are needed (–284). Michael replies. Sin makes law necessary, though law cannot cure sin (–299). A better covenant will be needed for that (–307). Hence Joshua, not Moses the Lawgiver, will lead the entry into Canaan (–314). There eventually the royal line of David will produce the Son who will reign for ever (–330). Meantime Solomon, the building of the temple, the Babylonian captivity, and the return are glanced at (–358), and then the birth of Christ foretold (–371).*

Rejoicing as he does at hearing of the coming of the day of Christ 'in whom all Nations shall be blest' (277) – a privilege for the human race quite undeserved by himself – Adam nevertheless fails to understand why so many laws need to be laid down for a people among whom God himself condescends to dwell (281: the reference is to God's presence in the tabernacle). Surely God cannot reside with a sinful people? Michael tersely reminds Adam that his descendants will without question be subject to sin. Law will demonstrate ('evince', 287) their natural corruption ('pravitie', 288) by provoking their sinfulness. When they see that law can

reveal their sinfulness but not lift its burden, except by
unreal sacrificial acts of expiation with the blood of animals,
they may realize that blood more precious must be offered,
just life for their unjust lives, before the righteousness they
have lost can be reclaimed for them. The argument is that by
such exchange, of life for lives, a faithfulness can be credited
('imputed', 295) to sinners, which of their own capacities
they could never attain: thus they might find themselves re-
established in a justified (not merely *tolerated*) relationship
with God, and thereby enabled to taste inner peace of
conscience. The law's prescriptive rites could never restore
such peace to them; and its regulations – by virtue of their
ingrained weakness – they could never morally live up to
(289-99). Thus law is shown to be inadequate, and established only with the intention of assigning its subjects in due
course to a 'better Cov'nant', when they have been disciplined by gradual understanding of symbolic practices and
prescriptions to a full grasp of the truths they represent –
disciplined, in other words, to an insight into the spiritual
realities that the physical practices and external constraints
of the law prepare them for. Freed, then, from the sense of
prohibition, they enter the sphere of unconfining grace where
the dread of the slave is transmuted into the loving respect
of the son. What is righteously done under this dispensation
is done not because law commands it but because faith wants
to do it (300-6). For all these reasons it will not be appropriate for Moses, the great lawgiver, to lead his people into
the Promised Land, but rather Joshua (i.e. 'Jesus' – 'the
Saviour'). Christ, like Joshua, will bring the human race
from their long wanderings in the world's wilderness to the
promised land of 'eternal Paradise' (314). The traditional
symbolic correspondence between Heaven and the Promised
Land is here explicit. We have touched already on associative
analogies that accompany it.

We see that Michael's extended prophecy is not an attempt
to *summarize* Jewish history. Rather it is a series of glances at
the Old Testament; and the episodes selected are those that
make clear the situation of fallen (as opposed to innocent)

mankind, and those that stand as symbolic anticipations
of the coming redemptive work of Christ. Perhaps everything in the long prophetic interlude, stretching from XI. 376
to XII. 551, could be subsumed under one of two headings:
The evil released on the world by the Fall; God's active
work in delivering man. Two great deliverances have domi-
nated the story so far: the deliverance from the Flood in
Noah's ark – and the covenant of the rainbow; the deliverance from Egypt – and the symbolic summing-up of the
renewed divine guarantee to men that is represented by the
construction of the Ark of the Covenant. All instances of
the 'one just man', all deliverers, are so many anticipatory
pictures of the Saviour who is to come. The traditional
parallels between leading the Israelites out of bondage in
Egypt and freeing man from bondage to sin are fully exploited. It remains to hint briefly at the establishment of the
royal line of David from which an everlasting kingship shall
arise in 'the Womans Seed' (327) promised to Adam
(x. 179–81); and also to tell how, during the reign of
Solomon, the Ark of God, no longer carried about by a
wandering people, comes to rest in the 'glorious Temple'
(334) of the Holy City.

The second great deliverance is no more conclusive than
the first. Sin and idolatry have not been finally conquered,
and as their grip is renewed God once more allows his
people to be chastened, this time by exile and captivity in
Babylon. After 'seventie years' (345) they are brought home,
for God in his mercy remembers his sworn promise of salvation to come from the house of David. The Jews again live
more righteously for a time, but once more prosperity produces factions and corruption even among the priests, and
David's lineage is ousted from the throne, so that the
Messiah king is born 'Barr'd of his right' (360). Nevertheless
a new star marks his birth and brings the wise men from the
east to offer their gifts to him. The shepherds, too, are called
to worship him by a choir of angels. He is born of a Virgin,
but he is fathered by the 'Power of the most High' (369:
see Luke I. 35).

372-551 Adam rejoices, and asks about the final struggle between the Deliverer and Satan (-385). Michael expounds the doctrine of atonement (-410), foretelling Christ's crucifixion (-419), his resurrection (-435), his founding of the Church (-450), and his ascension (-465). Adam rejoices again, and asks what happens to the disciples after the Ascension (-484). Michael tells of the coming of the Holy Spirit and the growth of the Church (-507), then of its later corruption (-537), till the Second Coming of Christ in glory (-551).

Michael has paused, because Adam is so overcharged with joy that, without the relief of words, his feelings would burst out in tears. At last Adam sees why the hoped-for deliverer is called the 'seed of Woman' (379). 'Virgin Mother, Haile' (379), he cries, renewing the correspondence between first Eve and second Eve (v. 385-8; see p. 133). Godhead will be united with manhood in the Son of God born of her womb, and the time will be right for the *capital* bruising (*fatal* and *in the head*) of the serpent. In what way, then, will the victor's heel be bruised and the other half of the prophecy fulfilled?

Michael warns Adam against too literal an interpretation of the prophecy in terms of physical conflict. Satan cannot be weakened by physical defeat, for his fall from Heaven, a much deadlier blow, did not incapacitate him from giving a mortal wound to Adam. The Saviour will cure this wound, not by destroying Satan, but by wiping out what Satan has effected in the human race. And this can be done only by doing what Adam failed to do, only by cancelling out Adam's disobedience. Since God's law of obedience was imposed on penalty of death and that penalty still remains unpaid in respect of Adam and all those his successors who share his sinfulness, the payment of the penalty can alone meet the demands of justice. The Saviour will meet the full demands of the law in obedience, yet out of love – though love is the only ultimate fulfilment of what the law exists for. The Son will endure Adam's punishment by coming in human flesh, leading an innocent life, and accepting a 'cursed death' (406). All who believe in his redeeming work will by their faith have his own obedience credited to themselves and his deserts likewise, so that they are saved in him, not by any deeds of their own done in obedience to the law.

Thus the Saviour will be hated and crucified by his own people. In being nailed to the cross, he nails man's enemies, that is the law that would pass judgement on guilty man, and the sins of men that have made them guilty. These enemies die in his dying, for they can never more be cited in the arraignment of those men who trust in 'this his satisfaction' (419) of their demands. The Saviour rises to life again on the third day. Adam's ransom is paid, which redeems man from death – those men, that is, who accept the life offered to them, making its benefits their own by a faith that is not uncorroborated in their deeds. The sentence of death passed upon Adam is annulled: Satan's head is bruised in that his power is broken, for sin and death, his two 'maine armes' (431), are defeated. Their stings are deeply sunk in his own (Satan's) head, while the 'temporal death' of the Saviour is a mere bruise on the heel. The same applies to those whom he redeems: their temporal death is a temporary death – a sleep that wafts one to eternal life.

After the Resurrection, the Son will make a few appearances to his disciples, charging them to teach all nations what they have learned of him, to baptize them in running ('profluent', 442) water as a sign of their cleansing from sin, and to adjust their minds to self-sacrifice unto death, if need be, after the pattern of their Saviour's lot. The disciples shall take this teaching to 'all nations', so that all can become in faith, though not in physical lineage, the Sons of Abraham (cf. 125–6). The Son will ascend to Heaven; as he moves in triumph through the air, cleansing it by enchaining Satan, the 'Prince of aire' (454). He will enter into glory, and return, when this world is ripe for dissolution, to judge the quick and the dead. The faithful will be received into bliss.

The last section of Michael's prophecy, dealing with the Incarnation, Redemption, and Ascension (393–465) covers roughly the same theological ground as does part of God's decree in Heaven (III. 281–343).

Adam marvels at the way good is to be brought out of evil. The work of divine redemption (the new creation of man in Christ) seems now more wonderful than the first creation. Adam even begins to doubt whether it is more fitting to repent of the sin he committed and the fall of man that it brought about, or rather to rejoice that it should have become the occasion for this greater outpouring of God's goodness, abounding in grace to men and glory to God himself. Having touched thus lightly on the theme of the *felix culpa*, he asks about the earthly lot of the disciples left behind at the Ascension (479–84).

They will, of course, be persecuted, Michael admits, but the Son will send a 'Comforter' to them, to fill their hearts with faith and love, to guide their minds in truth, and to strengthen them in spirit against the assaults of Satan and against the hostilities of men. They will be so rewardingly supported inwardly by the consolations of the Holy Spirit that their sufferings and martyrdoms will amaze their persecutors. Moreover, the outpouring of the Spirit on the Apostles will endow them with a wonderful gift of tongues and with the power to perform such miracles as their Lord performed. They will thus convert many peoples. At last they die, leaving their doctrine and their story recorded in writing. After their death 'Wolves' (508) succeed them (cf. *Lycidas* 114 ff.) – supposed teachers who make profitable careers out of the sacred mysteries of religion, corrupting the purity of scriptural truth with superstitious accretions. Michael adds parenthetically that the Spirit's guidance is needed for understanding of the New Testament (514). The unworthy successors of the Apostles assume titles and offices, and mix secular power with their ecclesiastical authority, though keeping up the pretence that they act as men whose impetus is spiritual; and indeed they appropriate to themselves a monopoly of divine spirituality, which in fact is promised and given to all believers (515–20). On the basis of this pretence regulations about things spiritual are imposed on individual consciences by exercise of worldly power – laws that no one can find among what has been authentically inherited by these false teachers, or among what the Spirit inwardly dictates to the individual (520-4). What are they about, these people, but to control the spirit of freely given divine grace itself – in other words to unbuild the living temple of God that every Christian is in himself (1 Corinthians III. 16-17) by virtue of his own faith, not by virtue of someone else's? No earthly power can claim infallibility over against this authority of personal faith and conscience. Nevertheless, many will try to arrogate such right to themselves and bring persecution upon those who stand firm in true spiritual worship. The rest, the majority, will take it ('deem', 534) that the requirements of religion can be properly answered by superficial external practices. Thus the truth shall be hidden and acts of faith rare; the world will go its way, bringing evil to good men and prosperity to evil men, till the day of revival ('respiration', 540) for the just shall come ('the times of refreshing', Acts III. 19), the day of vengeance on the wicked, at the return of the 'Womans seed' (543), first mysteriously foretold (x. 181), then more fully known as the saving Christ, and at last fully revealed as the Son of God in the full glory of the Father, who shall come to obliterate the perverted satanic world and from the burning mass, 'purg'd and refin'd' (548) to make new Heaven and Earth, an eternity of blissful righteousness, peace and love.

552-649 *Adam sums up what he has learned* (-573); *Michael gives his last advice* (-587), *and bids Adam return to Eve* (-605). *He does so, and finds her comforted by her dreams* (-623). *The cherubim take up their station while Adam and Eve leave Paradise* (-649).

Adam marvels at the speed with which Michael's forecast has surveyed the course of temporal history to its conclusion. Beyond that conclusion lie the mysteries of eternity, which the eye cannot penetrate. Adam realizes that the insight and knowledge he has been granted are as much as the human mind can cope with. He has learned that he must obey, love God, walk 'as in his presence' (563), adapt himself to God's dealings with him ('observe/His providence',

563-4), trust only in him whose 'tender mercies are over all his works' (Psalm CXLV. 9 – line 565), always overcoming evil with good (cf. Romans XII. 21), accomplishing big things by attending to small things, turning the tables on those who have worldly power and wisdom by concentrating on what is ostensibly ineffective in meekness and simplicity of purpose. For he has learned, too, that in bravely suffering for the truth one achieves the greatest victory, death itself being the beginning of life for those who are firm in faith. All this he has learned from the Son whom he now acknowledges as his 'Redeemer' (573).

Thus we may observe how the world's whole future and past, our future and Milton's past, have been swept together to a point at which the first man proclaims himself, by prospective forecast and historic retrospect, a Christian. One of the most pressing problems of theology is happily solved by Milton.

Michael assures him that in his knowledge he has attained to the summit and maximum ('summe', 575) of human wisdom, and cannot advance beyond it, however much factual information, worldly wealth or power he may gain. But he must match his knowledge with deeds; with faith and the moral virtues, love especially. Then he will not be loath to leave the external Paradise because he will possess a happier inner paradise of the spirit. (We must remember that these words are addressed to *fallen* man; and that Paradise is not what it was.)

Let us go down, Michael says, from this hill of prophetic vision ('Speculation', 589; cf. XI. 377-80), for the appointed time demands ('Exacts', 590) our departure. The guards are waiting on another hill for the signal to move into position with a flaming sword before them as a sign of the clearing of the Garden. Go and waken Eve. I have brought her to inward composure and acceptance by dreams full of good promise. At an appropriate time you must share with her what you have learned, especially on the matter most relevant to her faith – the future deliverance of all mankind to come from her own 'Seed' (600). So you may live long together, single-minded in your faith, duly grave ('sad', 603) in respect of the past evils, but even more heartened by reflection on the happy outcome.

They descend the hill. Adam eagerly runs ahead to Eve's bower, where he finds her already awake and cheerful. She has been divinely comforted by promising ('propitious', 612) dreams that forecast 'some great good'. She is ready to follow Adam's lead. (The angelically induced dream and the sequent obedience match the satanically induced dream and the sequent disobedience.) To go from the garden or to stay in it is not an issue at all for her as a separate individual; all that matters is that she should be with her husband who is 'all things under Heav'n' (618) to her. For her 'all places' are in his presence who is now banished from this place through her own 'wilful crime'. Yet she goes strengthened and consoled in the knowledge that though all has been lost by her, it is by her 'Promis'd Seed' that all shall be restored.

Our Mother Eve has the last word, for Adam answers not, well pleased at what he hears. Moreover the archi-angelic presence is near and the bright cherubim are moving down from the hill to take up their watch over the Garden. In their starry splendour they glide over the ground, like an evening river-mist rolling fast over a fen and pursuing the labourer on his homeward trek. High before them blazes the fiery sword of exclusion. Its fierce heat singes and vapourizes the ground and growth of the Garden to a desert dryness. The hurrying angel takes our 'lingring Parents' in either hand and leads them directly through the eastern gate and down to the 'subjected' (640) plain appropriate to their now accepted subjection. Then he disappears.

Turning, Adam and Eve see the whole eastern side of Paradise ablaze under the flame of the uplifted sword, and the great gate alive with fearsome faces and burning armour. It is natural that they should drop tears; not surprising that they quickly wipe them away. The world is 'all before them' (646) with all its freedoms, and God's providence is their accepted guide. They make their slow and tentative way through Eden 'hand in hand'.

Index